BANKING IN SILENCE

THE COMPLETE MANUAL ON HOW TO PROTECT YOUR MONEY

Dr WG Hill

Banking in Silence

Scope International Ltd,
Forestside House, Forestside,
Rowlands Castle, Hants
PO9 6EE, UK

1st Edition 1994
By Dr WG Hill
British Library Cataloguing in Publication Data

A catalogue record for this book is available from the British Library
ISBN 0 906619 47 5

Phototypeset by Barbara James Typesetting, Rowlands Castle, Hampshire
Printed by Hartnolls, Bodmin, Cornwall

CONTENTS

''Of all rights to the citizen, few are of greater importance or more essential to an individual's peace and happiness than the right of personal security, and that involves not merely protection of an individual person from assault, but exemption of an individual's private affairs, books, and papers from the inspection and scrutiny of others. Without the enjoyment of this right, all other rights would lose half their value. Today, in every major country of the world, individual rights of privacy have indeed lost half their value. What is needed today to regain these rights are a set of new workable blueprints for financial privacy, 1990s-style.''

Dr WG Hill

Introduction

A PERSONAL MESSAGE FROM WG HILL

Right now, as you read this, there is a war going on. In the name of everything that they think we believe is desirable, bureaucrats and politicians and other con-men and schemers are attacking our personal privacy. Their excuses nearly always sound convincing. The assault on your privacy is, without exception, proposed and executed in the name of efficiency to comply with fiscal regulations that they themselves have dreamt up to enforce tax codes (yes, *their* tax codes!) and so on *ad nauseum*.

Day after day we see examples where this blatant abuse and misuse of power is not enough to satisfy the politicians and their armies of self-serving pen pushers. These bureaucrats then turn to using threats, violence and similar heavy handedness to achieve some higher goal they themselves have set. Surprise: this is always done in the name of the "common good". A closer inspection reveals that the common good happens to benefit Big Brother and the particular political or ideological ideas of the politicians in power, and inevitably the government's coffers. Many laws have been passed to enforce tax codes, currency and monetary restrictions to fight illegal drug traffic, corruption and white collar crime. These laws are being used to erode what last bastions you may still have left to protect your privacy. Inhumane as they may be, they are necessary to stop international crime – *or so we were told!* What we are not being told is that they don't even attempt to deal with criminals. They were never intended to. The "let's stop crime now and forever" slogan is typical political window-dressing. The sugar coating on such a bitter pill that no free voter in the western world would ever swallow if he were told the truth, the whole truth and nothing but. So what do all these new laws do? Who are they meant to stop? Who needs to be afraid of them? To discover the real answers all you need do is cut away Big Brother's snake-oil rhetoric, then look closely at what effects these many new laws produce in day to day life in all OECD member countries. To discover the real answers look at who suffers. Look at whose money is being taken away and look at who has to turn up in tax court. Do you see any drug barons there? The enforcement of these laws does not net drug traffickers, corrupt kingpins, gangland bosses or top white collar criminals. The professional crooks are far too clever to get themselves caught in the bureaucratic traps. The true victims are the people who can least afford it.

THEY'RE SHOOTING AT YOU

In a time when governments and over-zealous bureaucrats all over the world keep passing more and more bad laws, lack of privacy is not a good thing. Although lack of privacy can never make an honest man into a criminal, it can expose him as a lawbreaker. A breaker of those laws which no man should ever be forced to live by. Ayn Rand in her classic *Atlas Shrugged* has her character Ragnar Danneskjöld say the following: "When robbery is done in open daylight by sanction of the law, as it is done today, then any act of honour or restitution has to be hidden underground". With silly laws making this or that harmless pastime illegal in many countries the world over, and with politicians using their homebrewed laws to steal from their most productive citizens, every truly freedom loving man or women has to resort to low profile and privacy tactics to live a decent life the way it was meant to be lived.

Even if you have nothing to hide, privacy is a good thing which you can never have too much of. Just as you can never be too rich or too good-looking, you cannot have too much privacy.

Once upon a time, two good friends, let's call them Henry and Howard, sat in the sitting room discussing architecture and the passing of the seasons while looking out into the big garden and enjoying the colors of the trees in autumn.

In the middle of their conversation while they were taking in the view of the trees and the falling leaves, five police cars shrieked to a halt in front of the house, all with flashing lights and sirens at full blast.

Howard opened the window to see what was going on. Two or three cops leapt out of each patrol car, whereupon they immediately sought cover, drew their guns and started firing round after round after round towards the house at full blast.

Howard threw himself down on the floor. But Henry kept still in his chair with his legs crossed and a glass of port in one hand. He was still enjoying the view when Howard yelled, "Get Down. Get Down, NOW !"

"Why?", asked Henry. "I didn't do anything wrong!"

This little tale is a fairytale. It could not have happened in real life. Any sane person will seek cover when others start firing bullets in his direction. It doesn't matter whether he did anything wrong or not, common sense dictates that protection be sought whenever there's a danger, no matter who's innocent or who's to blame.

Not all use common sense and rational thinking when the issue turns to personal and financial privacy. Most of those who will seek cover when the police start firing at them, do not seek cover when the tax man goes on the war path or when some other triggerhappy government bureaucrat feels like opening a case.

The fact of the matter is that you may not have anything to hide. But you would be unwise not to seek some measure of privacy. With a bloated government virtually bankrupt and out for blood-money, even the most honest taxpayer can find himself in the line of fire. Not seeking some cover is dangerous to your financial health. If you manage to annoy the bureaurats enough you could find yourself at the receiving end of a phoney criminal case. This has happened to thousands of US tax payers who could not prove their innocence when they were charged with scheming to defraud the IRS. All received jail sentences of at least one year. They didn't commit a crime, but they had to do time. All had their property attached even before the case got to court. Eventually their assets were confiscated and later sold at auction to fill the tax man's coffers. Do not think this won't ever happen to you. In criminal tax cases, unlike other criminal cases, the defendant is assumed guilty unless he can prove otherwise. This flagrant piece of human rights abuse is accepted not just in the USA but in most European countries as well. An OECD special session, as reported in the *Wall Street Journal*, even drew up a model treaty on ways the government could take your property away from you *without prior trial*. The way the treaty was implemented in at least one country, means that failure to file just one of some forty-five different forms automatically puts your entire assets worldwide at risk. So do not think that privacy is only for those who have something to hide. Do not claim that low profile is for those whose dealings cannot bear scrutiny out in the open. It may have been like that in Utopia many years ago. Today the world is simply not so. Privacy and low profile is an urgent necessity for all of us. Take steps today to lower your profile and increase your privacy. Don't put it off. No one likes to be under surveillance. And no one likes to live with the fear that one day a vicious law that never should have been there in the first place can wreck your life.

THE USA 1970 BANK SECRECY ACT

Whatever future steps you take to safeguard your own hard-earned money you should always assume that bank secrecy does not exist.

Once upon a time, something resembling bank secrecy used to exist tucked away in various corners of Planet Earth. Today most countries use their bank secrecy merely as a marketing gimmick. Several countries do have bank secrecy acts on their statute books. Even the United States in 1970 passed the Bank Secrecy Act (which was updated in 1979 with a similar act).

Bizarre as it may sound, the loss of bank secrecy inadvertently quickened with the passing of the 1970 Bank Secrecy Act. It required all domestic banks to maintain duplicate records of their transactions. This unleashed a host of government fishing expeditions. The act was termed a misnamed piece of legislation if ever there was one by Robert Ellis Smith, publisher of the respected *Privacy Journal* newsletter. George Orwell would have liked the act, as it demonstrates clearly what he meant by his "Newspeak", a language whereby totalitarian regimes alter the meanings of old words so as to render language (and thus reason) meaningless.

While it euphemistically sounds as if the USA 1970 and 1979 Bank Secrecy Acts might be offering protection to clients of banks, its purpose is exactly the opposite. The Bank Secrecy

Act requires banks to keep records of customers' deposits, withdrawals and financial statements. And to make them available to the Department of the Treasury, or any agents who come calling. In *US vs Miller* the Supreme Court ruled that bank customers whose records are sought by the government for whatever reason have no right to ensure that access is controlled by an existing legal process.

Other countries have similar measures. Some claim they are necessary to combat crime. But criminals seem to get away with anything, as the recent years' rises in crime figures all too clearly show. So government must be lying. Either their statistics are false and crime is on the down or they are lying when they claim that electronic bank surveillance is catching criminals. You spot the Big Lie, then ask yourself what kind of regime finds it necessary to lie to its own citizens time after time.

Britain has implemented guidelines based on the US legislation and put them into place with more than a steering hand from the Inland Revenue. The same procedures are followed by Revenue Canada.

IS IT TOO LATE TO RE-CLAIM YOUR RIGHTS?

As you study this report you will need to evaluate your own situation. Some of the techniques to tax freedom are only for a select elite of the world's population. Likewise, some of the paths to privacy are not for all. Depending on where you live, local laws may prevent you using all your options.

To reclaim your right to financial and personal privacy you will first need to move some of your assets out of your present jurisdiction. Readers of the two *PT* volumes are familiar with the "five flags" theory and the A+A freedom formula. The "five flags" are five different countries. One is your business base (make your money in a jurisdiction different from your personal, fiscal domicile). The second is your citizenship (make sure you have at least one passport from a country which doesn't care what its non-resident citizens do outside its borders). The third flag is your domicile (officially and legally in a stable, secure tax-haven with strict bank secrecy laws). Flag number four your asset repository (stash your assets somewhere from whence they may be safely and anonymously managed by proxy). And your last flag, number five, the playgrounds (where you physically spend your time). You are best off if all five flags are planted in different countries. Those who do not yet have all five flags in place have found freedom taking their A+A (Ass and Assets) out of their country.

Are you living in the same country where you were born? Are you making your money there? Are all your assets tied up there? It may already be too late for you to win back some of that precious privacy your government has been taking away bit by bit during the last 20 years.

Your first step will be to set your assets free. The more liquid your wealth is the easier it is to move it across borders. The most liquid form of wealth is, of course, untraceable cash. Moving it by hand Big Brother will have a hard time stitching together a paper trail later on.

Law-abiding citizens are finding it harder and harder to keep their own money safe from government confiscation. Increasingly they are coming up against newly-erected walls. Barriers put there to stop them from sheltering their assets in safe places.

If you want to put a little aside for a rainy day, beware. This may already have been made illegal in your country. Sure you can invest at home, earning an interest rate on your deposits that does not keep pace with the real inflation (real inflation, always two to three percent higher than the official government-cited inflation figure. If you doubt it, start putting your own yearly inflation index together and follow the way prices truly rise. Official statistics cannot be believed).

As if it wasn't enough that the money you make at home hardly keeps pace with inflation, your government expects you to pay for the privilege of having been suckered. They want tax on homegrown interest, thirty per cent to fifty per cent, depending on your country and the nerve of its politicians. Whichever way you slice it you end up with a hole in your pocket. There is simply no way you can win with the chips stacked against you. You will lose no matter what you do. Unless you move away from your home turf. And start Banking in Silence.

The first thing you have to realize is that all governments, not just your own, are after one thing. Revenue. Some of them have scruples, but more often than not governments simply don't care much about what pretense they use to get their clammy hands on your cash. The reasons are many, but when you trace back to the roots of every one, you will find the same old dirty word. Socialism. Look at the Americans with Disabilities Act for a case in point of how socialism in action compels government to come up with ever more cash (*your* cash). Or look at the Clinton Administration's health care plan. A large down payment on socialism with future instalments certain to be larger than advertised, whether measured in money or in lost freedom to make your own decisions about medical care that are literally questions of life and death.

Once you understand that this is a real-life game of you against them, and that they play dirty, you are better equipped to plan your strategy.

Governments in industrial countries the world over are on a collision course. What's even worse, they are – with the possible exception of New Zealand – long past the point of no return. This point is reached when it is no longer economic to turn back but only to continue on your chosen path. Unfortunately for those of our readers who live in one of these countries or pay taxes to one of these countries, the chosen path, as they no doubt have found out, is the wrong one.

In the United States, what some see as the beginnings of virtue is nothing but make-up to camouflage the fact that government control is getting bigger every minute. In Europe the battle has been lost long ago. Leading authorities liken Europe to the *Titanic* flirting with disaster, calling Europe a sinking ship (*The Economist*, volume 329, number 7839). Among European governments the average budget deficit has rocketed to a frightening seven per cent of GDP, Gross Domestic Product. The highest level ever since the second world war. And this number is arrived at using the governments' own fiddled figures. The true picture may be grimmer still. And with all rich countries going down together, no outsiders will gallop in to save the day. For the schemers and the politicians leading these countries, the sad truth is that their foreign friends are just as much bogged down as they are themselves. Therefore, the only way out of this mess is the same old tried and tested racket. Put the squeeze on Johnny Lunchbucket. We all know what that means. If Mr Lunchbucket does not pay voluntarily he is threatened with all kinds of ills. Blackmailing the electorate to pay up even when no one has money to pay is still the favorite tactic of the morally corrupt Big Brother governments and their cash-hungry armies of public service sector leeches.

Governments would do well if they would realize their past mistakes and, like communist parties of the past, shut themselves down. By firing each and every one among their own ranks who has never done an honest day's work, more than 90 per cent of the public sector payroll could be eliminated from one day to the next. This holds true for all rich countries. Taxes could come down to something resembling humane levels, and even then your government would run a current account comfortably above five per cent of GDP.

But this is no way to run a railroad. What bureaucrats want and what bureaucrats get is an endless stream of cash that absolutely nobody would fork over willingly if given a free choice.

As tomorrow becomes today, the problems of financing a huge and outdated extortion racket do not go away. On the contrary, all numbers show that these problems will, without exception, grow bigger in the future. The free lunch, governments' future liabilities from unfunded pension schemes, will swell as populations age. When you couple these liabilities with a ratio of public debt at already well past two-thirds of entire GDP it becomes clear that something will have to change. Calculations by the OECD suggest that even on favorable assumptions the present value of promised public pensions net of future contributions amounts to 216 per cent of France's GDP and 160 per cent of Germany's. Three times as big as their existing public debts. Since politicians are the ones playing the game and making up the rules at the same time, fitting them to suit their own interests, you can only be sure of one thing. They will never lose. Who will be the loser? You will. Unless you hide your cash where no one can get it . . .

Questions, comments, corrections? Contact WG Hill at Scope International.

PART 1
CREATING YOUR OWN BANK SECRECY

Chapter 1

YOUR MONEY IS IN DANGER

The biggest lawbreakers of them all are governments. They routinely expect you to follow every petty decree they lay down, even while they themselves at the same time break laws faster than even the most hardened of criminals.

Look to the so-called leader of the free world. The United States. They invade other countries illegally, kidnap foreign nationals, torture them, drug them and bring them unconsciously and against their will to the United States where they may or may not face a trumped-up trial.

"Kidnapping by Government Order" is not exclusively a US phenomenon, unfortunately. Most governments, if they think they can get away with it, will break the law. If you think Third World governments head the list of offenders before the International Court of Human Rights in Strasbourg, think again. Top defendants appearing before the judge again and again and again include such "free" countries as Britain, Denmark and Germany, all on human rights abuses.

When they claim innocence, don't believe a word of what these bureaucrats say.

In the July 1990 copy of the *American Journal of International Law,* volume 84 no. 3, Andreas F. Lowenfeld (Charles L. Denison Professor of Law, New York University) wrote on page 712:

> *I urge that no great faith be placed in assertions by the US Government that abduction of persons who ended up in American custody were carried out solely by the police of the foreign country, that the United States had no knowledge of or participation in torture, or that the foreign country really consented to the operation, though it could not say so publicly.*

That you have been dragged out of your bed in a foreign country, kidnapped by government order, then tortured and drugged by foreign agents is no defence either. In the *Argaud* case France argued that the accused had no standing to raise any international law argument, which was for states only. This, of course, rings well with the traditional Latin line of thought that when push comes to shove, a citizen is simply property of the state. Cattle, if you will.

In our view, no one is more sovereign than yourself. Even if some fool shows up at your door calling himself "the State" and frantically waving papers in your face, claiming them to be the law, you should have the right to slam the door in his face. We know the world ain't so. If it was we wouldn't have to write this book showing you the ins and outs of maneuvering safely through shark-infested waters. In an ideal world, what you choose to do with your own money should be your business and your business alone. Throughout this book, we will be defending your right to do anything you wish with your own money. After all, it is your money. You made it. Anyone who tries to tell you otherwise usually has an ulterior motive. Watch them closely. He, she, it or they are trying to get you to fork over part of that cash.

In a perfect world, would-be Duck McScrooges can build a tank full of green stuff and go swimming in it every day. If such Disneyesque behavior is not your style, go march to the beat of your own drum. Light cigars with your cash. Stuff it in a pillowcase. Bury it, burn it, pile it high . . . or launder it. The choice is yours. It is your money. What you want to do with it, or what loops you want to put it through, should be your own decision; no one else's. If you want to channel your cash offshore, then through a foreign company or two, investing it in turn somewhere else, who should object? What you do with your money should be up to you. Where it goes and what it does is your business.

THE MOST EFFECTIVE FINANCIAL INVESTIGATION UNIT IN THE WORLD

Because you have money, you are automatically guilty until proven innocent. That is the view of FinCEN.

Fin-who?

FinCEN stands for Financial Crimes Enforcement Network, a quasi-secretive federal US sleuthing operation whose brief is to unearth money secrets. Since it was launched with a low-key champagne reception at the US Treasury Department in April 1990, FinCEN has become the most effective financial investigation unit in the world. It is a state-of-the-art computer-snooping agency so effective that when Russian president Boris Yeltsin needed to locate stolen Communist Party funds, he asked FinCEN for help. Today the US government is constructing a system to track all financial transactions in real-time, ostensibly to catch drug traffickers, terrorists and financial criminals. This should scare you out of your wits. Because the builder of this network is FinCEN. The "Big-Brother-Is-Watching-You" arm of the Treasury Department.

Using the Freedom of Information Act, we have managed to pierce together a sketch of what FinCEN is up to.

FinCEN was established by top IRS tax-cop Brian Bruh a few years before his retirement in October 1993. In 1991, FinCEN wrote classified reports on 6,000 individuals. In 1992, that number was 12,000 individuals. The 1993 total hit 20,000 individuals. Few ever knew that their financial affairs were being investigated by a branch of the US Treasury Department with ties to the Pentagon and the CIA.

The CIA? Yes. Brian Bruh refuses to discuss his agency's association with the CIA, but he doesn't deny there is one. His own background, besides his IRS experience, includes time spent at the Pentagon.

In addition to the more than 40,000 confidential snoops conducted to date, FinCEN has also completed what is called "longer-term Strategic Analytical Reports" for 715 investigations involving 16,000 other individuals and entities.

When facing the public, Brian Bruh claims that FinCEN is all about mapping the digital trails of dirty loot. As examples he lists profits from drug sales, stolen Savings and Loans money, hidden political slush funds, or the financing conduits of terrorists. In reality what FinCEN does is far more down to earth. It involves all of us, not just terrorists, drug dealers or crooked politicians. It systematically collates and cross-analyses public databases on a day to day basis. It is the only US federal unit devoted solely to this kind of work. The reason it is so secretive about its operations is that if the public knew what FinCEN was up to, the public wouldn't stand for it. FinCEN breaches civil liberties on a day to day basis. In the eyes of Brian Bruh and FinCEN you need to break eggs to make an omelette. Breaking privacy and peeking into personal information is necessary to catch criminals, or so the excuse goes.

A list of the 40,000 or so "criminals" that FinCEN has netted, shows that less than ten per cent of them are bad guys in the moral sense of the word. And 90 per cent or some 35,000 people were merely trying to keep a bit of their own money outside of the tax-man's knowledge. They didn't succeed.

If you ever find yourself the target of a FinCEN investigation, chances are slim that you'll know about it. FinCEN works in secrecy. The agency is located in a luxurious high-rise office building in "Spook City", down the road from the Central Intelligence Agency (CIA) in Vienna, Virginia.

You will be up against the following forces, all pooled together by FinCEN acting as coordinator:

- The Internal Revenue Service (IRS)
- The Federal Bureau of Investigation (FBI)
- The Drug Enforcement Agency (DEA)
- The Central Intelligence Agency (CIA)
- The State Department's Bureau of Intelligence and Research (INR)
- The Secret Service
- Customs Agents
- Postal Inspectors

According to senior intelligence officers, these investigative units can access the resources of the CIA, the Defense Intelligence Agency and the National Security Agency. The latter is important. As part of its routine brief the National Security Agency intercepts all data on electronic currency movements into and out of the United States. This data then makes its way into FinCEN's analyses.

Testifying before Congress, Peter Djinis, Director of the Treasury Department's Office of Financial Enforcement and one of the few Treasury officials close to FinCEN's activities, said:

> *It's the first ever government-wide, multi-source intelligence and analytical network brought together under one roof to combat financial crimes.*

In his view a financial crime would be to help your neighbor repair the leak on his roof and then let your neighbor do you another favor in return, with neither of you reporting this as income and paying tax on the value of the work received.

Bureaucrats love FinCEN. It's the best thing that has happened to them since sliced bread. *FinCEN is absolutely necessary*, says a senior General Accounting Office (GAO) official, who audited the agency but skirted emerging concerns about privacy, civil rights and the appropriate role of the CIA and other spies spying on their own citizens.

FinCEN will not reveal how it works or what it is capable of doing. The few examples that have surfaced have all been very routine run-of-the-mill jobs utilizing only a fraction of FinCEN's computer power. One concerns a so-called money launderer called John and was reported by Anthony L. Kimery, covering financial industry regulatory affairs as an editor at *American Banker Newsletters*. Here, with the kind permission of the publishers, is his report verbatim.

HOW TO BUST A JOHN

There wasn't much to go on. The police salvaged the slip of paper that a small-time East Coast criminal tried to eat before being arrested but on it they found scribbled only a telephone number and what appeared to be the name "John". This frustrated the police. They had anticipated more incriminating information on the man they believed was the supplier not only to the dealer they had just busted but also to dozens of other street corner crack peddlers. With two slim leads, the police weren't technically equipped to do much more than antiquated detective work that probably wouldn't yield evidence they could use to indict John. So they turned to FinCEN for the digital sleuthing they needed.

Less than 45 minutes after receiving the official police request for help, FinCEN had retrieved enough evidence of criminal wrongdoing from government databases that the district attorney prosecuting the case was able to seek indictments against John on charges of money laundering and conspiracy to traffic narcotics. The local police were impressed.

The whiz kids at FinCEN are good. Very good. That's why state and local police have come to depend on FinCEN to pull them out of the electronic-sleuthing quicksand. The case of John is a good example of one of their less complex assignments, and it illustrates the adeptness with which the government can collate existing financial data.

Seated at a computer terminal inside FinCEN's command post, a FinCEN analyst began the hunt. He started by querying a database of business phone numbers. He scored a hit with the number of a local restaurant. Next he entered the Currency and Banking Database (CBDB), an IRS database accessed through the Currency and Banking Retrieval System. CBDB contains roughly 50 million Currency Transaction Reports (CTRs), which document all financial transactions of more than US$ 10,000. By law these transactions must be filed by banks, S&Ls, credit unions, securities brokers, casinos, and other individuals and businesses engaged in the exchange of large sums of money.

The analyst narrowed his quest by searching for CTRs filed for transactions deemed suspicious. Financial institutions must still file a CTR, or IRS Form 4789, if a transaction under US$ 10,000 is considered suspicious under the terms of an extensive federal government list. There was a hit. A series of "suspicious" CTRs existed in the restaurant's ZIP code. Punching up images of the identified CTRs on his terminal, the FinCEN analyst noted that the transactions were made by a person whose first name was John. The CTRs were suspicious all right. They were submitted for a series of transactions each in the amount of US$ 9500, just below the CTR threshold of US$ 10,000. This was hard evidence that John structured the deposits to avoid filing a Form 4789, and that is a federal crime.

Selecting one of the CTRs for an expanded review, the analyst got John's full name, Social Security number, date of birth, home address, drivers license number, and other vital statistics, including bank account numbers.

Plunging back into the IRS database, the analyst broadened his search for all CTRs filed on behalf of the suspect, including non-suspicious CTRs. Only 20 reports deemed suspicious popped up on the screen, but more than 150 CTRs were filed in all. A review of the non-suspicious ones revealed that on several, John listed his occupation as the owner or manager of the restaurant identified by the telephone number on the slip of paper taken from the arrested criminal. The connection between the name and the phone number originally given to FinCEN was secured.

The FinCEN analyst then tapped commercial and government databases and turned up business information on the restaurant showing that John had reported an expected revenue for his eatery of substantially less than the money he had been depositing, as indicated by the CTRs. Fishing in a database of local tax assessment records, the analyst discovered that John owned other properties and businesses. With the names of these other companies, the analyst went back into the CTR database and found that suspicious transaction reports were filed on several of them as well.

As routine as such assignments as this case may be, the chumminess between FinCEN and the intelligence community raises serious questions about the privacy and security of the financial records of citizens John and Jane Doe, considering the intelligence community's historic penchant for illegal spying on non-criminals. Given the vast reach and ease with which the government can now tap into an individual's or business's financial records on a whim, these questions have received far too little scrutiny.

BEWARE OPERATION GATEWAY

It started in July 1993, a hot and dusty summer day in Texas. Since then, ''Operation Gateway'' has spread throughout all American states. In the process, lives have been wrecked and families torn apart. Before 1995, this menace will be present in foreign countries as well.

Gateway is inherently prone to abuse and provides, in the words of one banking professional, a ''disturbing indication of the direction in which the government is moving''.

Gateway gives state and local law enforcement officials direct access to the massive federal Financial Database, a huge mountain of personal financial details known in Federal Agent speak as the FDB. All of what the enormous FDB contains can rightly be classified as sensitive information. It contains, among other things, *all* the records that financial institutions have been filing under various acts for the last 24 years. In case you're worried, here's the partial list:

- CTRs (Currency Transaction Reports, filed by banks in every transaction involving more than US$10,000)
- suspicious transaction reports
- International Transportation of Currency or Monetary Instruments reports
- Foreign Bank and Financial Accounts reports

Operation Gateway will be expanded with direct access, so every local trooper or sheriff's hoodlum can tap into the database of Forms 8300. These are reports of payments over US$ 10,000 received in trade or business, not necessarily filed in connection with banking matters. From the massive FDB, state governments can download hardcopies of documents principally containing information on deposits, withdrawals and the movement of large sums of currency. All Americans are in the base, and quite a number of foreigners too. The FDB has nothing to do whatsoever with the war on drugs or catching criminals. Beware Operation Gateway. It is Big Brother's electronic eye watching you. Keeping tabs on every move you make, no matter how legal.

FinCEN state coordinators will handle the log-ons. They think they're the only ones smart enough to surf the electronic waves. In their eyes, the 50,000 federal agents and 500,000 police officers would otherwise wreck the sensitive circuits in no time. Under Gateway, results from all queries are written into a master audit file that is automatically compared against other requests and databases to track whether the subject of the inquiry is of interest to another agency or has popped up in a record somewhere else. If you think this is bad, hold your horses. Your worst 1984 nightmares have only just begun . . .

BEWARE OF THE DEPOSIT TRACKING SYSTEM

While the FDB mainly contains records on major money movements (the rich), foreign transfers (the foreigners) and suspicious transactions (the criminals), the Deposit Tracking System (DTS) shoots in all directions and not just at the three minorities that federal agents love to hate most.

In the understatement of the century, a computer magazine recently called the Deposit Tracking System "a potential menace". We quote:

> *If implemented, the estimated US$12.5 million computer system could be used to penetrate the security of bank accounts belonging to you, me, and 388 million other bank account holders in the US.*

The Deposit Tracking System is at the drawing-board phase so far. The American Congress has yet to approve the US$12.5 million price tag. When this happens, it will still be 1996 before a full-blown DTS is operative and running at capacity.

In the American media, little has been heard about DTS. Liberals like it, but professionals in the banking sector raise serious concerns. According to Diane Casey, executive director of the Independent Bankers Association of America:

> *The Deposit Tracking System would fundamentally change the relationships among banks, consumers, and the government in ways that have implications beyond banking policy. Our open and democratic society would be changed profoundly if any agency of the government maintained the scope of information on private citizens described in this proposal. It raises questions about our democracy that would have to be addressed by the highest policy-making levels of government.*

This is heavy-duty stuff coming from people who usually keep their voices down and prefer to stay out of the political fray. But other bankers are very much against DTS, too. The very conservative ABA, the American Bankers Association, said outright that

> *We doubt whether there are privacy safeguards that would be adequate to effectively protect this database from use by government agencies and, eventually, private parties. It is inconceivable to the ABA that such a database could be used only by the FDIC in deposit insurance coverage functions. Such a database . . . would provide a wealth of information for investigations being conducted by the FBI, the Drug Enforcement Administration, and the IRS, to name but a few. Like the baseball diamond in* Field of Dreams, *build this database and they will come. Eventually, whether legally or illegally, they will gain access to this database.*

The government argues that such a system is necessary. It claims that the FDIC needs the database. The Federal Deposit Insurance Corporation Improvement Act of 1991 says so. And the DTS database will only be used by the FDIC, or so the government claims.

Funnily enough, the FDIC doesn't even want this database. In a 234-page draft report it submitted to Congress in June 1993, the FDIC argued forcefully *against* the Deposit Tracking System. So why is the government still committed? An open secret making the rounds in intelligence circles is that both the CIA and the top of the IRS are clamoring for the system, blatantly disregarding privacy issues and matters of civil liberties. And totally forgetting price, the hefty US$12.5 big ones to get the ball rolling and then an estimated US$20 million a year required for facilities, salaries and benefits and routine hardware and software maintenance.

The CIA wants the Deposit Tracking System because it will boost the much-hyped role of economic intelligence gathering. The spooks think that DTS is a boon to their ability to monitor foreign financial dealings.

The IRS, of course, wants the Deposit Tracking System because every one of the 388 million American bank accounts will be open to detailed scrutiny at the touch of remote computer keyboard. Big Brother wants to look into your bank account, from any IRS office, any time it pleases.

Can anything be more frightening? You may be forgiven for thinking no. But think again. Enter, the real-time financial Robocop.

THE SYSTEM TO END ALL SYSTEMS

FinCEN's AI/MPP system should make you seriously question the role of government in today's society. It will be the mother of all databases.

AI stands for Artificial Intelligence. The FinCEN AI capabilities currently exploit the Financial Database for what is called proactive targeting of suspicious activity. The system automatically monitors the entire FDB database, constantly identifying suspicious financial activity in supercomputer-aided, rapid-response time. In addition to the FDB with its mountains of sensitive data stretching back almost 25 years, FinCEN is applying Artificial Intelligence to the newly created Criminal Referral Forms that must be filed with FinCEN whenever banks, examiners and regulators uncover financial activities they "suspect" are illegal.

In the near future, all of these government databases will be interfaced by way of AI/MPP technology. MPP, or massive parallel processing, will then be able to perform real-time monitoring of the entire US electronic banking landscape. The database of databases will have been created: FinCEN's AI/MPP system. The system will be tied into the private computer vaults holding all credit card transactions of Visa, MasterCard, American Express, Diners Club and other companies. This, the government argues, will become necessary "so that we could have nearly instant time-tracking capability".

Hooked into the Deposit Tracking System, the FinCEN system will be able to identify financial movements the minute they are carried out. If something looks suspicious the government-computer will automatically alert the computers of the receiving bank, thus red-flagging and halting the payment before the customer even knows that the transfer has arrived.

FinCEN has a hush-hush US$2.4 million contract with the US Department of Energy's Los Alamos National Laboratory to develop what can best be described as a powerful "money flow model", a piece of software that will use Artificial Intelligence to look for unexplained, atypical trends and money flows, then single them out for further examination by humans assigned to monitor the system.

The almost 2.5 million dollars spent at Los Alamos will be recouped when FinCEN leases its software to other countries. OECD in Paris is said to have a list of nations eager to get their hands on the snoop-technology. This is according to Bruce Hemmings, a former CIA operative whose specialty was financial investigations. When the government, or any government for that matter, is cornered and has to face questions about the ethics of what it is up to, it always turns to the old line about catching money launderers.

But look who their antics net. Money launderers get off scot free. They know how to beat the system. Instead, the little guy, who chisels a bit off his taxes gets caught red-handed.

Politicians the world over don't have the guts to own up to this plain truth. Social democrats and bureaucrats, dishonest thieving scum of the earth collaborate. This is how they rake in their paychecks. By lying, spying and abusing their power.

The shortsighted view that a free society protects its citizens from monetary and fiscal abuse no longer holds true when society itself is the one carrying out this abuse. Citizens of ex-Communist nations have known this for a lifetime (the rest of us are just learning it now). In the Slovak lands, no one trusted the state to ever tell them the truth, not even after the supposed fall of socialism and the split from the Czech neighbor. So in 1993 when Slovak authorities warned against a certain investment fund, no one listened. The fund promised to double all dollar deposits in a month. The Slovak government was right to warn, because the fund was nothing but a 'Ponzi' scheme. An ever expanding spiral where the promotors were using new depositors funds to pay off old depositors *ad infinitum*, until the inevitable burst of the bubble. Yet no one heeded the warnings. They all thought that this was just the usual "government speak" of apparatchiks railing against the evils of the free market. A few economists and mathematicians stayed away because they were smart enough to draw their own conclusions. But the rest of the Slovaks eagerly invested. In one large town, more than 95 per cent of the population had money in the investment fund at one point. Some sold their real estate and their cars to raise cash to invest. When the fund crashed, many were left destitute.

Chapter 2

THE LAY OF THE LAND

You're alone on a dusty desert road. You've just run out of water. A hot sun is baking relentlessly from above. Your mouth is dry and you don't know how long you can keep it up. The nearest town is a mirage on the horizon, ten miles away.

It will be a long walk, and you may not make it.

In one hand, you have your car keys. Your car is parked right next to you. It is a beauty, it works, it is full of gas and it runs like a dream. Even the airconditioning works.

There is just one problem. The year is 2008 and eco-wackos have taken over this particular stretch of the desert. They don't like technology, they don't like money and they don't like cars. They haven't outlawed cars completely, that would be inconvenient, for they use cars a lot themselves. Without them the world would come to a halt. But for all realistic purposes, cars are banned. You can only drive one if you fill out a form in advance. Gasoline can only be purchased if you state your purpose on a special form. Private ownership of cars has not been made illegal but the local media runs stories of eco-criminals. As a result, most cars are kept at home, hidden in the garage. When people venture out, they do so on foot.

Here's the choice you are facing:

Do you hop in your car and zip into town like a breeze? Or do you start the ten-mile walk on foot, with no water and only a baking sun as your companion?

If you walk, you may not make it. But if you drive, the townspeople may label you a criminal because these days anybody driving a car is said to be a bad guy . . . or so government propaganda has it.

If you think this little tale borders on the absurd, consider what Tom Paine would think of today's regulatory environment were he, by some wonderful time capsule, to arrive at a western financial institution.

Tom Paine would want to start a second American revolution immediately if he ever heard of Currency Translation Reports.

Thomas Jefferson would join him before he could comply with the IRS reporting requirements and file a form 8300.

And Benjamin Franklin would demand his face removed from the US hundred-dollar bill, then lecture on the civil liberties of free men and women to handle their money in every way they see fit, with no outside interference.

To the founding fathers, the fact that you can no longer freely do what you want with your money sounds as outlandish as our 2008 eco-wacko story, where you're forced to leave your car behind or risk being lumped in with bad guys, simply because of public ignorance and government indoctrination.

Yet, today, if you transfer money offshore, you risk being called a criminal. If you don't report your transfers, you will be fined. Repeat offenders go to jail. A time traveller arriving today would think it natural to place his money where it earns the most interest and is subject to the least tax. If that place is in a foreign land, so be it. He wouldn't think twice before transferring his holdings offshore. Upon learning that there are people who are against his doing so, he would simply laugh, shrug them off as lesser-informed beings; idiots even. He would continue doing his thing. After all, the money is his.

Soon, however, our innocent time traveller would be in legal trouble. Just because some law or government decree is silly, an utter waste of time and talent, doesn't mean that it is not enforced. On the contrary. Instead of using logic, government planners take the old socialist trick of appealing to your "emotions" and relying on "feelings". Then, like all true socialists, they denigrate and demonize political opponents.

At the heart of the socialist vision is the notion that a compassionate society can create more humane living conditions for all, through government "planning" and control of the economy. Anybody who dares to disagree is automatically Evil. Just look at how the Democrats in the US regard their political opponents as somehow less pure and less clean at heart. Or look at the name-calling all Social Democrats in western Europe turn to when they run out of logical arguments to throw at their enemies.

Yet Marxism as an ideal continues to flourish on American college campuses, as it does nowhere else in the world. In *Forbes*, the scholar and author Thomas Sowell wrote how even in hard-line communist countries like China and Cuba, Marxism is simply an instrument in a system of totalitarian power and control. "With China, especially, it is clear that Marxism is used instrumentally – and is disregarded where the regime thinks it can allow market activities to generate economic benefits without losing political control. 'Only in America' are there substantial numbers of adherents to Marxism as a creed for its own sake."

Most of the closet socialists of American campuses turn up in government a few years later. Don't be fooled by the fact that they now wear a tie and talk rosily of "working with the market". What they're after is power without earning it, money without working for it.

With America leading in what will surely soon become a One-World government, this trend is dangerous. Closet socialists and Marxists running the United States federal bureaucracy believe that they have some sort of moral obligation to impose cryptic ways of thinking onto the rest of the world. Deep down inside they hate capitalists or anybody with money. To them, money, as long as it is not in the government's coffers, is bad and evil. Just look at some of the laws they have enacted to stop so-called white-collar criminals. Laws that most other countries, so far, have had too much common sense to enact.

Under the new One-World government, the United States bureaucrats are telling everybody else what to do and how to behave. American federal agents have conducted seminars for Polish, Czech and Hungarian public sector employees, demonstrating how to investigate so-called economic crimes. There are also training programs abroad, such as a three-year Justice Department operation to boost the skills of Bolivian prosecutors. Who pays for these far-flung schemes to massage the ego of closet Marxists in the US administration? American taxpayers with hard earned tax dollars that could be better spent at home. Big Brother confiscates your private earnings, then goes on a wild spending binge stretching from Eastern Europe to the jungles of South America. In doing so, your freedom is dissipating. Real freedom is inevitably linked to your wallet. To protect your wallet from bureau-rat attack, you need to bank in silence. You need to bank in a Marxism-free zone, far away from the prying eyes of the rats.

DID MONEY DIE?

No, it merely moved into cyberspace. To better understand the lay of the land, start by looking at how fast the economy has changed in the last couple of decades. Money as we know it is dying. Some say money is dead already, because the money you carry in your pocket is no longer what matters. The money you imagine as "real" because it is imprinted on real paper and used to buy real commodities, bread or butter, scissors or screwdrivers, a measure of comparative values. But the economy in which I hand you my US$10 and you hand me the screwdriver of my choice is no longer where the action is. That economy of butchers, bakers, screwdriver salesmen and candlestick makers is where most of us live most of our time. But it's now exceeded by the screwdriver-economy of just, oh, futures contracts, to which nothing tangible can be attached. Nothing, that is, save spreadsheet numbers.

Exceeded, moreover, by – hang on – a multiplier of 30 to 50. That's the extent to which phantom trading exceeds trades in anything as real as a screwdriver or a plain pair of scissors. So forget screwdrivers, urges author Joel Kurtzman in his book *The Death of Money* (US$21 from Simon & Schuster, ISBN 671-68799-9). Forget screwdrivers and consider how we all exist amid "a network of financial networks." Unless we speculate personally every day, these networks do not touch our daily transactions at all. But they touch us, year by year, as they devalue our cash holdings. That's because the money markets on the screen, according to Kurtzman, have lost all contact with tangible commodities. Figures bounced about in cyberspace and on "virtual reality markets" by speculative fervor can be obsessed with mere seconds. Humans do not have so short an attention span, let alone reaction time. But, yes, trading programs have.

Joel Kurtzman is right in pointing out that the cash economy is a tiny insignificant entity when compared to the amounts floating around the world's data screens. He is wrong, however, when he believes this computer money to be free from the restraints of applied market logic.

Traders, too, use common sense and usually a whole lot of it is built into their trading software. If anything, the market liquidity created by heavy computer trading makes for a more efficient market. The old "invisible hand", that Adam Smith pointed out guided commodities to find their optimum price, is still at work. Now more than ever. When politicians tried to turn logic and common sense upside down in the European commodity market, the market cut them down to size. For a while at first, they succeeded in sacrificing rational thinking for their vain dream of the ERM. But the built-in flaw of maintaining currency parity and even exchange rate between currencies with different inflation rates was bound to fail. Newton proved why when he demonstrated gravity. Any second grade math student could have told Europe's pig-headed politicians the same. Some second grade math students probably did. But since when has Brussels been known to listen?

When planning your future personal financial affairs, try to move as much as possible of your transactions into untraceable cash. Some PTs operate on a cash-only basis. Since government investigators and snooping bureaucrats are generally lazy and rely on their computers, they find it hard to believe that some people even today in the age of the electronic cyberspace economy can manage to work solely with cash. But some can. You may be one of these people already. Or you may be able to plan your affairs so that within the next six months, you become one of these fortunate few.

The pros of operating on a cash-only basis are that you are not watched by the eye in the sky. No computers store your name, nor your financial details. The big plus that no one knows who you are (and no one is looking for you) can, however, in some cases be a negative. You won't have a credit history, for instance, neither a good one nor a bad one. But the headache does not loom too large. Every day in every country the world over, credit histories are being built. In the United States, one underground publisher even sells a do it yourself kit showing you the speedy way to build a credit history, and you can do so in a controlled fashion, letting the computers see only what you want them to see. You hold the reins and you know what enters the circuits.

If you ever get to be the subject of a criminal investigation, be aware that the fact you have been running a cash-only economy looks incriminating in itself. Investigators see mischief in even the most common daily acts. An ambitious and ruthless public prosecutor will then dress up his story even further, making it look like you are a big time mob hitman or the leading drug trafficker of the western world, simply because you prefer cash to a computer-generated paper trail of electronic money. Please do not shrug off this very real threat. A criminal investigation can hit any of us from out of the blue. You do not need to be a criminal. Today, criminals are the ones that go free. The easier victims to nail are hard-working citizens who prefer to be low profile in their daily dealings and don't like to share their salary with a government or a political system with which they cannot sympathize. An unfounded out-of-the-blue criminal case can be opened on even the best of us. Usually the reasons are flimsy. Sometimes all it takes is to get on the wrong side of local government or mildly upset a petty bureaucrat. At other times, it does not even take that. One reader in Spain tells us that he was falsely accused of a VAT-scam by professional informers, who earn large cash rewards under the Spanish *denuncia* system. Other southern European countries operate similar squeal-for-cash programs. As a result, many foreigners today are locked up on groundless fantasy-charges in the jails of Italy, Greece, Portugal and Spain. If you do not speak the language, you will be convicted. Do not count on your court assigned local lawyer to help you.

In today's society, every prudent citizen will want to obtain the maximum possible secrecy, privacy and confidentiality. Our reports may help. We set out to give you the absolute truth about the loss of privacy a citizen of any major country today causes to himself if he blindly believes in everything his government says and stupidly continues to follow the beaten path. One major mistake that almost everybody makes is to concentrate all personal and financial affairs in one country only. By opening a checking account at home and placing your name on the deadly signature card application, you could be signing away half of your money as well as what we believe is your right to financial privacy.

THE NAME GAME

What's in a name? As reported in *The Passport Report* (available from Scope International) a name change, even a temporary name change, is a very real possibility that you should at least consider from time to time. This is not illegal, provided you do it by the book. And even if you don't, you still may not necessarily be breaking the law. Using an assumed name is not in and by itself automatically illegal. It all depends on the circumstances. As a rule of thumb, only if you are doing so with an intent to defraud, can you ever be convicted for having used an assumed name. In a victimless situation, with no one hurt and no one defrauded, using a pen name or a stage name will not lead to anybody pressing charges against you for anything.

There are those who, for personal reasons, will not or cannot participate in the low profile parlor game or "name dropping". You may be one. If you still feel queasy about signing with a pen name, go ahead and shield yourself behind a corporation instead. Corporate shells can be purchased in many countries for a few hundred dollars and upwards. For added secrecy, buy outside any countries where you live or make your money. As long as you just need the "name", you don't necessarily have to buy corporations in tax havens. In fact, doing so could raise a red flag. If your corporation will not be income producing and will only be used to shield your identity, you can safely incorporate anywhere, even in high tax countries, as long as you don't do business there and have no other ties to that particular country. The United States, United Kingdom and Ireland are all players where lawyers and "company mills" sell ready-made shelf companies for just a few hundred dollars, already formed. With an anonymous sounding company name, you don't need your own to do business. Bring the documents with you next time you visit your favorite corporate tax haven, then open an account in the name of your foreign corporation. Just as foreigners (physical persons) can keep bank accounts abroad, so, naturally, can foreign corporations (legal persons). Shielding yourself in any way possible will give you added confidentiality in all of your personal and business affairs.

Start slow. You don't need to do everything all at once. If this is your first venture into the world of foreign banking, and if you have never before banked in silence, it is only natural that you are timid. Some of the procedures may seem a little foreign at first; in fact, that is precisely what they are. Having said that, you won't know how easy it all really is until you go ahead and do it. "It is just like learning to swim", says one leading privacy expert based in a Central American country. "At first you have some deep reservations but once you are in the water and your feet are wet, you are almost home free."

Chapter 3

WHAT ALL SMART MONEY MUST KNOW

THIS YOU ALREADY KNOW: Taxation, especially direct taxation, is used as a means to control each individual. Today, with most governments the world over technically broke, taxation is also necessary to keep Big Brother and his brutal bureaucracy afloat. Taking your money through taxation allows the government to spend and spend, not just on itself but in elaborate politician-managed giveaways.

Those people who truly appreciate their freedom and liberty know that the time has come to cut off the purse strings. To stop paying more taxes to dishonest governments the world over. Many individuals and businesses located in countries with high, unjust and unfair tax rates feel treated like mere milk cows. Law after law has been created by immoral politicians, only so that they can claim they have a legal right to milk you for all you've got. These politicians extract hard earned cash from *you*, the producer, then give this money away to various domestic welfare programs, the foreign aid give-aways, bank loan bail-outs and various bonanzas designed to either line the politicians' own pockets or stuff their private pet projects full of cash.

Today, politics is regarded by those too lazy to work for a living as an easy way out. Politics is simply a profession and politicians speak of their careers as if voters didn't exist. Some of the worst crooks inhabit the US Congress. They have failed their office miserably. Where else can someone write 532 bad checks for over US$800,000 and not go to jail? It seems that most are only interested in the prestige of the office. Getting the boot won't necessarily mean a drop in living standards. Most former politicians take to lobbying, an industry where they find themselves making even more money than when they were in office. Tradeable commodities such as influence peddling and clout have paid for many mansions in and around such cities as Strasbourg, Brussels, Bonn, Geneva, Paris and of course the old standby, Washington, District of Columbia.

THIS YOU MAY KNOW: In theory, if no one knows your true financial position, no one can accurately tax you. With no one knowing the amount of money you earn, no one can effectively extract (through tax and other confiscation techniques and tactics) what legitimately belongs to you. In the real world, the truth is not as simple and clear-cut. Victims of government confiscation and seizure of assets have found that if government wants to, government can take everything you own away from you, even without a trial.

THIS YOU DON'T KNOW: In many cases, the bureaucrats don't even have to prove you did something wrong. One acquaintance, let's call him Victor, once lost a luxury yacht to government seizure. He was using it just a couple of weeks a year. The rest of the time, he turned it over to a charter company, which in turn – to earn commission – advertised and rented it out by the week to anybody willing to pay the rental. The yacht was an income-producing asset when Victor was not using it. All parties were happy with the arrangement. One week, a nice-looking young couple rented the yacht, claiming they were going on their honeymoon. In reality, unknown to both the boat charter company and to Victor, they headed to Mexico and loaded the yacht with marijuana. When they returned, the US Coast Guard searched the yacht, found the dope, then arrested the couple and seized the yacht. Victor only learned about this when government agents visited him and told him to sign over the title to the yacht. "It is not your yacht any more", they brutally informed him. "It has been used in a federal crime, therefore it is now by law the property of the US Government". Victor couldn't believe this. He hadn't known anything, yet he had lost his yacht. Insurance didn't cover him. All of a sudden, he was almost a million dollars poorer, without having done anything wrong or broken the law in any way. A few years later, Victor packed his bags and emigrated. Today, he is living as a PT, not subject to any government's jurisdiction anywhere. Others like him, having had almost similar experiences, are leaving too. It is becoming clearer and clearer that even in the free western world, we are living in almost totalitarian dictatorships where socalled rule of law is a sham designed merely to placate civil rights activists.

IT'S NOT TOO LATE TO TAKE BACK YOUR FREEDOM

Leaving, and taking your money with you, is the way to hit 'em where it hurts! Without you to kick around anymore, government bureaucrats will lose revenue. You, on the other hand, will have regained something much more important than money, your freedom.

The United Nations Declaration of Human Rights tells you that you can leave any given country if you want to. This is all very well and fine. The same declaration forgets to mention whether you are allowed to choose where to go, or whether you are allowed to leave with your money and other assets.

In fact, you can't leave freely. At least not if you are a resident of the inhumane western democracies. The United States of Abuse will keep you on its tax rolls forever, at least as long as you are an American citizen. The age-old international principle that taxation relates to territory is conveniently forgotten by the US, a country where grabbing your money using every available excuse is a lot more important than mere moral principles. Those leaving Germany will still have to pay tax unless they can satisfy the German Fisc by showing that they pay (similar high rates of tax) to some other blood-sucker. Sweden actually has an emigration-tax, holding back all except the most fed-up from leaving. In Denmark, the government produces a list of approved countries each year. Only a fraction of the world's countries are approved. If you defy the bureaucrats and decide to move to one of more than 190 non-approved countries or territories, you will be punished with what in all respects amounts to a fine. You will have to pay four years' of income tax to the Danish *skattevaesen*, the tax department.

Despite this (or maybe because of it) many productive citizens from leading countries all over the world are determined to leave. The best brains and the smartest money makers have already left. As a result, even more governments are now drafting legislation combining some of the draconian principles of the Danish, the Swedish, the German and the US tax laws restraining emigration. They think this will keep their hardest workers from leaving. It may. Few want to leave if they are not allowed to take their wealth along. Instead, they reluctantly stay put. But the price will be too high. Countries as prisons are not worth living in. Who wants to be a millionaire in a gulag?

As the People's States of Europe have passed law after law making it expensive to emigrate with your money, this very same money has simply gone underground. It has disappeared into a netherworld of shady deals, where bureaucrats cannot control it. It has been forced to. "When robbery is done in open daylight by sanction of the law, as it is done today, then any act of honor or restitution has to be hidden underground".

WHY MOST MONEY MOGULS EMIGRATE EVENTUALLY

In today's society, many branches of your government spend the better part of their time each day spying, snooping and prying into the personal and business affairs of its citizenry. Business enterprises are having an especially hard time. Businessmen and entrepreneurs, the new serfs slaving for self-serving bureaucrats find themselves harrassed almost every day, having to put up with an incredible avalanche of paperwork and with unannounced visits from nosey government inspectors. As a result, the best brains among the self employed are moving away. Some of them simply disappear. They refuse to slave any longer for a government they neither accept nor respect. In America, the businessmen and other self employed individuals are today treated as cattle. Yet it was these very same people who made and built America.

WHERE DOES THE TAINTED MONEY GO?

Beauty is in the eye of the beholder, goes the saying. And so, should we add, is taintedness. What you would call tainted money may be lillywhite to the next guy. The first tainted money existed even before banks. The House of Medici lent to finance English war efforts, knowing full well that it would be paid back with the spoils of war – blood money, or the first tainted money.

So the concept of tainted money is all relative. What we call tainted money is money that the tax man has extracted by force. But what he and his cronies call tainted money is money that has, somehow, escaped his tax. Liberated money.

Where does this liberated money (or tainted money) go?

If it is organized in some way, it finds its way into the money markets. For years, so-called private placements have been the main outlet for this money. Today, with computers and more liquid money markets, and a financial scene devoid of borders, the importance of private placements has diminished. But they still exist.

Back in the 1970s when currency controls were the norm rather than the exception in most countries, private placements were handled by highly secretive individuals. They only catered to very large investors and they did not ask any questions. You had to have millions before they would even let you in the door. Once in, you could trust them to do their job. One, Michel Sindona, invested in US banking. This eventually brought him down. Another, Commander Broberg, sat high in his ''House on the Hill'', a fortified building in London. His private placements found their way to at least three western governments. Their taxpayers paid more than ten per cent per annum interest for the use of the funds. This interest, less the Commander's tiny commission, ended up in the pockets of the anonymous owners of the money. The governments never asked any questions. They may have known where the money came from and they may not have cared.

Old-timers such as Sindona and the Commander have been replaced by younger men in fancier offices. But private placements still exist, probably more than ever.

Drive through downtown La Paz, Bolivia these days and you will think you are in a LA. La Paz, Bolivia, is flush with money. We drove through in early 1994 and had a hard time believing what we saw. For a country supposed to be the poorest in South America, the Bolivians sure had a lot of building going on. Everywhere you turned, US-style high rises were sprouting up. Bolivian yuppies complete with cellular phones were directing foreign architects where they wanted the marble to go and how to fit the fountains. After hours, we went cruising with them to top-dollar *nouvelle cuisine* restaurants and chic night spots that made our recent outings in New York look poor by comparison. And here we were in La Paz of all places! La Paz, Bolivia, hell-hole of the Andes. Surrounded by Latin yuppies with slick Ivy League American accents living in an eighties timewarp. They all drove '94-model four wheel drives. Most of these young builders are connected with finance, in some way or other. Some are bankers. Others help invest, which is why they are always out nagging imported architects on the building sites. Whichever way you look at it, there is no escaping the fact that the Bolivia we visited in 1994 was a country overflowing with cash. Where does this cash come from? Have the bowler-hatted Indian women finally decided to come down from their mountains to invest the household surplus in real estate? Or are the many new malls the result of some lucrative trade in highly illegal substances? None of the Bud Fox lookalikes we met in La Paz probably had anything to do with drugs. But ask them, and they will wink. They, too, know where the money is coming from. And for a cut, they don't mind handling it. It pays for their brand-new jeeps, their wristphones, their Jacuzzis, their monoplanes and their dream homes. And it doesn't stink.

If Bolivians are having apartment high rises, shopping malls and all their new hotels financed by laundered drug money, other South American countries are too.

Colombia is a case in point. Most of the leading daily newspapers and weekly magazines there are in favor of legalizing drugs. They see the money drugs bring in and the jobs they create. But they resent the wealth being kept in the hands of criminals. They also resent the violence, the breakdown of law and order and the daily bodycount that is a direct result of prohibition. Even after Pablo Escobar was gunned down in a hail of bullets on a Bogota rooftop, these papers kept running emotional pleas for drug legalization.

Colombian president César Gaviria argues that as long as there is a market for drugs, it will be hard to convince the Colombian people that they shouldn't benefit from this commodity. Colombians have already grown accustomed to the good life. Today, foreign bank accounts are legal. Inside Colombia, there is no longer a black currency market. In Colombian banks you can now keep accounts in US dollars or any currency you choose. It is common today to see Baccarat chandeliers worth hundreds of thousands of dollars, castles in Spain, Swiss chalets and Caribbean hideaways worth many millions of dollars advertised in Colombian magazines and newspapers. Colombia has become a major international market and a showcase for luxury items from furs to automobiles, jewelry to high-tech appliances. The country has even invested in the most sophisticated telecommunications system in Latin America. If all of this is the result of something illegal, everybody seems to think, what won't the future bring if we start legalizing it all. And rid ourselves of the deaths and the violence.

In Peru President Fujimori knows that if drugs are made legal, terrorism cannot survive in his country. He will no longer have to fight the Shining Path or other so-called terrorist organizations. Without income, Marxism will lose its appeal and the Sendoro Luminoso will wither away and die all by itself. Through lesser aides, Fujimori has been advocating drug legalization for almost three years now.

In Asuncíon, Paraguay, the new democratically elected president Juan Carlos Wasmosy, whom I met in March 1993 during his election campaign, states quite openly that legalizing drugs could be the best solution. He would be willing to at least try it, providing other countries would go along. Wasmosy knows that the inhabitants of Asuncíon are sick and tired of the United States DEA ruling their city as if it was some American fief. The DEA headquarters for South America are based in Asuncíon and federal agents treat the locals like monkeys. The locals, thinking human beings with eyes and ears and independent thoughts, naturally resent this. They would like to kick the US federal agents in the butt, and Wasmosy knows it. He also knows that he will be up for re-election in a few years' time.

All over South and Central America, local people as well as their politicians are in favor of at least discussing the legalization of drugs. Sometimes, they will not say it openly. But if you travel in the region, like this author, then get the top brass aside for an off-the-record chat, with no tape recorders running, they are willing to tell you what they feel. One thing is certain, from

Caracas to Buenos Aires, from San José to Santiago, they all resent the high handed US war on drugs. And they all know that this war is a phony, if ever there was one.

WHERE YOU ARE GUARANTEED TO MAKE FIVE TIMES YOUR NORMAL RATE OF INTEREST

Private placements are far from the only outlet for tainted money.

If you have a bit of cash, but not enough for a private placement, take it with you on a plane to Taiwan. In Taiwan, what is called the *parallel economy* may comprise 40 per cent of the whole economy, according to government officials speaking privately. Taiwan has an underground futures market, an off-exchange stock market, a black-market foreign exchange network and an underground banking system – all highly efficient.

The return is government guaranteed because most black-market loans are made against post-dated checks; your money is in effect, government guaranteed. To a point. Like most EU countries Taiwan has adopted the practice of guaranteeing small-amount checks. Regardless of whether there are funds in the account or not, the bank on which the check is issued will redeem it up to a maximum value of NT$ 5000. For larger loans, protect yourself with several NT$ 5000 checks. Or put your trust in the borrower. Before 1987 failure to pay at maturity was a criminal offense punishable by imprisonment. Today, bouncing a check is only a civil offense, as long as intent to defraud cannot be proved.

The black-market lending industry is so well established that Taiwan's Central Bank of China publishes monthly statistics on the prevailing interest rates!

Currently, black market interest rates are around two per cent a month, according to central bank figures. But reports in Taiwan's newspapers, backed by market sources, say that rates can range up to six per cent a month. When we visited, we placed some of our "suitcase cash" on the black market, government guaranteed. After a month, we got it all back, plus a nice three per cent interest. According to the concierge of our hotel, had we been willing to venture into unsecured black market lending, he could have got us six per cent. Have you got your calculator handy? Six per cent a month equals a cumulative annual interest rate of roughly ninety per cent. Few other places worldwide can beat that. And none can offer at the same time a stable government, low inflation, sound money policies and no real exchange rate exposure.

The Taiwan secret for doubling your funds in a year, tax free, is probably our best advice for those who want to venture into the black market. In all other countries, the black market is a shady, unregulated and very risky place where newcomers routinely lose their shirts. In Taiwan, it is highly efficient (more so than the official markets) and so open that everybody knows what's going on. Choose between the underground futures market, the off-exchange stockmarket, the black-market foreign exchange network and the underground banking system. All highly efficient and all run by reputable firms that don't go bust overnight and don't cheat innocent foreigners.

If you want to operate on your own, not dealing through middlemen, you can always open a nightclub in Taiwan. Don't laugh. For one thing, everything remotely western is bound to bring in the crowds. But even if you fail to attract a single soul, fear not, you will still make a bundle. Fact is, nightclub owners in Taiwan make most of their money being illegal bankers. This is done on the club's credit card account. The nightclub simulates a purchase but instead gives the "customer" cash, then collects from the card issuer. Using this system, your money will be banking in what amounts to the safest country in the world. You will be making five times your normal rate of interest. And with a local partner, a Taiwanese or an expat living in Taiwan, you don't even need to stay on full time to look after your funds. This one little secret netted us US$ 90,000 last year alone. When in Tainan, Taiwan, ask American expatriate Kevin Nelson for advice. He is married to a stunning Taiwanese doll, speaks the language fluently, has been living there since the mid-eighties and has lots and lots of connections.

THE UNKNOWN ROUTE TO SECRECY

In most countries they are not allowed to advertise. Governments fear them. Tax departments are scared, too, but powerless. As a result they ban all advertising. What are we talking about? Mutual funds based in other countries (read: based offshore). FOREIGN mutual funds. These funds are not allowed to solicit your business. But here's the loophole. If you can find them, dig up their address all by yourself (with no active effort on their part), they are in turn allowed to take your money. You will not be breaking the law and nor will the mutual funds. This, for many, has proved to be an unknown route to low profile, high yield secrecy.

Buying into a mutual fund outside your own country is a popular alternative to plain vanilla banking. It is also, in most countries, an area lagging behind when it comes to official attention and reporting requirements. Fund managers don't ask where your money comes from. Funds catering to expatriates usually manage to steer clear of all reporting requirements. They are based in Luxembourg, Gibraltar or in the Caribbean, but often sold from London. *The International*, a Financial Times magazine for investors based outside the United Kingdom, carries ads for these funds. Mention WG Hill and order a sample copy from: *The International* (subscriptions department), **Financial Times Magazines, Central House, 27 Park Street, Croydon CR0 1YD, England.** These funds are not allowed to invest in the United States, UK, France and more than ten other countries, but as long as you use a non-UK return address you will get the magazine. Once you know about the funds, they will take your money if you seek them out. This is not illegal. What they cannot do, however, is openly solicit your business.

Don't think these mutual funds are all small. Some are operated by the offshore divisions of the largest US fund management groups. Fidelity, for one, is making more money offshore than on. And offshore, you have a choice just as wide as with domestic funds.

People invest in mutual funds for the same reason they invest in money-market funds. There is strength in numbers. Top investment advice can be hired. With many investors participating, a diversified portfolio can be created and stocks also have liquidity.

THE BOGUS WAR ON DRUGS

Although the United States has the harshest drug-trafficking and money laundering laws and regulations, drug consumption is soaring and major crimes continue to rise. What should this tell lawmakers? More importantly, what does it tell any intelligent individual? One thing is certain, that the laws and regulations do nothing to deter professional, ruthless criminals. Instead they nail the wrong victims, little people who do nothing wrong and who are certainly not crooks. This unknown side of the coin reveals that those caught in the net of reporting requirements, computer database surveillance and other spin-offs of the money laundering war are common folks, usually in import-export or with some other form of self employment. Small independent businesses are the victims. Criminals go free, but under the phony cry of war on drugs, neighborhood firms, mom-and-pop stores, cottage industries, private professionals and small business owners are having their arms twisted to pay for government spending.

There is no dirty money, there are only dirty people. Every thinking person agrees that blaming money for all the world's ills is mystic superstition. After all, money is only a piece of paper or a coin, a commodity to trade with. Yes, there are evil people who do evil things with money. The most evil of them all are those who believe that they have some unearned right to other people's money. These people believe that if you don't hand over your money voluntarily, they can grant themselves, by some higher and totally inexplicable virtue, the right to take your money from you by force, then use it to line their own pockets. If you refuse and hide your money where it cannot be found, you are called evil. A reversal of logic because in reality those who want your money are evil. You are not bad for wanting to simply keep what is yours.

The United States made money laundering illegal in 1986. Since then, thousands of Americans and foreigners have been charged in US Courts under Title 18 of the US Code, the section that deals with money laundering. A few countries have since followed suit.

In 1993, at least 400 banks in the United States were under investigation for money laundering activities. A veil of secrecy shrouds these actions. And no wonder. Reputations are at stake, as are astronomical sums of money. The large number of banks involved is testimony to how difficult it is to define money laundering. After all, what separates a transaction which a banker views as a series of perfectly normal, legal movements, from what an investigator will then turn around and call money laundering? Because proof is elusive and most banks know that the government always wins when it goes to court, they prefer to settle out of court. After all, US courts will indict a ham sandwich (in the famous words of federal prosecutor Sol Wachtler). Big Brother knows full well that most banks settle out of court. Which is the reason for the secrecy in the first place, and the reason for the large number of banks under investigation. US banks routinely pay millions of dollars to the government in restitution (or penance, to be more precise) to the US government as the outcome of money laundering cases. Which leads us to believe that seeking fairness and justice was not the reason for the 1986 clampdown on money laundering. The real reason? Big Brother was short on cash.

The victims of the bogus war on drugs are not swarthy Latin Americans. If you think so, think again. Since the passage of money laundering legislation in the United States in 1986, the US charged over 290 accountants, 151 CPAs and 225 attorneys. And they are only the figures up till 1991. Most were convicted, according to the special internal IRS survey revealing these previously secret numbers. Add to them more than 5000 tax-paying Americans who found themselves audited and later sent to jail by the IRS. Again, this was solely as a result of money laundering, supposed to stop drug barons but in reality squarely aimed at Mr and Mrs Middle America.

How to protect yourself? Lower your profile. Start banking abroad and in silence. After all, you are better off safe than sorry.

THE SILLY PAPER TIGER

Financial freedom fighters often refer to their enemy, the government, as a Silly Paper Tiger. They are right about the Paper Tiger part. Government bureaucrats feed on paper and, increasingly, on computer files. They think that a piece of paper, such as a new decree handed down from an almighty politician, can solve all the world's ills. They also think that everything is well ordered and on computer. If it is not in the computer records, it does not exist. With increased use of computers and cross referencing, governments all over the world think that they are hot shot information overlords. Fact is, by staying off their computers, you obtain a very real freedom. The freedom of invisibility. These Paper Tigers rely so much on their computers that if you are not on file, you don't (they think) exist. Which is probably fine with you!

What about the Silly part? Is that true as well? We are increasingly inclined to believe so. Federal agents have, in a confidential memorandum to local US law enforcement, stated their silly beliefs that big time drug barons and other bad guys have a certain 'look' and that it is simply enough just to look out for a few key tell-tale features, then arrest these individuals. Bonkers. But they believe this! So watch out if you are a single male wearing black attire and driving a car with out-of-state license plates. US agents are hot on your trail. The pokey will be your next stop. This memorandum, a prizewinning example of how stupid some of Big Brother's foot soldiers can be has been making the underground rounds for a few years now, especially among nation-to-nation gun runners and others in the covert arms trade. As a result, one Colombian banker, Eduardo Martinez Romero,in a meeting with two of his money launderers on the island of Aruba, instructed them that when working in the United States " . . . we have to keep the people who make the rounds alert . . . they have already been told to dress properly, not to wear Bermuda shorts, to try to refrain from wearing gold watches, jewels . . . nothing flashy. The idea is to look like business men, well dressed . . . "

WHERE DID ALL THE MONEY GO?

In 1994 when researching this report, we contacted several central bankers to ask if they could account for their cash. The experience was a true epiphany. Everyone we spoke to knew where their money was. Everyone knew who had held the exact percentages of it and why. Everyone thought the question was stupid. The problem was: everyone consisted of only four people. The rest, claiming state secrets or not even bothering with an excuse at all, refused to be made accountable to the public. This made us realize that perhaps not all was as it was supposed to be.

Most countries are able to track down about 80 per cent of their national currencies at any given time. The US Treasury can account for only 18 per cent *at best*. Of course, the Treasury didn't tell us this. In fact, the Treasury refused to speak to us, preferring only to answer questions in writing and through its press relations office. Anthony Rowland, writing in the *Far Eastern Economic Review*, quotes Tomomitsu Oba, a former Japanese financial adviser who addressed the annual meeting of the Asian Bankers Association in Kuala Lumpur with the following words: "This situation leaves a projected financial gap of over US$100 million. This shortfall is traditionally financed by what the International Monetary Fund calls 'errors and omissions'."

Of the errors and omissions, a large part is thought to include money which has gone into hiding. Where have all the missing dollars gone? In many Third World countries, the dollar has supplanted local currencies. This has created a worldwide artificial shortage of US currency. Which is why the Treasury can only account, at best, for 18 per cent. We have come full circle.

Franklin Jurado is a sophisticated financier with homes in Paris and Luxembourg and a degree from Harvard. His master's thesis was on money laundering. Later, he put theory into practice. While he was researching new opportunities in Moscow, like any go-getting modern capitalist, the Luxembourg police charged him with laundering US$36 million through 33 banks.

Money laundering, the act of transforming tainted money so it can be used in other businesses, is a high tech business. When Franklin Jurado was arrested, Big Brother seized his computer networks and learned enough to convict. They also seized his fax with numbers of major banks and other contacts. His advice now to others: "Don't keep any papers in hard copy. Keep everything on the computer. Then make sure your computer is secure so outsiders have no way of entering."

A low profile discipline also known as PC Privacy.

THE GODFATHER OF MONEY LAUNDERING

How do you do, asked the polite little man while softly shaking hands. Meyer Lansky was his name, by many called 'the Godfather of money laundering'. Lansky, a Jew with ties to the old American prohibition-era Mafia, was a master of concealing the source of his, and other people's money. His techniques were used not only to hide his money's origins, but also to legitimize it. He developed the technique of layering account records and of using offshore bank accounts, primarily in the Bahamas and in Switzerland. In 1959, when Fidel Castro took over Cuba, he also took over Meyer Lansky's Riviera Hotel in Havana. Lansky wrote off his loss and promptly moved his operations to Nassau, capital of the Bahamas. "It's better in the Bahamas", he told friends on several occasions. Today, the island chain is using those very words to promote its tourism industry. Witness posters and leaflets extolling how, like Meyer Lansky found out, it's better in the Bahamas.

No one disputes that Meyer Lansky developed, refined and nearly perfected the techniques used even today in the Bahamas and other tax havens to confuse foreign government investigators. He used mainly banks in Switzerland, the Bahamas and Panama. Disguised profits often found their way back to the United States as "clean money", sent, especially, to Miami banks. When Meyer Lansky died he left behind The Lansky Legacy. The stratagem of hiding behind and operating through otherwise legitimate enterprises, thus blending in and avoiding detection. Like Darwin, Meyer Lansky believed that invisibility offered the best protection of all.

Lansky was not prone to strong-arm tactics. His genius was in understanding the power of money. All the methods that Lansky invented are the very same methods employed today by those with something to hide. For more on Meyer Lansky's larcenous genius, read Robert Lacey's biography *Little Man* (published October 1991). Not just in Bahamas, but in other countries, too, the device Lansky set in place in the early sixties has evolved into an awesome machine. Bureaucrats, fearful that they are losing their power of control in the face of free-flowing money, are desperately scrambling to fight back. They may still win the war. That depends on whether or not freedom loving taxpayers fight back to protect what little is left of financial privacy. The enemy is stupid, but it makes the rules and has strength in numbers. The outcome of the game is still undecided.

THE WAR ON FREE-FLOWING MONEY

Money, luckily, flows freely and disregards national boundaries. With the development of computer and communications technology, the old concept of jurisdictions is losing importance. Electronic fund-transfer systems whiz billions of dollars around the globe within seconds. In 1990 and 1991, the United States Congress held hearings on the money laundering problem. Officials and bureaucrats testified to the politicans. As the hearings dragged on, it became embarrassingly clear that these public employees quite simply don't do any work for the money we pay them. They did not have the faintest idea of the extent to which money was being laundered. All their figures were pure guesswork, picked out of the blue and ranging in size from zero dollars to one trillion per year (that's US$1000 billion dollars or about five times the entire GNP of France!). Making themselves look even more stupid, these silly bureaucrats bickered about the basic definition of money laundering. In doing so, they revealed the articifial concept of making money laundering a crime in the first place. We followed the hearings in depth. Anyone with just a little insight soon became overwhelmingly convinced that the whole idea of making money laundering illegal was nothing more than an excuse to use the law as another shake-down racket. What everyone did in the sixties right through to the eighties has now been outlawed. A whole host of perfectly sound and legal business transactions has now been made subject to rules and government decrees. Many have, at the stroke of a pen, been made illegal. If you do business the way your father did, and your grandfather before him, you are now committing a felony. This state of affairs has spread from the United States to most of the other democracies in the world, fuelled by a phoney proganda-created fear of drugs.

Is the fear valid?

It may be. Drugs are bad, as everyone knows or at least is supposed to know, considering all the establishment propaganda. Depending on the type of drug you take, you may become addicted. At the extreme, drugs can turn your life upside down.

Having said that, there is no forgetting that many legal drugs are also bad for you. At the very least, everyone would admit that too many cigarettes, too much alcohol, too many beers or too much coffee is no doubt unhealthy. Some of these drugs kill too. Nicotine is already responsible for far more deaths than all illegal drugs combined. Yet few are talking about banning Marlboros or shutting down the money laundering arm of the Philip Morris cartel.

The plain truth is that drug villains make for a convenient enemy. Such an enemy is needed, especially now that the "evil enemy" and its threat of Soviet-style communism dominating the world is a dead joke. Sixty years ago, Goebbels, Adolf Hitler's genius in charge of propaganda and misinformation, demonstrated to the world the effectiveness of inventing a fictitious enemy. With all hate directed at the Jews, and all ills blamed on their make-believe international conspiracy, he scored public support even for the more unstomachable of Hitler's policies. In novelist George Orwell's *1984*, his science fiction Britain uses the focus on one enemy to keep its inhabitants in line and to make them accept less than savory deprivations. These same techniques are being perfected in the US today. Federal agencies and the US government use establishment media to whip everyone into a frenzy about the drug-menace. When everyone is scared out of his wits the war on drugs is used as an excuse for taking away civil liberties, banning personal freedoms, stealing private money and property, tearing down financial privacy and generally making everyone serfs in their own land. Serfs, that is, to the government and its hordes of do-good bureaucrats who need every last dollar you made to pay for the war that they are clearly losing, if they were ever really seriously fighting it in the first place.

Going behind the headlines and the soundbites, most intelligent followers know by now that the war on drugs is nothing but a hollow, empty excuse. It should really be renamed the "war on citizenry". Its supporting tenets and its philosophy have been around long before such things as Colombia or Bolivia even existed. Its implementation started long before the United States considered drugs its number one problem. That the war on drugs is not even remotely about drugs is a point made by Professor Leonard Peikoff in his study *The Ominous Parallels*, subtitled "The End of the Freedom in America". This book shows just how far down the road

America has gone to establish what is, in all important respects, something closely resembling a totalitarian dictatorship. The ominous parallels that Professor Peikoff refers to are with German Nazism. The deepest roots of German Nazism lie in three philosophic ideas – the worship of unreason, the demand for self-sacrifice, and the elevation of society above the individual. Read these three ideas again. Does any of this sound familiar? It should. The same ideas are now influential in America, says Peikoff. They are shaping politics, economics and cultural trends. As a result, America today is betraying its founding fathers and moving toward the establishment of a Nazi-type dictatorship.

To those brought up on the *Time* magazine version of America as ever the land of the free, this sounds like a kooky shooting off his mouth. But Professor Peikoff is not a fringe loony or some ignorant extremist. He is Ayn Rand's longtime associate and her legal intellectual heir. His book is supported with a host of examples and backed up by in-depth research. A recommended read for those wanting to know who controls public opinion and why. This book is sold in major US bookstores (US$5.95). Or order by mail from the publisher, Mentor, via the **New American Library, PO Box 999, Bergenfield, New Jersey 07621, USA** (Ask for title 0-451-627407 and send check or money order with US$1 enclosed for postage and handling).

And where does our favorite author, the venerable Ayn Rand fit into all of this? Her bestselling underground classic novel *Atlas Shrugged* is a must. Read it to see that government terrorists need not be named Fritz or Jürgen to be abusive. They are just as likely to be called Skipper, Chip or Marty, drive American made vehicles, enjoy Saturday BBQs, take their kids to Disneyworld and flick the remote control to the same TV programs we enjoy. That does not change the fact that when they go to work, they work with the same ruthless cold-heartedness the Gestapo was notorious for. *Atlas Shrugged* is set in the heart of the American dream, and Ayn Rand based all her work on true life examples. *Atlas Shrugged* (Signet, US$6.99) is a shocker. It may change your life. Some made the decision to move their assets abroad after reading Ayn Rand's pages. Others left the country for good, to seek a life in freedom overseas. If nothing else, *Atlas Shrugged* will open your eyes to what goes on in Europe and in the United States once politicians, scheming intellectuals and over-ambitious bureaucrats are given too much of a say in your life. It will also open your eyes to the fact that when the politicians declare War on Drugs, they are in effect declaring War on Your Privacy. They are ignoring the fact that you are not using, buying, selling or abusing the stuff.

JOYCELYN ELDERS'S OFF-THE-CUFF REMARK

She is more red hot and Liberal than her President, and her son is in jail for selling cocaine. Her name is Joycelyn Elders and she is the first black to serve as the United States surgeon-general. Of the pack Bill Clinton appointed, she is probably the one who makes most sense when she opens her mouth. She talks about issues that make sense to every thinking person. Such as a woman's right to control her own life and, most recently, the need to at least *discuss* legalizing drugs.

This is something that Bill "at least I didn't inhale" Clinton can't accept. We feel differently. In *PT 1* we wrote in 1989 that when a solution fails time after time after time, the only intelligent alternative is to try something else.

Prohibition has failed before in America and it is clear to everybody, even those sheltered behind a White House hedge, that the war on drugs is failing now. The cost of prohibition is enormous: violence between drug traffickers; crime caused by addicts having to pay prohibition-inflated prices for their habit; overdoses and poisoning from contaminated illegal drugs; the spread of HIV and other infections through contaminated needles; overcrowded jails. And the worst, the constant erosion of *everybody's* civil rights by those claiming to fight drugs.

In the name of the war on drugs, investigators who have never had the slightest interest in pot whatsoever, gain secret access to your bank accounts, examine your credit card files, review your phone records, study all the checks you've ever written. Drugs used interchangeably with money laundering, as if the two things were the same, is an excuse that can convince anybody to forget about your civil rights. When government agents claim that they are fighting a Holy War in the name of all that's good they can convince even your closest family that you are a bad guy. If not a drug runner, then a money launderer.

This is not fiction. We have court transcripts. We have files and full details of family turning against family, testifying in bogus money laundering cases fabricated by the United States Drug Enforcement Agency. If you don't fancy your spouse turning State's Witness in a dummy-case orchestrated by US human rights violators, you need to:

1) Become a PT; 2) Bank in silence; 3) Pray that someone starts to take Dr Elders seriously.

The legalizing of drugs, since every other effort has failed, is an issue that at least ought to be studied. Champions of legalization argue that if it is done properly governments could take the world's largest untaxed industry out of the hands of criminals and start to exercise workable controls.

What will happen to the over-zealous DEA agents and their busy-body brothers in other countries? Once drugs are legal, they will be forced to look for other employment. Some of them will actually have to start working for a living, for the first time ever. But don't expect your civil liberties to be reinstated all at once. After all, the war on drugs was only meant as an excuse in the first place. No one actually expected it to be taken seriously. The pretense that the government still has the right to snoop on your financial data will be kept up, even when all other walls have fallen. Thus, all the money laundering laws that were ostensibly put in place to combat those ever-so-evil traffickers, will not fail. This is a promise. Tax enforcers simply like these laws too much to want to let them go. For every one *bona fide* drug trafficker the war on drugs money laundering laws netted, they also caught between 100 and 150 others. The actual number depending on the country surveyed. They include people who simply don't know how to fill out triplicate forms, but the majority are tax evaders. When drugs become legal, federal agents do not become human. Nor do they vanish. They will still be there and they will still have their mean streak, every one of them. Having lost their phony war may even make some of them even more nutty upstairs. The DEA may undergo a face-lift, even a name change. Some of its most evil and trigger happy staff may be relocated to other federal positions. The targets may change, but at heart you will still have the same evil government with the same diehard goal: to catch your money. In this quest for money and power, government agents force all banks to help them. The banks who will not play along but take a firm stand and prefer to protect their clients are promptly closed down.

A MONEY LAUNDERING INSTITUTION?

Enough has already been written about the failed BCCI, the Bank of Credit and Commerce International. On 1 July 1991, at 1pm Greenwich time, BCCI was shut down by the Bank of England. By this time, it ran 430 branches in 73 countries. Those interested in a full history of the 19 year old multinational can find plenty of serious and not-so-serious narratives spinning tales of woes and criminal wrongdoing within BCCI. Today, there is no doubt that the BCCI did not observe all laws of all the countries in which it did business. Some commentators have even called the bank a corrupt criminal organization (in the words of New York's District Attorney General Robert M Morgenthau, a politician). Whomever you choose to believe, there is no escaping the fact that BCCI evaded taxes and tried to escape government supervision whenever it could. Whether or not this is necessarily a bad thing is for each individual reader to decide.

Agha Hasan Abedi structured BCCI so as to avoid basing the bank in any major country. It was offshore everywhere. A pure PT type strategy that helped it avoid scrutiny by regulators. "We were an international bank with a worldwide network. And since we were not carrying any specific flag, we were a purely international bank," said the former director of Global Marketing for BCCI, Abdur Sakhia. In BCCI, you had a bank which would go that extra mile for its clients, disregarding silly government regulations or local banking practices. A Pakistani client who fancied a car he saw on a short visit to London said, "I wanted it immediately, so I called BCCI and a man turned up carrying £25,000 in a plastic bag". Now, be honest, who wouldn't want to have a bank as friendly and responsive as that?

Many politicians would. Among BCCI's best promoters, you found Jimmy Carter (US), Carlos Menem (Argentina), Alan García (Peru), Javiér Pérez de Cuéllar (the UN and Peru), Lord Callaghan (UK), Julius Nyerere (Tanzania), Indira Gandhi (India), Willy Brandt (Germany), Mohammad Zia ul-Haq (Pakistan), Ferdinand Marcos (Philippines), Saddam Hussein (Iraq) and Manual Noriega (Panama). Not all of them laundered money through BCCI. But some of them certainly did . . .

HOW POLITICIANS LAUNDER MONEY

In most countries, the biggest crooks are found in the government. Politicians, not mafia bosses, are responsible for more ills in any one country than all bandits put together. No amount of "clean hands" inquiries will ever change that, as the Italian experiences since 1992 have shown. Two years of police investigation and almost daily arrests still didn't deter the incorrigibly corrupt. Politicians of all stripes still regard the notorious *bustarelle* (envelope stuffed with cash) a birth-right.

The envelopes are often invested in local businesses. This is done through others, usually friends or family members. Clever politicians invest in other regions of the country. Usually, this is done with little paperwork. Investigators of corruption, those that are not corrupt themselves, have a hard time finding a papertrail. One tactic, widely used in Campania and Calabria, is to boost the value of an inheritance. There, somebody always seems to be dying. And surprise, when the heirs look into the financial matters of the deceased, they find that they stand to inherit a lot more than everybody expected. Unknown bank accounts turn up. Or a secret safe full of dollars suddenly comes to light. In nine times out of ten, this newly-found loot is invested in a local business. Thus, policians manage to launder their *bustarelle* money.

Even though it cannot be proved, the local community usually has an inkling of what is going on. In a 1994 survey by Pino Arlacchi, one of Italy's top Mafia experts, he asked 800 members of the industrialists' organization Confindustria the question: "Are there companies in your area financed with money of dubious origin?" Almost 62 per cent of the sample said Yes.

William Dean Barrow, or Wig to his friends, used to be Florida state senator. A former president of the local bar society, he had a fondness for "grass". He also felt it natural to help his friends, so when some of them needed proceeds from the sale of marijuana transferred from Florida to Texas, Wig obliged. As a result, this lawyer and big-shot politician was charged with money laundering. He was also charged with structuring deposits so as to avoid filing CTRs, currency transaction reports.

Wig is far from the only US politician caught by his own system's silly laws. However, politicians always receive far more lenient sentences. When a foreign-born American received a 505-year sentence without parole, Robert B Anderson was sentenced to one month in prison, five months house arrest and five years probation. Anderson, former Treasury Secretary, Navy Secretary and Deputy Secretary of Defense in the Eisenhower administration (1957-61), was sentenced for tax evasion and for operating an illegal offshore bank, the Commercial Exchange Bank and Trust in the Caribbean sun-spot of Anguilla. On behalf of drug traffickers, Anderson and his bank laundered large amounts of cash. Later, it folded, losing US$4.4 million of its depositors' money, still unaccounted for. Jim Wright, former Speaker of the House was one of the more influential political chums who wrote to the court on Robert B Anderson's behalf. In 1989, the very same Jim Wright was forced to resign following a House Ethics Committee investigation stemming from charges of ethical misconduct.

A LOOPHOLE

From the Big Sky country of Montana to the polluted horizons of Germany's Ruhr district, privacy minded individuals and businessmen have tried to beat the system by opening checking accounts right at home, using fictitious names, phony social security numbers, etc.

As a general rule, in high tech countries it will no longer work. The computer systems are now too sophisticated to beat. They cross match and you may get caught should you wish to try the same.

Europeans know that in most countries their home banks automatically report all accounts to the government's tax computer at year's end. This automatic filing tells the government the balance of each account as well as the (taxable) interest made during the year. Why the automatic filing and the automatic exchange of data files? Ask the government and it will tell you that this is necessary to make sure everybody pays his proverbial fair share.

Loophole alert! Who are, legally, not supposed to pay their fair share in western European high tax countries? Who are, with full government consent, exempt from paying anything? Foreigners. Plus nationals living outside their home country (expatriates). This loophole not only gives tax freedom to foreigners and expatriates banking in a particular country where the automatic exchange of data with the government tax computer is in place, it also gives, amazingly, a sort of limited bank secrecy.

When a resident national opens an account, he will have to give his national ID card number. In countries where no such card exists, or where it is voluntary, he instead gives his national tax contribution number. In the blueprint drawn up by government planners, theoretically there is no way for a resident national to open a bank account without giving a number that can then later be cross-referenced with the tax computer files (to check that everybody pays his fair share, of course). Now ask yourself, what happens when a customer shows up wanting to open a bank account but doesn't have any number? In some countries (Spain, for instance) he is told to go get himself a tax contribution number, even though he does not pay tax nor is supposed to pay tax. But in most countries, governments and banks alike think this is plain silly. Only tax payers are, after all, supposed to be on the tax roll. He who is obviously and without a shadow of doubt exempt because he is a non-resident foreigner or a national now living abroad will not be coerced onto the tax rolls. It will not be required of him to get a tax contribution number. Instead, he will be allowed to open his account *without any citizens ID number at all.* At year's end, only accounts with tax reference numbers are sent to Big Brother's central tax computer. Exempt accounts are not reported at all. This is all legal and the way the government wants it. There is no point in automatically reporting the account balances and interest earnings of foreigners or expatriated nationals since they are not supposed to pay the slightest tax anyway.

Because no automatic filing or central reporting takes place, you will have some semblance of bank secrecy as long as you yourself can keep the account a secret. Don't let anybody know about it, not even inadvertently. The bank will tell anybody everything if asked. But if no one knows that the account exists, how can anybody find out who or where to ask? Even in the Haunted Houses of high tax nations, the local banks of the world record holders Sweden, Denmark and Norway will keep your name and address out of government computers.

For a bona fide foreigner or expatriate living outside these countries, it shouldn't be too hard. But if you are a national (and a resident) of such a country, while at the same time wanting to keep a foreigner account that won't be reported to your government, you come up against an obstacle. How do you prove something which is not true? How can you make the bank believe that you are an expatriate, not living in icy Sweden but residing in sunny Spain? In fact, you are a Swedish Swede from Sweden, living in Sweden and supposed to only be able to open accounts with your Citizen's ID number and the subsequent automatic government computer cross-reference. The bank will not take your word if you simply claim to live abroad. It will want some sort of proof. But nor will it check with government records if the proof you give them is accepted and a foreigner account will be opened for you on the spot.

The proof you give the bank is your residence permit, the card showing that you have the right to live in the foreign country that issued the permit. The bank will accept your claim to expatriate fame on the spot. But do bank clerks know what a residence permit from another country looks like? Of course they don't. Which is why you, with a little finesse, can get all the so-called residence permits you want.

HOW TO GET RESIDENCE PERMITS TO USE FOR MICKEY MOUSE BANKING IN YOUR HOME COUNTRY

First off, you don't really want to get yourself a residence permit. You can, but then the purpose should be to live in another country (advisable, although PT style is always better) or to start the clock running on a citizenship-cum-passport program (also highly advisable – read *The Passport Report* for further information). If you only want to get a residence permit so you can go back to Sweden (or wherever) and claim to be an expatriate, our advice is: Don't. Obtaining a residence permit is a headache. You need a bunch of papers and you will be running around from government office to government office for weeks. This will take place in a foreign country where the chances are you don't even speak the language. You go to see your embassy. They are not helpful. Then you see lawyers who rip you off and can't do much, because red tape is red tape. When you have finally lined all your papers up, you sit back and wait. For photographs, fingerprinting, Interpol checks, embassy checks, crime certificates, proof of X, Y, Z, employment, education, parentage, all translated into some foreign language and stamped by your embassy there. After an interview, you finally get an OK. Now all you have to do is transfer XX zillion Dinars through the official channels, filling out a currency form and letting the Central Bank rip you off because it exchanges your funds at a ludicrous below-market rate. Having accepted that, you sit back and wait. And wait. Then, three months or even a year later your residence permit arrives. A smart looking card that gives you the right to live in X-land. With the card, you cheerfully enter your bank in Sweden. "Hi there, I am an expatriate, see for yourself. Now, I can open a foreigner account and no one can tax my interest, nor report the balance, since I won't have to give out my citizens' ID number."

Is there an easier way to banking nirvana? You wouldn't be reading these pages if you didn't think so. How would you like to get the easiest documents in the world, obtained simply by filling out one easy form, then snapping your fingers? These documents are called "Fancy Cards That Look Like Residence Permits, Smell Like Residence Permits And Feel Like Residence Permits". They are not quite residence permits, but for all practical purposes, they will pass muster in any Swedish bank. Or any other bank anywhere else requiring you to prove that you live in another country than the one you are actually living in. Introducing: The WG Hill Shortcut to Smartlooking Official Cards.

Go on a holiday. Most charter tour packages will do. Stay a week or two. Choose one of the world class playgrounds, Spain, for instance, or Brazil, or Portugal (read more ideas in *Sex Havens* for some pointers on how to have a good time).

While on holiday, sign up with the locals. Normally a PT makes sure he stays off computers. But now is the time to actually get on one or two, voluntarily. If you are never going to return anyway, what does it matter . . .

In Spain you can get a tax contribution number even though you are not, nor will ever be, a tax payer. The number itself is just your file number in their system, it does not mean you have to pay them anything. What it does mean is that if you ever decide to do so, the Spanish authorities will know who you are and your payment, we should assume, won't go missing, as has happened in the past in almost all Latin countries. Partly a result of poor office keeping and filing procedures and partly the result of corrupt officials. To get your tax number, you have to give a Spanish address. Any address will do, even an *Apartado* (a post office box) that you yourself have rented ten minutes earlier. If you don't want to rent a PO Box, simply give your hotel's address, or make a deal with a lawyer or a mail drop. They advertise in English language papers such as *The Entertainer* on the Spanish Costa del Sol.

In Spain you get the tax contribution number at the *Hacienda*, the Spanish tax office. To prove it later you are issued with a smart looking card bearing a lot of officialese in Spanish, an impressive looking seal, your new number and, as the most important bit to you, your name.

Now you're ready for phase two. Return to Sweden or wherever you live. Enter a bank in a city where you are not known. All bronzed and expatriate-looking, you tell them your true name because they will want to see your passport anyway before opening an account. You then tell them that you are an expatriate Swede now living in Spain, and that you want to open an account. "I still have a few business dealings back here in old S.," you tell the bank, "so I figure it would be convenient for me to keep an account here too. Of course, the account will have to be a foreigner account, since I am an expatriate now. And as we all know, expatriates and foreigners don't pay tax to Sweden, nor do we get our accounts reported automatically every year to the Swedish government tax computer."

The bank will want to know your Spanish address. Use the hotel, your lawyer, the mail drop there or the *Apartado* you opened at the post office. Next, the bank will want to see proof of your expatriate status. So acting like a million dollars, you whiff out your snazzy-looking new Tax Contribution Number ID card from Spain. The bank teller is almost blinded, a more official looking card is seldom seen on those shores.

"Ah yes," you say. "It just so happens that I have here my residence permit. I assume that will do. Of course I am an expatriate," you say.

Any Swedish bank teller will buy your story. We know. We have tried. So have many before us. No Swedish clerk has the faintest idea what a Spanish residence permit is supposed to look like anyway. The document you shove over is a jiffy thing with seals and official signatures, and, most importantly, your name on it. Depending on the country, it may even carry your foreign address "proving" that you are an expatriate.

Most holiday destinations have some version of the Spanish tax contribution number card. The Latin countries are the easiest, as they will sign up all comers, then issue the cards fast and free of charge. You won't get it on the spot, but it will be sent to your address there in a few days or a week. Ask about this when you sign up. In Portugal, you want the *numero contribuente*. In Brazil, you want an NIC-number. Greece, too, has cards, as do Cyprus and Malta plus all the countries of South and Central America.

Chapter 4

THE STING

Did you hear the one about the guy who got 505 years without parole? For a crime which is legal in more than 180 countries in the world?

It sounds like a sick joke. Regretfully, it isn't. It's a true story about Big Brother locking up people for victimless crimes, just because they refuse to pay to a corrupt system they firmly believe has grown too big.

Big Brother's very own computer spying center, FinCEN is constantly spying on the American people. It claims to do so because spying on the American people is necessary to combat drugs and the laundering of drug money. To be fair, some of FinCEN's most publicized successes did involve drug strikes against organized drug-money laundering. In Operation Green Ice, the US government seized US$54 million in cash and assets. In Operation Polar Cap V, FinCEN's computer tracking documented more than US$500 million in financial activity by 47 individuals who have since been indicted on drug trafficking and money laundering charges.

One of the harshest prison terms ever imposed in the United States. Five hundred and five years without parole, owed a great deal to FinCEN for having identified and targeted money laundering activities via computer . . .

The sentences, three in all, came down in August 1991 against Vahe and Nazareth Andonian, Los Angeles jewelers of Armenian descent, and private banker Raoul Vivas, their Argentinean partner.

Did the three murder babies in their sleep? Did they sell nuclear bombs to Saddam? Did they try to assassinate the President? Or did they flush the LA drinking water with poison gas? None of the above. Their crime, selling and buying gold and thus, in the process, helping to launder criminal money. Their old, respectable and in all other respects totally legal jewelry business got infiltrated by undercover agents. As a result, in late December 1990, they were each convicted of 25 felony counts of money laundering and conspiracy, with each count drawing a ridiculous 20 years imprisonment. In August 1991 they were individually sentenced to serve 505 years without parole. Prior to conviction none had a criminal record.

Had they been doing business in Germany they would have got two years. In Britain, perhaps three. France would probably have given them four years in jail, while it is doubtful whether Italy even would have bothered to prosecute at all.

Did they do something wrong? Not according to the penal codes of more than 180 countries worldwide. In by far the majority of all countries, the crime called "conspiracy" does not exist. Nor is money laundering a crime in itself. It all depends on the circumstances. And as circumstances have it, the two jeweller brothers and their friend from Argentina would have got off scot free in almost every country in the world. Their bad luck was that they did business in the most oppressed nation on the globe, human rights abusing USA. Because of this, and nothing else, they will die inside a maximum security prison, innocent victims who were simply born ahead of their time.

THE CASE OF THE DEAD AUTHOR

Your own government will lie to make banks lift their secrecy.

In 1991, a 50 year old author and consultant was giving a lecture in a private London gentleman's club. His words were highly critical of some specific government blunders. The next day he was gone. He turned up in France, having fled England in the middle of the night by boat wearing a wig and a hastily issued passport.

A few months later he was dead, to some. To others he had simply retired. And to the government investigators looking for this freedom fighting hero, he had disappeared from the face of the earth.

His crime was that of a dissident. From his self-imposed exile outside the United States, he had written books highly critical of his government's army of bureaucrats. As an author he dealt with words. But he followed up his words and his true convictions with actions. As a consultant he helped other dissatisfied Americans transfer not just their assets but in many cases even themselves abroad to sunnier climes, to countries where taxes were low or non-existent. Where quality of life was high. Where good food was cheap and abundant. Where the local authorities would readily issue citizenships and legal second passports to all-comers.

As a consultant this author helped many people regain their freedom in an unfree world. He always made sure never to deal with criminals, but there is never a way to 100 per cent safeguard yourself. In 1990 he unwittingly advised a person who later turned out to be a drug dealer. When the crook was arrested, police found the name and the unlisted phone number of the author in his personal address book. Although the author had not been involved in drugs, and although there was no evidence whatsoever to that effect, this was an excuse to start the hunt.

The author had to give up his life's work, flee a newly-purchased penthouse, and stop receiving his mail, since his mail drops readily turned over his correspondence to the US authorities. One foreign service operator even travelled to the United States to assist federal agents in the fraudulent investigation. When the authorities confiscated the author's mail, they found statements from banks and brokerage houses and immediately set out to attach these assets. Their theory is without money a man can't run very far. To learn more about how the author made his money they tried to get Switzerland to lift its bank secrecy. Switzerland wouldn't. At least not until the United States claimed that "we have evidence that this person is the brain behind a large drug running operation". Then Switzerland obliged. Combined assets of close to US$3m were frozen. These funds are still frozen. If the author surrenders to the United States, then manages to prove his innocence, he can get his money back. But wisely he does not trust government to play fair. And prudently, he had other funds hidden elsewhere, stashed away in banks that didn't send any statements out, ever, and thus gave the US no clues when the confiscated mail was read.

Life goes on, but an innocent author lost a fortune because his government lied and falsely tied him to a crime he didn't commit. Our author fears that if he shows up, although he may clear himself of drug involvement as the government can't have evidence of a crime he didn't commit, he *will* be convicted of lesser offenses, even though everyone familiar with the case knows that his real crime consists of simply having written angry words exposing the scam called government.

THE CASE OF THE GOVERNMENT-MADE MONEY LAUNDERER

When there are not enough criminals the government will create them.

Or so it seems, at least to everybody who bothers to examine the long list of sting operations that various US agencies can be held responsible for during the last ten or so years.

José O. López, born, raised and still living in Los Angeles, belonged to a Spanish-speaking minority of Americans. He had a good job and a great future. He had never been involved with crime and he detested criminals. He also felt very strongly about politics. He knew that the world was not black or white, as newsprint would make it out to be. And he knew that more often than not, government was in the wrong. As a loyal citizen he paid more than his fair share in taxes, but he longed for some breathing space and just a tiny little bit of tax free income on the side.

As a supervisor at the Security Pacific National Bank, he worked with the central cash vault. After having seen years of abuse by heavy handed federal investigators, he eventually got fed up. If there was any way he could help the "other side", he would.

So when he received an offer to launder US$364,000 through the cash vault for a five per cent commission, he agreed. The money, however, was clean. It had been given to him by undercover IRS agents. Unaware, López opened bank accounts using fictitious names on behalf of his clients, so they could withdraw their profits at will. Poor López had to plead guilty with four of his bank associates involved as well.

THE CASE OF THE PHONY MOB

Friends are not always what they seem to be.

In 1987 the firm of Brown and Carrera, based in Atlanta, Georgia, was poised to make the big league laundering money. Partner Jimmy Brown appeared to have ties with the New York Sicilian Mafia. He was a fast-talking Irish-American blessed with a grasp of accounting and a shrewd business mind. Partner Alex Carrera appeared to be street smart and confident. He was a Cuban-American who spoke English and Spanish with equal ease. Within a few years, millions in US funds were rolling through into the offices of Brown, Carrera and Company, who promised low profile and privacy to a number of clients who all wanted money transferred safely abroad without a record of the wire transfers and without their own names appearing anywhere.

Whenever the two did business they had a backup. They carried a weapon. And they were wired for sound. Weapon? Wired for sound? Backup? Precisely. Carrera was not called Carrera, his real name was Cesar Diaz, a special agent for the Drug Enforcement Agency. Diaz's partner Jimmy Brown's real name was Johnny Featherly, also a federal agent. By pretending they had underworld connections, the two lured both crooks and legitimate business people into thinking that with Brown & Carrera untaxed money could be whisked out of the country safely and with no one finding out. If you found yourself in Atlanta in the late 1980s, with a divorce case or a greedy ex-wife breathing down your back, you would probably not have thought twice about asking Brown or Carrera to hide a bit of your cash on a sunny island abroad. Be glad you didn't. Had you done so, this money and more would be the property of the United States bureau of extortion and trickery.

The two lured many people into their trap. Foreigners as well as Americans. Along the way, they made friends with freedom-loving bankers all over the world. Some gave them helpful advice and valuable tips to use back home. Many swapped names of contacts in the US, including contacts in US banks. Some of these bank officers were then visited by the undercover agents wearing wire and taping whatever revelations they could get their hands on. In a typical case, Cesar Diaz and a special agent of the IRS, working undercover of course, interviewed a bank officer at the Continental Illinois National Bank located on Madison Avenue in New York. The bank officer taught the undercover agents how to set up an account for wire transfers without arousing the suspicion of her bank's legal department. She rightly believed that the government's intrusion into the financial privacy of American citizens had gone too far. From her post on the inside, she was trying to do her little bit to help the fight for financial freedom. She was acting on her convictions. Merely fighting back and trying to regain long-lost privacy and civil rights. But all the time, without knowing it, she was being recorded by slimy scum.

There are things we would love to be able to write in these pages. But we can't. If we spell out some of the more elaborate How-To instructions in too much detail a lot of useful and helpful schemes will be closed down immediately by government investigators. We try to give as many hints as we feel we safely can. Some things simply cannot be written. Read between the lines. Reading this report over again three or perhaps even four times will help put everything in perspective. Meeting with a privacy consultant for a personal one-on-one discussion could be another solution. Either way you do need to draw your own conclusions as to some of the things we simply cannot spell out. The door is ajar. If we give away all the details and openly advertise the last remaining loopholes, the door will shut.

ADVENTURES IN THE DARK WORLD OF EVIL MONEY

Bruce Perlowin used to enjoy a joint or two on occasion. But he was fed up with having to pay inflated prices to crooks and criminals. "Why don't I skim the profits myself?" he thought. He decided to buy direct from the wholesalers, cutting out the middlemen.

This was in 1975. Ten years later on his way to a yoga course in Detroit, Bruce was arrested on board an airplane. Slight and self-effacing, bespectacled Bruce Perlowin liked yoga. He also liked to do things right and he loathed his colleagues in the drug business. So to avoid capture he retained a research firm in Berkeley, California, commissioning it to determine what mistakes major drug dealers made. And reveal the weak spots of law enforcement tactics. Using the results, he erected a counter-intelligence barrier with state-of-the-art electronics, including antennas, beepers and radar to evade detection. He even built a US$3 million fortress in northern California's Mendocino County, complete with bulletproof walls, an electrified stairway and a sophisticated communications center connecting him to his marijuana businesses in other countries. Bruce Perlowin was helped by lawyers and accountants who laundered money mostly through Panamanian corporations, banks in the Cayman Islands and a trust in Luxembourg. According to an article in the *Chicago Tribune,* he attributed his downfall to " . . . an addiction to greed. I wanted to own everything." Bruce Perlowin was paroled in 1992. Looking for a job he sent around his resumé advertising his organizational skills and his experience in import-export as well as being a manager of "a fleet larger than most countries' navies . . . and a money laundering ring that extended from Las Vegas to banks in the Cayman Islands." This experience helped him land a US$25,000 a year job with California-based Rainforest Products Inc, an importer of nuts from the rainforests of South America. Bruce Perlowin still smokes pot.

Another purveyor of illegal substances whose downfall can be attributed to greed is Thomas Mickens. Only 24 years old when he was arrested in 1990 in New York, Thomas Mickens already owned a fleet of expensive cars including a Rolls Royce, 20 real estate holdings, among them houses, stores and condominiums, and a yacht anchored in a secluded California cove. Today, he is serving 35 years for trafficking, cleaning his money, then evading tax. He laundered his money by burying cash in legitimate investments. Often with the complicity of lawyers, accountants, merchants and real estate agents. Mickens had diamonds, sapphires and emeralds implanted in his teeth. Had his tastes been less ostentatious, the police conceded, he may have gone undetected – mainly because no one bothered to file any Form

8300s, even though all merchants are supposed to do so when they receive more than US$10,000 in cash. The Rolls Royce was purchased for US$165,000 cash with the dealer not filing anything. He justified his action, or rather lack of action, to the IRS by saying, "I am not a cop. My business is to sell cars". Fair enough. We would have told off the IRS the same way, a sort of "You mind your business and I'll mind mine" attitude.

By the end of 1991 a survey revealed almost 60 per cent of US car dealerships failed to comply with IRS requirements to report cash transactions exceeding US$10,000. If this is the number the government will admit to, the true figure is much, much higher.

These dealers are not charged, simply because an all-out effort to "do justice" would make the IRS look ridiculous. And because the hidden weapon of always being able to persecute someone is enough to strike fear into the hearts of those who would otherwise be hard to keep in line. For the benefit of the press and the cameras, the IRS will occasionally put on a road show. In New York, fifteen people representing five Manhattan car dealerships were arrested in just one such show trial, involving Mercedes-Benz, Ford, Nissan, Acura and Mazda. The dealers accepted cash without filing the required IRS Form 8300. All except one were willing to accept pen-names and homemade IDs on papers. You can still do such deals, almost everywhere in the world, as long as you deal directly with the owners and don't discuss anything with a floor salesman.

Whatever your skill, be careful about advertising it. If you have found a good and quiet little money spinner, keep it to yourself. Share it only with PTs you know and trust. Don't ever help criminals and don't ever help people you don't know well, no matter what hard-luck stories they claim to have. Never reveal any of your secrets. Not even to friends. And as the old saying goes, beware of strangers bearing gifts. If someone approaches you and offers you money to help him out, you could be talking to an undercover agent. There is no way of knowing until it is too late, as Nancy So, wife of New York Chinatown jeweller Richard So found out. Approached by an undercover agent she offered to transfer money from New York to Hong Kong in 48 hours without leaving a paper trail. Her fee: a five per cent commission.

THE EARLY WARNING SIGNALS OF GOVERNMENT STINGS

No one wants to be the target of a government sting. How can you avoid one? Don't do anything wrong. Unfortunately, this advice is not much good today when in the eyes of pigheaded bureaucrats, perfectly normal business transactions are all of sudden made criminal. So what is one to do? Be careful.

If there is a strange delay in getting your money followed by vague excuses and your counterparts stalling for time, you may be under investigation.

One case involves Eduardo Martinez Romero, a cattle rancher and financier who made money during the 1980s lending his name to fellow South Americans so they could launder money through Panama's Banco de Occidente. In 1987, some US$5 million of Martinez's money was somehow tied up in North American banking red tape, or so his "laundry" claimed. In reality, his laundry was a sting operation and the people helping him stateside were all US federal agents. The real reason for the hang-up, the DEA was photographing every 10 and 20 dollar bill to keep track of the money's flow through the world's financial network. This painstaking operation took time, since US$5 million in cash is quite a bit of money. But according to one source, although photographing money is not standard procedure it is something that the DEA indulges in quite often.

Beware of people acting like B-grade movie gangsters. They may not be as bad as they look, if you know what I mean. People helping you bank in silence are not bad guys. They are not crooks, but simply professionals doing their job with a loyalty to you, the client, and not to the enemy. They are not big bad crime figures. Yet government agents seem to think so. Which is why when government agents try to impersonate a money launderer or privacy consultant, they usually overdo their act. They play by a gangster-script, whereas in reality, they should be using a Freedom Fighter script. An example: Federal agent Johnny Featherly, pretending to be private banker Jimmy Brown, met a courier in the bar of an Atlanta hotel where the courier handed over US$94,000 for deposit. A true privacy consultant would write a receipt, then cordially thank the courier. Instead, federal agent Featherly pretended he was a high-up hoodlum and improvised as if Hollywood cameras were rolling. He acted outraged. He told the courier that he did not work in bars much less take money stuffed in shoeboxes like some lowlife street peddler. He added that he never touched cash personally. That was the work of underlings. Besides, he fumed with an air of disgust for an amount that was hardly worth the trouble.

If your bank orders you to close down your account, it is time to not only do just that, but to seek cover as well. The legal departments of large banks are terrified of unwittingly assisting what some future government crackpot at some point down the road may or may not determine is a so-called crime. Because several countries have followed the USA lead and have adopted laws whereby the banks are fined for the help, even though they didn't know what was going on. In one federal suit filed in New York, nine banks and three foreign corporations were listed as assisting in the laundering of US$433 million. None of the banks was found guilty of illegal activity, but under the suit the money was the property of the US Government and the banks were instructed to make full restitution. We repeat. None of the banks was found guilty of anything. Yet the US Government told them to pay US$433 million. This request, of course, was made under threat of otherwise using brute force to close down these banks. If an American bank does not comply with a government order, it loses its banking license and thus its right to do business. Foreign banks have to pay, too. Abroad, the US Gestapo cannot take away their licenses because they don't operate in America anyway. So instead of hundreds of millions of dollars, the trend so far has been that foreign banks are "only" asked for a fraction. In one such case on 14 August, 1989, a Panama bank was ordered to pay US$5 million for alleged away. But so far, all have paid. If they don't, the United States has the power to tell correspondent banks in the US to freeze all US-based assets and accounts belonging to that bank *and* to its clients. This will inevitably cost the foreign bank more than what the US asks for in the first place. The US is a master of dirty dealings. Home banks are told to pay hundreds, sometimes millions of dollars to the US government in what in blunt terms would be called pure blackmail. Fines and restitutions are always levied in the US$1 million to US$10 million range when foreign banks are concerned, simply because the United States has less muscle to flex against foreign counterparts. There is evidence to suggest that before the US settles on an amount, it looks into the total value of assets held stateside by the foreign banks and its clients, usually dollar-denominated accounts operated by American correspondent banks. The government then hits on a figure roughly 10 to 20 per cent below that amount.

Beware of anybody asking you to meet them outside your own country. If they want you to travel, make sure that you choose where you go. Many countries conclude stings by napping even foreigners on their own soil. The United States is, as ever, the market leader. But many countries are learning a little too quickly that playing dirty pays.

Whenever you meet somebody, try to meet on your own territory and in a location you know. If this is not possible, and if your partner has chosen the site, ask yourself if he could have wired the site for sound and/or video equipment prior to your meeting. Taking a stroll through the park even at night when cameras only work with hard-to-procure nightscopes is advisable if you are inclined to be paranoid. You can always check for sound, although due to tensions, it is our impression that this job is usually left to an associate. In advance, think about what to do *if* wiring is found. It probably won't be. Wiring these days is mostly for the movies. Tapping equipment is now so advanced that sounds can be picked up at great distances, even through several walls.

Undercover agents prefer to work in pairs. Whenever you can, meet one-on-one.

If you find strange creatures rumbling through your trash at night, that too should serve as a warning signal. So think about what you throw away. Buy a shredder, then use it. Look out for new faces on your office cleaning crew. In Operation Polar Cap, Big Brother placed undercover agent Nellie Magdaloyo in a cleaner's uniform. At the end of her shift, stealthily and with great aplomb, she systematically stole the trash that other workers had gathered and placed it in the service elevator. During several months of these odd findings, the government agents carefully picked through the discarded bits and pieces. They found tags from two bank currency bags, indicating a total of US$480,000 all in 20 dollar bills. They also found account numbers, matching dates of cash deliveries, couriers' numbers and cash invoices made out to Canadian customers. When checked with the Royal Canadian Mounted Police, none of the names matched with the addresses. Either these cash paying customers didn't exist or they themselves had given false information to conceal their identities. Beware of the trash patrol. It is far more efficient and far more widespread than we have been led to believe. Anyone using the Freedom of Information Act to obtain vital documents of tax and other cases involving so-called financial crimes will learn that evidence obtained from office or household trash is presented in court with greater and greater frequency.

Chapter 5

IS IT YOUR MONEY, OR . . . ?

You have never felt better. This calls for celebration. You have just closed the contract of your life. By the stroke of a pen you made yourself £90,000. What a guy! You're really *going* places. You pop open the champagne, pass the expensive bottle around, smile, grin, laugh. You are on top of the world. You have just made some serious money by virtue of your own skills, talents and hard work. But . . .

Stop. Wait. Is it your money, or . . . does someone else own it? Of course it's yours, you reassure yourself. But the doubt still lingers on, nevertheless. Because in the back of your head, you know that out there in the cold hard jungle of the world, the rodents don't agree with you. "Yes," they say. "You made the money. But it is not yours until we have been paid off. What little is left is your money. Yours to keep. Or sort of, because we, the rodents, reserve every right to pass a new law at any time confiscating even more of your money should we feel like it."

According to Big Brother, your money is his. Only when he has been there and grabbed what he wants can you enjoy the remaining crumbs. He has the first call on your money. Worse, he enforces his shake-down racket like a mafia chieftain with threats and use of force. Don't think there is such a thing as paying taxes voluntarily. What happens if you refuse to file? You get assessed and ordered to pay some arbitrary figure before a certain date, or else . . . If you still don't pay, your assets will be seized and sold off to pay what Big Brother has the cheek to claim that you owe him. Owe? What for? You never bought any of his services of your own free will? If a door to door salesman were to come around selling the "services" Big Brother is selling at the price he is charging you would slam the door in his face. If he still wouldn't leave but kept pestering you, you would call the police and have him arrested for vagrancy, trespassing or loitering. Then, if he sent you a bill even though you made it clear you weren't buying, would you pay it? Of course you wouldn't. Yet Big Brother sends you a tax bill every year and readily expects you to pay up, or else . . . If you don't you lose what you own. The tax man helps himself to all your assets. If you are lucky you will be left in the gutter, destitute. If you are unlucky you will be thrown in jail. Today, in several countries, such government-invented victimless crimes as "failure to file" or the prizewinning "tax evasion" are enough to get anybody put behind bars for several years.

The public does not know it and the newspapers keep silent. But there is an underground movement afoot, especially in the United States, promoting the discontinuance of the filing of income tax returns and the paying of income tax. The movement consists of several fragmented organizations, none yet well organized. Most seem to be naïve but they mean well and they honestly believe the income tax to be illegal.

If you can, support these groups anonymously but don't get too involved. Their struggle is brave but it is a losing struggle. You are better off keeping a low profile and banking in silence on your own and abroad. If you become too much of a tax activist you will end up on a mailing list that one day falls into IRS hands. Then you will be audited. This is a danger, especially if you have listened to some of the more nutty anti-tax gurus and followed their advice because it is always tempting to believe in fairytales. At some later date, in the worst case scenario, you could find yourself being dragged to Federal Court and charged with a felony. You may think the solution is to simply not file. If so, wait until you are a resident of a foreign country. Americans still living in the US, and not filing, have found themselves charged with "Wilful Failure to File Income Tax Returns". This rarely happens to expatriates. Even though they are supposed to file, only around a quarter actually do so every year.

When sociologists discuss democracy they talk of the social contract. Listening to them, it sounds as if the social contract was some sort of magic instrument; sometimes a cure-all potion, sometimes a secret super-weapon that we all have to fear and respect.

Truth is, no one has ever seen this social contract.

For all we know, it may not even exist. Nevertheless, just as old priests of the past used to invoke the Fear of God in disbelievers sending them shivering from the inferno, so today the social manipulators cite the Social Contract as your obligation when you tell them to stick their tax bill where the sun don't shine. This social contract, some strange sort of dues that you owe to society (whatever that is) and never can pay off, is the modern-day version of the proverbial mill-stone around your neck. Yet no one has ever seen it. The politicians and the intellectuals have never bothered to write it down. They won't do it. Because they know that if they ever put pen to paper and formulate this social contract into words, *few people, if any, will ever want to sign it.*

The social contract is a one sided scam. In theory, it goes something like this. You were born into our midst. You share our language and our culture. We taught you what you know (in return for your daddy's tax dollars, but that's another story). Because of this shared past, we hold an I-O-U on your future. You have an obligation to pay, whether you like it or not, not according to how much you took out, but according to how much you are able to put in. In the social contract, your debt to society has no limit. And for good measure the social contract is not just about money. It also gives the rest of us the right to tell you what you can and cannot do. To cap it all, you were never asked to sign this contract. By virtue of having been born, you are automatically signatory to this one-sided deal.

So runs the social contract.

It is in the name of this screaming lunatic nonsense that politicians and social engineers claim that they have the right to legislate, even if it takes away freedoms that you regarded as personal and precious. They cite the social contract. The only sane answer is to ask them to prove in court your obligations under said contract. That will expose their scam because the contract simply doesn't exist. And if it does, you surely never signed it.

Properly written a social contract is not a bad idea. In fact, it is probably essential to every truly free society, laying out your rights and obligations and those of your counterpart government; eternal friend and foe. In such a society, victimless crimes would not exist and arbitrary justice would become a thing of the past.

Will the perfect world ever exist? We doubt this. Which is why we try in our own way to create a stress-free, government-free way of living, not change the world for everybody else. A perfect world is a society that ensures the maximum possible liberty for all. Such a society is libertarian, as author and visionary Robert A Heinlein described it in his bestselling "Future History" series of books. In his future world no possible act or mode of conduct is forbidden to anyone as long as that person's action does not damage another. Even an act specifically prohibited by law cannot be held against someone unless the state is able to prove that this particular act harmed a particular individual.

In Robert A Heinlein's world, even if one should wilfully and knowingly damage another, the state does not attempt to sit in moral judgment, nor to punish. As one judge says: "We have not the wisdom to do that, and the chain of injustices that have always followed such moralistic coercion endangers the liberty of all."

Instead, he can choose between treatment or expulsion, having the state withdraw itself from him by going voluntarily into exile. This system of society, based on a pact that each citizen signs of his own free will, is a thousand times more free than the freedom you get by being born into a system and never asked whether you wish to join it on premises that already exist and that everybody else seems to take for granted. In Heinlein's *Coventry*, a fictitious future land lending its name to the title of his novel, the very limited government does not impose itself on its citizens. Instead, it says: If you want to be part of society, you can join us on these following simple terms by signing what we call the Covenant. It is a social contract spelling out your rights and your obligations, both of which are fairly limited. If not, we will leave you to your own devices. Today, at the close of the millenium, few governments take this enlightened stance. Instead, politicians and bureaucrats are busy thinking up new ways to mess with your life and get their hands on your money. You can strike back by refusing to serve them as a sacrificial lamb by hiding your money legally, and from now on banking in silence. Part two of this book is your survival kit. Consider it a toolbox full of ideas. Use the ones that appeal most to you. All will help you achieve tax freedom and freedom from outside interference. You have the *right* to bank in silence.

PART 2
HIDING YOUR MONEY

Chapter 6

HOW INTRUDERS PRY OPEN FOREIGN BANK SECRECY

For all practical purposes you should assume that bank secrecy does not exist. At least you won't be caught unaware. In some foreign countries a semblance of bank secrecy *does* exist. However, *every country in the world* promising bank secrecy has lifted its veils to local or foreign investigators at one time or another. Some do it on a daily basis. If you rely on your foreign bank protecting your account from outside scrutiny you should at the very minimum have some backup plan. In a tax case you may be saved in the last innings because your foreign banks refuse to let others look at your bank records, financial statements, etc. But more often than not foreign banks readily waive bank secrecy. You must understand the following: all banks and tax haven jurisdictions advertise their oh-so-strict bank secrecy when it comes to getting customers and attracting deposits. If they are asked to open the lid they may do so out of courtesy to another country. You, as an individual, do not mean a whole lot to governments. If the foreign country wants to stand up for you and protect your right to bank secrecy by refusing to divulge information to your home country, your home country has ways of getting the information anyway. France has bribed bank employees. Greece was involved in a scheme buying stolen records from Swiss banks. The USA routinely lies to a whole lot of countries. If Switzerland refuses to lift secrecy in a tax case, because tax evasion is not a crime under Swiss law, the United States suddenly discovers "new evidence". Officers then return to the Swiss claiming that the case has escalated. The suspect is not merely a tax evader any longer. No, just last week, by a stroke of luck, federal agents also found evidence that he was dealing in drugs (or was a child molester, a murderer, a stock swindler or any other number of things illegal under Swiss law). Lying is accepted practice and may even get an IRS agent promoted. In a similar vein, the Supreme Court has ruled that evidence obtained illegally by the IRS can be used to convict a taxpayer. This decision will no doubt encourage future covert action and government misconduct against suspected citizens.

How then, does foreign bank secrecy protect you? First of all, this depends on the country. No country is immune from pressure and no country has 100 per cent airtight secrecy.

Banks know that if they fight, eventually they will lose. So they usually cave in to pressure from their own government and even from foreign governments. It wasn't always like this. In the 1980s, several banks still thought that laws actually were worth the paper they were written on. In one landmark case, the Bahamas branch of the Bank of Nova Scotia, a Canadian-owned bank, claimed that it had to follow Bahamian bank secrecy laws. It repeatedly resisted subpoenas by a US federal grand jury investigating the activities of one of the bank's customers. The bank protested, claiming that local bank secrecy laws forbade them from revealing any information, which was true. Did that stop the Americans? It didn't. The US put pressure on the Canadian owners. Eventually, US prosecutors won themselves a court decision that forced the Bank of Nova Scotia to pay US$1.8 million in fines. In the face of such powerflexing all banks would rather betray their clients. Some have gone even further, accepting only smaller clients. Another Canadian-owned bank in the Bahamas, the Canadian Imperial Bank, no longer accepts cash deposits of US$5000. Elsewhere, banks have simply stopped taking cash.

Don't rely on foreign banks to provide effective bank secrecy. Give it to yourself! How? To get such secrecy depends on *you* not giving your game away. This is not merely a matter of keeping your trap shut and not bragging about your offshore account. You'd be amazed at how few people can actually keep themselves from telling others about their brilliance and their financial genius. But you will have to. Don't share it with anybody, not even people you trust. What for? Does your wife need to know? In nine cases out of ten she doesn't. So don't tell her.

Maintaining bank secrecy is not merely a matter of controlling your own big mouth. You need to avoid all contact between your foreign accounts and computer networks, at home or abroad. Your bank may be the kind that does not send out any statements. Fine. But if it sends out statements, have them sent to somewhere else. Many Americans establish mail services in Canada to receive sensitive mail. Mexicans knowing how their government used to confiscate all foreign mail with the word "bank" in the sender's address, always established a mail drop abroad when they opened the account. This is how we have done it for years. Before opening a foreign account we always went to a nearby lawyer, usually in the same country, sometimes even in the same town. After introducing ourselves we explained to him that we were perpetually travelling. Thus without a fixed address. We also told him that we were about to open an account with Bank So-and-So down the street, and that the bank would expect us to give some sort of address. Would it be possible, for a fee, to receive mail care of his law firm? In the course of several decades and a large number of bank accounts, we only had two lawyers turn down our polite request. One was on the verge of retirement and would be closing his office by the end of the year. The other only dealt with established clients, he claimed, and didn't service newcomers. We left and went to one of his colleagues in the same Luxembourg street. A lawyer has been receiving and holding mail for more than five years now, billing us one hour of work per year for his service. If we ever get the urge to see some of the bank statements, we visit the lawyer in person to collect the mail, which is always a good idea if you are in the country anyway. Visit him prior to visiting your bank. Or we call, anonymously and never from home, to have him forward the mail to where we happen to be staying. If you do the same, never have any mail forwarded to your home address. Not even from a lawyer using non bank envelopes. Receive the mail while you are on vacation somewhere else. Or use a mail service under a different name. Our book *PT 2* tells you how. A more complete work on low profile and privacy techniques does not exist in the world today. Grand words, but true.

Let's get back to bank secrecy and how it can be pried open if you are careless. Financial transactions are coming under careful scrutiny. Every time you cash a check, apply for credit, purchase an insurance policy, seek employment or attempt to enter a facility with controlled access, you are asked to provide information regarding your personal money matters. If you are reading this, privacy is of primary importance. Your author believes that it is an inherent right of each person to keep his finances confidential. And not just a right, today sadly, it is a necessity. If you don't you could spend the major part of your life battling lawsuits and negativity. We don't. We travel, enjoy good food, agreeable company, pleasant beaches and all the other great things this little planet has to offer. If you want a healthy stress-free life you need to spend time thinking about bank secrecy.

In today's world privacy is virtually nonexistent. Under modern law, creditors or litigants or private detectives are given the right to find out how much money a person has in the bank. With a little effort a private investigator can uncover your entire affairs and expose you in an embarrassing lawsuit.

The logical solution is to keep silent about all personal and financial affairs. But this is far easier said than done, especially where the questions come from a government that has taken authority over much of your life. Don't keep too silent, either. If you find yourself in a court case and refuse to talk, you could in some countries be held in contempt of court. This in itself carries prison time. In other countries bank secrecy is lifted by yourself, acting under stress. A tax haven has a statute on its books whereby banks are only allowed to divulge information to third parties (foreign governments) if either:

A) a local court orders the bank to do so or

B) the account holder orders the bank to do so.

In both cases this must be done in writing. A phone call or a fax won't suffice.

How then does your government pry open this bank secrecy? Often local courts in small tax havens are easily manipulated. Sometimes they are bribed. Sometimes they are pressured into cooperating. Sometimes they are duped and lied to. Either way, getting a local court to tell your foreign bank to lift bank secrecy is almost never hard. Judges are bureaucrats themselves and prone to side with bureaucrats in other countries. The bank doesn't care one way or the other.

If your own government, for whatever reason, decides that it won't get a local court in the foreign jurisdiction to order your bank to release your records, your government will expect you to authorize the bank to release the records instead. WHAT?! Yes, your government, carrying on a case against you, will expect you, the suspect, to incriminate yourself by ordering your own bank, in writing, to turn over all your records to your enemy. This is how it is done. Your files will be claimed essential to a trial. Until you turn them over you will be held in custody. Custody before trial is common practice even in non-violent cases where the crime is a white collar crime such as alleged tax evasion or insider trading. Few countries have a set time limit on how long you can be held in custody. After a year or two, chances are you will sign a release instructing your foreign bank to breach bank secrecy and open the lid. If you still don't Big Brother has means of messing with your mind. He will put you in solitary confinement until you suffer a nervous breakdown. In western democracies this is the most common method of torture. It is ideal, the authorities believe, for breaking the will of a free spirit. We recently learned of a case in Europe where a harmless family man and, so the government claimed, a white collar criminal, had spent more than a year all alone tucked away in solitary confinement, while waiting for his trial to begin. Locked in while no one knew whether this realtor was even guilty. He had no TV, no human contact, no letters and only access to one book (of the Barbara Cartland variety) per week. Like everybody else, his resistance and will to fight finally broke.

In most tax cases the burden of proof rests upon the tax payer. You have to prove what you are saying, backing every word up with solid paper records. Worse, you often have to disprove what the enemy claims. You may not like it but that's reality for you. It's stark.

To pry upon foreign bank secrecy with your help your own government will open a tax case against you. Remember, in tax cases, you have to prove your innocence, it is under no obligation to prove your guilt. Having opened the case, it will then proceed with some outrageous claim. This is merely the opening gambit. Usually you are hit with something too wild to believe. Why? Because. Multi million dollar tax evasion carries stiff prison terms in a lot of countries. In these initial stages, the enemy sometimes throws insider trading into the case for good measure, just to back you up into a corner. You naturally protest. This is what is expected. This is actually what the authorities want you to do. If they can get you furious so much the better. They want to see you go down fighting like a caged, crazed animal, because venting your anger you protest your innocence. You are not a multi million dollar tax evader, nor are you an insider trader or whatever else they've thrown at you.

A common ploy in more barbaric countries is to charge you publicly with all these crimes using front page headlines in the press and reconstructions on TV, before you even know anything yourself. You won't be given a chance to respond. One Danish friend of ours learned that his government was building a case against him when he saw his face splattered on the front page of that country's largest newspaper. No papers had been filed against him formally. He had a clean criminal record at the time. The lies in the paper, fed to it by misinformed government officials with their own axe to grind, were never corrected. No one had bothered to contact him first for comment. The USA, too, is such a barbaric country. In the United States, a public prosecutor with large political ambitions wrecks human lives without second thought, simply to advance his career. The more wins he can stick in his belt the better he will look in the press. And he will win votes. To you, it means a very real risk. If you don't look out for yourself and all that's yours, you can easily become a stepping stone in some bureaucrat's personal career-plan.

Once you protest your innocence you will be asked to prove it. "Lay open your records for us to examine," the tax man will urge you. "If you don't we have to assume that our information is valid. And that you, Mr Insider Trader, evaded tax to the tune of X million dollars". You are caught between the proverbial rock and a hard place. Your lawyer will tell you to go for the lesser charge and grant access to your foreign financial records. He will tell you to write to your bank abroad giving your consent to go ahead and let third parties from your country examine all your records. Your lawyer may be right. When you are stuck faced with having to fight some pretty tall lies coming from the other side, you don't have much of a choice. Unless you have already prepared for the worst.

PREPARE FOR THE WORST AND SAFEGUARD YOUR MONEY

Perhaps one of the biggest mistakes you can make is believing that bank secrecy is an impenetrable barrier. Even countries that are not partners with the US or with OECD members in an information sharing system will sell you out. Every two or three years the White House seeks to intimidate certain international jurisdictions by reminding them that the US government can, at any time, discontinue financial aid by terminating its Caribbean economic development plan. The Bahamas, the Caymans, Panama and the Antilles have all been threatened with the loss of annual subsidies should they fail to cooperate with federal tax investigations. Some of these small countries have been bullied into signing the MLAT (the Mutual Legal Assistance Treaty). Even more will sign in the future. They are signing away their independence and what little is left of their already tattered bank secrecy. The expanding tentacles of the MLAT allow more power for foreign officials, US agents, for instance, operating in another country to search and seize documents, properties and even funds. This treaty is an attempt for the United States to be able to track the funds of its citizens and confiscate them at will. The countries that have so far signed it are: Anguilla, the Bahamas, Colombia, Italy, Turks & Caicos Islands, Mexico, Montserrat and Switzerland. Just because a country has not yet signed MLAT, and just because it claims to offer you full protection behind bank secrecy laws, does not mean you are safe. Bermuda, one of our personal favorites, has now signed a double taxation treaty with the United States that includes exchange of information. This exchange is a one way street. Bermuda is a tax haven and few Bermudeans, if any, go to the US to hide proceeds from the Bermuda tax man. The Cayman Islands' current law now allows US tax authorities to examine bank records there, ostensibly in an effort to stop drug traffic.

Foreigners, beware too. Just because you are not American doesn't mean the United States is not interested in getting at your cash. Only if you have never had any dealings with the

United States, and have no assets in the country, nor have ever lived there, can you be relatively safe that the IRS will not open a file on you. But what about your own government? If your government is repressive, and most are, or a member of the OECD, which includes almost all developed nations in the world, you do have something to fear. The Interfipol, with the "fi" standing for Finance. Interfipol is the international fianancial police force, a new invention not to catch criminals or swindlers, but to combat tax evasion and to step up information exchange between countries.

Interfipol is only now coming into force. The treaty has been ratified by the USA and most European countries. All has happened in deep secrecy. A fact that the *Wall Street Journal* couldn't quite accept. In an article headed "An OECD Secret Session", the paper wrote: *We asked to cover the (OECD) meeting of the working party on tax avoidance. The answer was no. It's for member states' delegates only; it's not open to the press. The OECD claims the tax convention is not the subject of the meeting but won't state its exact purpose. It won't even promise to release a communiqué at the session's conclusion. This is an agency avoiding public scrutiny because the public wouldn't stand for what it's up to.*

The lesson to be learned is that no one is immune. It can be dangerous to trust completely in any location's secrecy laws, no matter how watertight they appear. Laws change, they are overturned or overthrown. Or they are forgotten in convenient ways. Look at how most countries treat their own Constitutions, for instance. Investors seeking privacy protection should build their own wall of secrecy, not expect some foreign bank to provide secrecy as a ready-made product. Make a habit of only sharing information on a "need to know" basis. Drop false hints so investigators will be led on a wild goose chase, should they ever pursue your cash later on. Every two or three years, move to transfer assets. Make sure you break the paper trail completely. Moving your assets before someone else moves in to seize them can mean the difference between poverty and prosperity in your future.

Too many more than we care to mention have had their assets seized, stolen or placed under a lien in a lot of countries. If you take your nest egg and diversify politically or geographically by going international, you can minimize this risk. Our original life-plan, *PT 1* shows you how.

Certain countries are less stable than others. The less stable the government, the more important it is to move assets internationally. For Joe Blow, already living the sweet life of a PT-expatriate in Monte Carlo, Monaco, financial privacy is an added luxury. For Mustafa Habid, on the wrong side of a political power struggle between ruling clans in Iran, financial secrecy becomes a lot more than a luxury. For him, it can mean the difference between freedom and imprisonment, even death. In these cases, banking *must* be done in silence. And it must be done by you, no one else. Banking in silence is too important to be left to lawyers, accountants or anybody else claiming to be professionals.

Use caution in choosing your bank. Deal with well established foreigners and make sure at the same time that your foreign bank has no branch in your home country. This could put pressure on them. Start slow. No matter what country you bank in, there is always a risk that a bank may go under. In tax havens this rarely happens. Yet the risk is there. If your bank folds you are normally not covered by any depositors' insurance. You lose all.

In one educated and well researched underground text that made the rounds in the early to mid-1980s, spooks and S&L looters learned how to set up banks abroad. As a result the mid-1980s saw quite a few banks that only existed in name and on paper, usually licensed to do business in Anguilla or Montserrat. Some, sold by Beverly Hills based WFI Corporation, brazenly bastardized the real world banks. Using familiar sounding names such as Prudential Bank & Trust or Chase Overseas, they sadly lured unsuspecting depositors into parting with their funds. The early 1980's underground text for S&L looters and CIA freelancers which told them how to establish their own offshore banks was called *A Bankers Trade* and mostly dealt with the Cook Islands. We have a tattered, dog-eared copy of the manuscript, photocopied several times over from other people's old photocopies, from which we quote one of the more innocent sections dealing with loss of tax haven privacy through breach. The section is headed "How To Avoid This Risk" and reads as follows:

1. Do not keep all pertinent international bank information in one place. It is important to develop methods of record keeping which will give you the financial information you need to have in order to operate your bank efficiently and profitably, while at the same time will protect the confidentiality of operations.

2. Deal with resident agents and directors on a "need-to-know" basis. Provide information only relevant or pertinent to effecting a transaction. At the same time, pay all employees or agents to maintain their loyalty.

3. Screen for loyalty persons entrusted with secret or proprietary information. Trust no one who has not been screened.

4. Use paper shredders when possible. This is a good way of eliminating useless or confusing financial records.

5. Constantly test your security

6. Do business in several international banking centers, thus diversifying disclosure risk, and, when appropriate, establish a bearer-share holding corporation to further insulate the identity of the bank's true shareholders.

A Bankers Trade indeed.

A TRUSTED INSIDE CONTACT

In the eighties, when the Central Intelligence Agency was looting money from American Savings & Loans associations to pay for some of their unauthorized freelance operations, we had access to several friendly helpers with their own banks and S&Ls. Some of these bankers didn't have a whole lot of business, so they didn't have a whole lot to do. One trusted inside contact sat in his office all day with nothing to do but pick his nose. His business could be taken care of in 30 minutes, yet he had to stay in the office eight hours a day. The rest of the time, seven and a half hours of boredom, he spent calling S&L owners with the same predicament. They then put together some of the deals that American taxpayers are paying for today.

Our friend would often help out if somebody needed a gold plated bank reference. Even if the client was a "ghost" (a fictitious name) we could count on our trusted inside contact to help us out. Other banks would call him up. "Sure," he would answer them: "I know Robin Hood. Mr Hood is a pillar of our local community here and he has been a customer for years." Helping out with our foreign banking, our trusted inside contact could usually fix matters whenever a mail order offshore bank in the British Isles wanted a banking reference on a new client. Our banker friend would find a piece of stationery, then write them a glowing reference going something like this:

August 28, 198X – Ref: ZZ

Village Bank,
Cash Flow Street
Jersey, Channel Islands (G.B.)

Confidential.

Re: DAVY CROCKETT

We hereby confirm that the above named, DAVY CROCKETT Esq., of 22 Homestreet, Anytown, USA, is a client with our bank, the Anytown Savings & Loan Association, license number XXXXXX.

Mr CROCKETT has been banking with this institution for the past eleven years, to our utmost satisfaction. He is known to us as an honest citizen of impeccable repute and financial integrity. He is highly regarded in the community and among professionals in the State.

We can unconditionally give Mr CROCKETT our best references. Should you have any queries regarding this or other matters, please do not hesitate to contact me personally by telephone, telecopier or mail. I assure you of my personal devotion.

Most sincerely,
Billy J. Banker, Jr.
Managing Director, "Anytown Savings & Loans".

We still have contacts in the international banking community. Depending on the circumstances, some of them can still be counted on to lend a helping hand in times of need. Friends are sometimes willing to go that extra mile for you. This is not a service anybody sells, at least not yet. We cannot advertise it. Study the classifieds in newsletters geared to freethinkers and PTs. One day you may come across an ad from a friendly banker somewhere. For a fee you may then be able to get the bank to testify how Mr Scoopy Doo has banked with them for the past number of years. This can then in turn help Mr Doo get a bank account opened, mail order, on the other side of the globe. Personalized check books (Scoopy Doo, Esq) and credit cards (S Doo) will be sent airmail once the account is opened and funds have been deposited. For plenty of room and to ensure that your applications are accepted, start by depositing £5000 sterling. You can always increase or decrease your balance later.

With a ghost account opened and operated strictly by mail, you can have your alter ego pay bills you don't want to pay yourself. Your alter ego can write out checks you don't want to clear at home. All of this, amazingly, is legal. No one will persecute you for using an assumed name when dealing with an island bank in some Channel in Europe. The bank doesn't even care one way or the other. As long as you don't defraud anyone (especially not the bank!), you can call yourself Mr White, Mr Brown, Mr Yellow or Mr Pink for all they care. Yet in doing so you are buying yourself the most precious luxury available in the international community today. Privacy. And best of all, it does not cost you anything. Whatever name you use, opening a foreign bank account is free. Even checks are free. A high interest checking account, dollar denominated and kept with a UK Channel Islands mail order bank can be opened *gratis*. Once it is opened you can structure your expenses so your paper trail at home only shows what you want it to show. When this happens you will have reached the point where you are effectively banking in silence.

PAPER TRAILING

From the information any government investigator can find in an average personal checking account, he can usually assemble quite a personal dossier. In most cases you will not know that you are being investigated. You will not know that the tax man is examining your private records held at the bank, because the bank always has orders not to blow the whistle. Your bank file of old and cancelled checks can tell more about you than your preacher or your doctor, sometimes even more than your own wife. Each little document tells where you have been, and when. What doctors you see, and when. What church you attend, how much you give. Who you do business with. What you buy. Get the idea?

Be careful about ever writing a personal check. No matter how innocent it may seem at the time you write it. Understand that every check you write on a personal checking account is 1) photographed, 2) microfilmed and 3) retained by your bank, so any government agency, even from another country, can get access at a later date. Your own act of simply writing a check can turn into evidence against you.

Without your permission branches of government can investigate your checking account. Even in countries with so-called bank secrecy, no one ever bothers to ask the account holder for permission in all the many cases where this bank secrecy is lifted. The court's explanation for this is often that the bank's records constitute third party records. In the US, such records are not entitled to Fourth Amendment rights which otherwise are said to give you the protection of your books, records and private papers.

From what the tax man finds in your checking account, he can determine if you are paying your fair share ie all of your required income taxes due. If not, you get audited. Fined. Penalized. Assessed. Attached. And we haven't even mentioned interest and delinquent and negligence assessments.

Even more worrying to privacy buffs, from what the tax man finds when he rumbles through the history of your checking account he and his fellow bureaucrats can determine your entire lifestyle. Think about this. Your habits, your religion, your travels, if you have other women, your income, your home operating expenses and a wide range of other details to make up your profile, a secret privacy intruding government dossier.

Your credit card account is even more revealing. Few people realize how often they use their credit cards. We have credit cards. We never use them. They serve as back up if we should one day find ourselves short of cash somewhere, and that's all. Everywhere we go we pay cash. If you find it hard to pay cash for a particular item (hotels, car hire, air tickets) use a middleman. This is not shady. Travel agencies act openly as middlemen. They broker airline tickets and will let you pay cash. Most will even sell you vouchers for car hire or hotels. And we have never heard of having to show a travel agent any ID when buying these vouchers. Vouchers are purchased with cash. When you arrive at your hotel, you pay with the voucher, same with car hire. This way, in almost all countries, you sidestep the credit card requirement. Elegantly. In some countries, using pre-paid vouchers is the *only* way to escape the otherwise firm demand that a credit card must be using when renting a car. You can usually buy travel agency vouchers even in the same country where you plan to use them. But to save serious money, plan ahead. Buy them abroad, at least a few days or a week before you are to use them.

Vouchers are not filed anywhere except in internal accounting. No reporting requirements exist, nor are governments informed that a cross border transaction has taken place. Anybody examining your checking account or your credit card statements at a later date will be non-plussed. Investigators won't be able to tell where you have been, whom you have been with, when you slept where, whether you rented a car. Banks routinely sell out their customers. Banks may want to tell the government all. But when the banks don't know anything about you, they can't tell anything to anybody. You have succesfully created your very own private version of bank secrecy. Banks are your Number Two enemy. Governments are Number One. Playing along with governments, banks are gaining more and more control over each citizen's daily life. Abuses of credit reports are commonplace. Just pick up any daily newspaper these days and start studying the headlines. No legitimate business reason exists for the banks to collect and store so much information about you. The filming and computerization has reached the point where you, the customer and the victim, need to stop it. How? Refuse to play along. Start banking in silence. If you don't have a bank account in your home country you have no place for your local tax department to go snooping and prying. You will have pulled the automatic computer link and made it a lot harder for the enemy to learn of your personal and private affairs. If you ever get in serious hot water the locals will have trouble confiscating your assets, your property, your checking/savings accounts etc over any disputed amounts they claim you owe. They may still harass you, but at least you can walk away from it all still smiling and thinking "He who laughs last . . . "

GIVE THEM SOMETHING WRONG TO GO ON

"Hell, this is even better than sex," roared an old friend we will call Warren Trumpet. We had just spent three days with him in Rimini, putting the final touches to a home-made D&M program. A deception and misinformation program. Warren had been through a nasty divorce case in his home country. On top of it came a tax audit. His wife, to get him where she knew it hurt, had given the local tax man some of Warren's very personal documents. Warren had decided it was time to fight back. He remembered Winston Churchill's golden words that "in times of war, it is necessary to shield the truth behind a veil of lies". As a result Warren decided to shield his own truth. In his personal war, the strategy was, Winston Churchill style, to manufacture a veil of lies. Once he had done so and put his lies in place he felt relieved. It was, to quote him verbatim, better than sex.

D&M, deception and misinformation, we feel is wholly justified if it's for a good cause and if you only deceive your enemies. Who lies most? Big Brother. All you are doing is striking back. Go ahead. Let him taste some of his own medicine. Think of who your enemy could be. You usually won't know that until it's too late. Government can be counted on to turn nasty. But even those you confide in today can become your enemies tomorrow. Your business partner can turn out to be not all you thought he was. Your caring loving wife may be sleeping with her tennis coach. Best friends could go wacky in the head. Anyone, anywhere, can blackmail you. Which is why you need to have sown the seeds of deception and misinformation. After all, if someone blackmails you with a piece of false information that you yourself created, what does it matter?

Now would be the time to tell you how to use foreign country addresses and low profile to orchestrate an effective campaign of D&M. But we have already written extensively on this in hundreds of pages of *PT 2,* subtitled "The Practice". If you haven't already done so, read this tome and learn its many secrets. Revealing crucial inside privacy information, this book was detailed with the help of a prominent intelligence operative. Before you consider doing any low profile business there are vital items that you need to fully understand for your own protection. You must read this book.

Once you have decided on a D&M program, drop false hints from time to time making sure they lead nowhere, but that they are at the same time consistent. True information should be shared only on a need-to-know basis. But those you share it with will think it strange if you don't fill them in on the full picture. Most people feel they have a right to know everything about you. This is why we never tell people more than they *need to know* to carry out their tasks or fit any other purpose in our lives. Sharing information only on a need-to-know basis applies to friends as well as enemies, governments, girlfriends, bankers, helpers, customers, clients, in short – everybody. In this way we protect our privacy. But unfortunately not everybody else sees it this way. They feel that you owe them more information. They will resent it if you don't let them view a full panorama of your current life. Maybe they feel safe if they "have something on you", knowing where you bank or where you live, how you live, whom you live with. We don't know. We just know that out there, very few people you will ever meet and deal with are rational enough to understand that they just cannot ask a lot of questions. And that whether or not you want to open up is your decision. Few people are intelligent enough to appreciate your respect to privacy. They are usually the ones who understand that respect is a two way street. Just like common courtesy and decency, it is mutual. And if they leave you alone you will leave them alone. Those who show you this respect can be taken into your confidence, gradually. You can build up trust with them and they will have earned it. As for the rest, that vast majority of the world, they are stupid, unthinking, uncaring blabbermouths. These pea-brains think that by some strange virtue they have a right to know and that you are obliged to tell them everything they would like to know, but strictly speaking don't need to know. Accommodate them. Feed them your D&M. It won't harm you and it will make them happy. Like us, you may have a hard time lying at first. But you have to. If you prefer to keep quiet and not say anything, the pea-brains will draw their own conclusions. And because the vast majority have a fixation with the dramatic, you can bet your hat that they will think of something unpleasant.

If you travel a lot, tell people where you go and why (but lie). If you don't say anything, they will think that you are a strange and mysterious character. From there, their next thought is, yeah, he's travelling a lot, ain't he . . . So he must be running drugs. Now you see why, even if you have difficulty telling a lie you are forced to pass out some fabrications from time to time. We once drove five different luxury cars in the span of four months. This raised some eyebrows. We had a perfectly legitimate reason for this, however. But we didn't feel like telling. The truth was quite an elaborate story and it involved a financier whom we were helping out while he was being written up in the newspapers. In our eyes, we saw no need for the whole world to know that we were helping this financier. There was nothing illegal about it, yet we also felt that none of the neighbors or our business contacts had any pressing need to know. So we didn't share this information. After a while people started drawing their own conclusions. Totally wrong and biased conclusions, of course. We learned about this through the grapevine. Rumors always filter back to you. If someone is talking about you behind your back, you usually get an inkling sooner or later. The rumors we had were scary. Because no one could come up with a better explanation, somehow somebody had gotten it into his head that a new luxury car every month was a result of our ripping off dealerships. We would buy a car on super-finance with no money down, the rumor had it. Then we wouldn't pay anything. Later, the car would get repossessed, but that didn't worry us, the rumor continued. Because by that time, according to the rumor, we already had another luxury car lined up the same way, bought under a finance plan with no downpayment. Soon after, we learned to protect both our good name and reputation and our privacy. How? By planting harmless deception and misinformation. The key to success is don't overdo it, don't defraud. And never misrepresent anything that matters. Outright lies should be avoided whenever possible. You are far better off just giving hints in the wrong direction.

HOW TO SET UP A FAKE PAPER TRAIL FOR THE ENEMY TO FOLLOW

Bobby Beaufort is a commodities broker. Sometimes he trades a little on his own account. He also has a ghost account he uses for trades that he does not want his company or his government to know about. Some of his most profitable buys and sells have been carried out through his ghost trading account.

Those gains he does not report to the tax man are kept at home in cash. Bobby prefers cash. Whenever he wants to buy something he can always pay in cash, and sometimes he can negotiate a lower price as a result, especially when buying big ticket items from private parties who, like Bobby, are most happy with cash. Last year when Bobby had some remodeling done inside his house, he paid most of the contractor's fee in cash. The contractor was happy because he was moonlighting in the "informal" or black economy (averaging 10 per cent in the US and Britain, 15 per cent in countries with more inflexible labor laws, such as Germany, and 25 to 30 per cent to locals who have a culture of happily cheating the tax man, Spain or Greece, for example).

Bobby kept his cash in his second floor bedroom, beneath a floor plank that had fake nails in it. No one else except his wife and a pal from the office had ever seen this hiding place.

Then late last year, right before Christmas, Bobby walked in on the two of them. He found his wife in bed bonking his best friend. Thus ended two partnerships at once. His cheating wife moved in with Bobby's friend and to get his mind off it Bobby decided he needed a vacation. He booked a trip to the Dominican Republic and right after Christmas he flew off for a week's holiday. When he returned his house had been burglarized. Worse, his cash was gone. The burglars had found his secret hiding place in the floor and had taken off with US$2300 in cash.

Bobby knew of course who had staged the burglary. His wife and ex-pal had thought they were smart, believing that Bobby never would dare to call the police to report the theft of illegal cash that for all official purposes didn't even exist.

Did Bobby call the police? Did he even get mad? No. He just laughed out loud. Because unknown to the whole world, except himself, his secret hiding place was a decoy. If the "burglars" had removed yet another plank they would have found another shallow opening deeper down. Here, more than US$30,000 rested, known only to Bobby. He had created a secret hiding place within another secret hiding place. His wife had known that Bobby always dug cash out of that little hole in the floor. She didn't know how much. And she didn't know that under the hole another stash was hidden.

Like Bobby Beaufort had his decoy-hideaway you should consider having a decoy papertrail. Then, when people demand that you turn your records over you can do so, knowing full well that what your records do not reveal is the existence of a secret set of records, known only to you.

Your enemy, an angry ex-wife or a vicious tax baron, can make your life hell once they have your personal financial records. But this depends on you. Fortunately, to a point, you are in control of what those records reveal.

Most of us have several credit cards. Most of us also have a PT friend or two, kindred spirits living either at home or abroad. Give one of your low-balance credit cards to a friend. Then give him your PIN code. You are still signatory, but with the PIN code your trusted friend can use your credit card *as if he were you*, at least in ATMs and other cash machines. In many countries he can even go shopping with your card, since he won't need to sign. Shops linked electronically to their own country's VISA or MasterCard center will let you purchase on "your" card just by punching in the correct four digit PIN. Most widespread in France, this practice is now spreading all over the developed world.

You are going to Gibraltar to visit your money. You don't want anybody at home to know, so you are giving them a bit of harmless D&M, telling them you're heading for the sunny French riviera. From a phone that can't be traced, you call up your friend in France and tell him that now is the time to use your credit card. The next day he withdraws Ff 1500 in cash from an automatic teller, simply by punching in your Personal Identification Number. He may even use your card to make purchases in a few stores. If he knows about low profile he will make sure not to withdraw cash where he is at the same time being videoed by a surveillance camera which is why in New York this little doddle won't work. There, by law, *all* ATMs are covered by an eye in the sky and *all* bank customers using their plastic are taped for all eternity. Worldwide, however, fewer than ten per cent of all ATMs are accompanied by surveillance cameras videotaping their use, as of 1994. A British study of built-in cameras and recorders rejected them on grounds of costs, which is why few banks are using them consistently with all ATMs.

A fake paper trail prepared by your friends and helpers at home or abroad, can be yours with very little work if you plan it in advance. When you next see them in person, friends will reimburse you the money they withdraw from ATMs on your behalf. Or you can let them keep it if you have no other way of returning the favors. Need invoices and receipts from places you have never been to? Ask your friends to gather them up. They will, especially since they don't need them to prove deductions they won't be taking anyway; As PTs, they don't file income tax returns. If your friends are short on certain rare papers, put an ad in privacy related newsletters such as the *Mouse Monitor*. Buyers of rare documents usually need to specify what they are looking for, such as *Sought: April 1994 Frankfurt memorabilia, especially restaurants*. Just like credit cards you can have several checking accounts, perhaps all of them secret yet (in your mind) some of them more public than others. They may be harder to use, or easier. It all depends on the circumstances your friends will be passing out your checks. Sometimes stores won't accept without ID. In either case sign in advance. If you leave blank but signed checks, also instruct your friends to use a typewriter when filling out the remainder of the information. We can't have someone else's handwriting go on your check. When it ends up among all other canceled checks in your bank records, that would stand out like a red flag. Whatever you do, compartmentalize your life. Put watertight walls and other barriers between each area of your life. In *PT 2* we tell you why you need not just one mail drop. The same principle holds true when it comes to checking accounts and credit cards.

No one likes to keep records but you may have to. If so, go ahead and purchase a three hole notebook, four hole for Europeans, to record those particular and important purchases and expenses that you may need to recall later for personal reasons, for business reasons or for tax reasons. Why a three hole notebook? A loose leaf notebook is simple and easy to maintain and more importantly if you make a mistake or put something in the records, then later decide to change it or modify it for whatever reason, you can easily do it. Your mistakes are correctable. Nobody will ever know about any changes, modifications, deletions or removals. Only you and your conscience, which is the way it should be. If you ever were to use the notebook in a government audit to prove a particular transaction, you could remove certain pages that you feel have no bearing on the case and that others shouldn't read. You can always place them back again if and when you decide.

Sometimes, as all PTs instinctively know, it is better to seek refuge in a safe harbor than stand up to lies and slander if some government somewhere is bent on wrecking your life. If ever you need to disappear for a shorter or longer period of time, trusted friends with credit cards and blank but already signed checks can throw the hounds off your trail for just enough time to give you a breather. Your persecution may come unexpectedly and out of the blue. If you don't already have friends in place who can use your PIN code with credit cards and checks with your signature to put out smoke and a fake paper trail, plan B is the Emergency Solution. It's fast and simple. Go downtown in any large city. Buy a subway ticket. Dump your credit cards in the subway, one card per train. Checks too. Sign a few of them for good measure. When you are ready to take off, drive your car into a bad neighborhood and leave it there with keys in the ignition. It will never be found. Your tax man and his pack of hounds or your ex-wife and her bloodthirsty private investigators will have a lot of fun chasing you via your credit card use and the bad checks you seem to be passing out everywhere . . .

Chapter 7

A HOW-TO GUIDE TO BEAT THE BUREAUCRATS

Assuming you are ready to tell the bureaucrats to mind their own business, this chapter will show you how. It is a four lesson course in lowering your banking profile. But first, a few basic pointers from various privacy experts:

1. For utmost privacy never cash a check where you are personally known. And, if you can avoid it (for instance by endorsing the check to someone else or by going to a private check cashing service), never cash a check in a bank. Never purchase a money order or a certified check and put your name on it. Don't leave audit trails.
2. Don't keep a bank account where you live. You probably alread, have one. Close it down so you won't be tempted to use it later, and open one in another country. It is possible to do without a local bank or checking account. You don't think so? Never say it's impossible not to use a checking account until you have tried it. Many people are doing it and finding it easy. Along with it comes your essential right to privacy.
3. If you don't like to carry around a lot of cash, don't worry. Buy what are fancily known as monetary instruments: put your cash in money orders, certified checks and/or travelers checks, payable to either yourself or a third party, then cash them when you need cash. Simple.

If you don't mind carrying a lot of cash around, fine. But be careful that this is not interpreted the wrong way by anxious, gung-ho customs agents. They may think you are a crook, when all you are doing is simply taking advantage of your right as a free citizen to choose whether you want to carry cash or carry credit.

Here is one way to handle large quantities of small bills. To avoid detection at airports, five, ten and twenty-dollar bills should be packed in carry-on luggage. Americans in the know then fly to Las Vegas where, for a four per cent commission, the money is changed into 100 dollar bills. Now, travel is easier and you are ready to go abroad. One plan looks like this. From Las Vegas the money is flown physically to Luxembourg, deposited in a bank account belonging to a foreign trust or a foreign company, then wired to Panamanian corporations or banks in the Cayman Islands, and put into legitimate non-taxable offshore bank accounts. You can borrow against these accounts for investments at home.

In an effort to beef up the war against taxpayers, most European countries now have schemes in place whereby the banks are required to report suspicious cash transactions.

To placate the United States and their scandal-driven popular newspapers, some Third World countries known the world over as money laundering centers have introduced controls on cash. One such country is Panama. It has laws requiring banks to identify transactions of more than US$10,000 if they look suspicious. But in Panama money laundering is said to be a national habit. Ebrahim Asvat, a former Panamanian police chief who likes money very much, cheerfully admits: "We have a culture here that believes money doesn't have any particular smell attached to it." In 1992, about US$180 million in anonymous US postal money orders cleared Panamanian banks last year. In 1993 the amount jumped to more than US$225 million. Whenever you are on the receiving end of a check or money order, consider clearing it abroad. All US checks will eventually be cleared via New York even if deposited in a foreign bank. So clearing it abroad could back-fire. This depends on your personal situation and how you use your foreign accounts. Using local check cashing services could be faster and just as low profile. In either case the checks you receive are being kept out of your own local bank account. If anybody at a later date inspects the goings-on of your local bank account, there will be no record of any checks having been cleared through it. This would apply to one or 100 or all of your checks being run through the check cashing system. However, it is recommended that you play the game correctly by only skimming and not being reckless and totally omitting all income. As the saying from the stock market goes, "Bears and Bulls make money. Pigs get slaughtered."

Of course there are those who do play the game hard and fast. They run all of their income through various check cashing services. They believe that all which is not traceable is not auditable. It is a very simple reasoning, but it works. There is no tax to pay because there is nothing to trace and nothing to audit, so they keep all the money which is theirs in the first place. Fortunately most of them succeed. The very few exceptions are mainly due to carelessness and not following the unwritten rules of the game. Once your income is cashed you need to look at your expenditures. Whenever possible try to pay in cash. Most private parties you will be dealing with will only be more than happy to take cash. Car hire firms and hotels demand credit cards occasionally. This is only a security precaution. Upon settling the bill simply pay in cash, then tear up the credit card receipt. All car rentals and hotels will let you.

Even when you pay cash you will sometimes need proof of payment. One popular myth is that a canceled personal check is the only acceptable proof. This is far from true. A copy of a money order will do nicely.

When cash is not possible, for instance, when you buy via mail order, use a money order. Americans can buy money orders for cash from the local 7-11 store or any other location that provides private money order services. You can use a US Money Order too. If you do you will be working with a government agency, but this is not as damning as it sounds, especially not if you don't put your name or any valid ID information on the money order. It is not required. Outside the US, money orders can be bought wherever travelers checks are sold. Post offices also sell money orders. The worldwide offices of American Express are yet another source. They sell US dollar money orders. Finally, a travelers check or a certified bank check is usually satisfactory, but again give no true ID as the remitter. A copy of the money order or certified check can serve as your receipt and proof of payment. This will allow you to maintain your privacy.

Do you have friends abroad? Think hard about using their accounts for receiving and dispursing funds. A friend in another country can cash your checks. He can also, directly from offshore, pay your charge accounts, credit card instalments and other items that you don't want to pay at home. If you don't have friends abroad, make some. Penpaling is one way of doing so. Ghosting is another.

If you are ready to beat the bureaucrats, start taking notes. Pick up some of the pointers the professionals are using. Copy the money launderers when they pull off a success. Imitate them step by step, playing a grown up game of "Simon Says". Not all of them are smart. As for the ones who fail, learn from their mistakes. Find out what they did wrong, then head in the opposite direction.

LESSON 1:

Many money launderers are hopeless romantics. They like intrigue and exotic places. They put their money where serious businesses would never dream of depositing funds in Nauru, for example. Since you don't want anyone to mistake you for a money launderer, stay away from colorful locales. Go where only blue-chip institutions would go. If you frequent Vanuatu, Nauru and other way-out places with too much enthusiasm, you could be mistaken for being a crook. Crooks are attracted to the odd-ball and the weird since they are hopeless romantics, often living in their own world of cartoon-style adventures. Behind his suit and tie, Franklin Jurado, now a resident of the pokey with Luxembourg footing the bill, hid a reckless streak. He was in many ways the prototype money launderer. Conservative on the outside but wild at heart. His lust for adventures drove him to place funds in banks so far off the beaten path that investigators felt themselves compelled to take a second look. Some of Jurado's moves simply didn't make commercial sense. IBM's finance department would never have made them.

So, lesson number one: Don't stand out.

Don't fall in with the bad crowd. Don't run with the money launderers copying their techniques blindly, because they may be wrong. We are telling you that the criminals are the ones most likely to find loopholes and get around new regulations. As a result you could do worse than follow in the foot steps when hiding your own non-criminal money. This is true. But they are not super human, so don't believe in them blindly. For best results use your own good common sense. If you want to bank in silence succesfully you don't want to stand out like a sore thumb. You want to blend in with the conservative, cautious "blue chip" business-crowd. Whenever you choose where to bank, always ask yourself: "Is this something IBM would do?" or "Would General Motors open an account here?" Islands like Guernsey and Jersey pass this test. Other islands like Nauru and Tuvalu, do not.

OUR BEST TIP: *Always work with cash when you can, but try to have a valid explanation as to WHY you are working with cash. Establishing a part-time cash-based business could be one solution. This offers a ready made explanation. You do need to have a story handy for all eventualities. As Eduardo Martinez Romero, financier, says: "It may not be good business to be moving money around in the street, but it's not illegal. If they caught me I'd say I'm sorry, I'd pay the tax, walk away and that's good. That's my cost of protecting that money and there's a lot of good ways to do it". Another business had the perfect front for working with cash and was only discovered for what it really was when a blabbermouth bragged to his girlfriend on the telephone. Her telephone was tapped on a totally unrelated matter. Later, when Big Brother's henchmen listened to the tapes, they learned that a famous Beverly Hills art gallery was fronting for money launderers. In March 1991 on a sun-drenched street in the heart of Beverly Hills, the government moved in and confiscated all assets of the art gallery. The scheme used by the owners had been simple. They would launder proceeds from other trades by overvaluing the art in the gallery. For example, a painting for sale with a US$60,000 sticker price tag was later appraised by independent art experts to be worth only in the region of US$800. Laundered money made up the difference.*

LESSON 2:

In a confidential 1994 memo prepared by the USA Drug Enforcement Administration, then sent out to other countries through the DEA-liaison of each American embassy, the USA tried to teach other countries how to spot a money launderer. At the heart of the memo was a list of countries used by money launderers to wash supposedly dirty funds.

Rumor has it that some countries took offense. Pakistan was not happy finding itself on the US list of money laundering centers. If it was a consolation the United States included four of its own cities on the list for good measure. To wit, all four are bastions of money laundering, Los Angeles, Houston, Miami and New York. What follows below is the list reprinted in full. Banks based in the money centers of the countries of the list all have experience with money laundering. Some are under surveillance. If you want to bank in silence you are better off going where the banks have had little experience with money laundering and can be counted on to be far less cautious.

MONEY LAUNDERING CENTERS WORLDWIDE

THE AMERICAS:
Canada
United States (in particular LA, Houston, Miami, New York)
Bahamas
Panama
Colombia
Ecuador
Venezuela
Uruguay

EUROPE:
Austria
Britain
Germany
Hungary
Liechtenstein
Luxembourg
the Netherlands
Russia and the Baltics
Switzerland

ASIA:
Pakistan
Thailand
Hong Kong
Nauru
Vanuatu

ELSEWHERE:
Nigeria

In the course of doing perfectly legal above the board business, every normal law-abiding international businessman would have to bank in some of the countries on the US money laundering list. That does not make him a money launderer by default. Just because Britain, for example, is on the list does not make every Briton banking in his own country a money launderer.

What the US list does do is make banking personnel in the countries above suspicious whenever a foreigner shows up. Foreigners wishing to open a bank account in mainland Britain will find it next to impossible. The banks, scared of money laundering and other abuse, simply do not want your custom. If you are a foreigner, simply try ''cold-calling'' next time you're in

London. Walk up to any bank counter and ask to open a current account. The experience is chilling. You will be turned down flatly, given the cold shoulder and shoved out the door with some lame excuse. This does not just happen to money laundering looking types, it hapens to most foreigners.

What the US list also does is make authorities the world over look extra closely at large money transfers to and from the countries on the list.

Try not to work too much with countries on the USA 1994 Money Laundering list. If you have to, like most of us, make sure that your business is legitimate and totally above-board. Make sure that should the need ever arise, you can explain the purpose of any transfer of money between accounts or between countries.

LESSON 3:

Exercise low profile in your daily dealings with your bank. And try to keep those daily dealings as infrequent as possible. In an ideal set-up you need never contact your bank at all. This author contacts each of his banks once a year.

Make sure that:

a) your bank doesn't know your address
b) your bank doesn't have a picture of you
c) your bank doesn't have you on tape (nor any government)
d) your communications are untraceable

A low profile is not that hard to achieve once you know how. No one banking in silence will ever operate from his home or from his place of business. Nor will he use a public post office box. His address is a mail service or maildrop, which *won't* open his mail but will let him collect it. The best of such services is the private box company where our silent banker is not known, and where he is free with a personal key to collect his mail from his box 24 hours. He never talks to his bank on the telephone. This way, neither his government nor the bank can ever record a tape of his voice nor of financial details, codes, account numbers, transfers and so on.

If speed is essential our silent banker uses a fax message, but never his own machine. Use a copy shop or a service bureau where you are not known. Or fax from gas stations. Germany, France, Denmark and Britain all have service stations with fax. Airports have coin- or card-operated fax machines in the US, Europe and Asia. If the machines are card-operated, use a prepaid phonecard. Never use a credit card. In Germany, even major railway stations have fax machines as part of the banks of phone boxes. No operator handles your fax and the fee is deducted from the credit of your prepaid phonecard. If you are in a country where services are not so advanced, use a hotel where you are not staying. Walk in from the street, ask for a favor and offer to pay for it. *PT 2* has a lot more information on how to use strange hotels as pit stops. Don't forget that a hotel fax has a sender's ID. If you don't want the recipient of your fax to know even what country you are in use the Nissei NX305 fax. This is a traveler's dream. A lightweight portable fax complete with a handle, a built-in rechargeable battery and an acoustic coupler for direct connection to *any phone.* Because of the acoustic coupler you won't have to mess with wires or foreign plugs. Your portable fax connects to any phone in seconds, even payphones and cellulars. We like the NX305 so much we bought two! The rechargeable battery means you can fax from the road, which we have done, literally, many times. Roadside payphones don't have power outlets but with the rechargeable battery your fax works anyway, both for sending and receiving. Your portable fax is compatible with all faxes everywhere, up to Group 3 standard. But because of the acoustic coupler and noise the NX305 is some four times slower than a normal fax, due to error-correcting. If you work internationally, which is the only work we do, note that this increases your phone bill. Yet this is a small price to pay for keeping a low profile. Olivetti of Italy has an OEM-version of the same portable fax machine, which is also sold by telecoms of several European countries, priced between £400 and £800.

Your lowest profile is obtained by living and working PT style in different countries, adhering strictly to the five flags theory of not mixing business with pleasure. In other words, keeping your citizenship different from where you make your money, which is again different from where you keep your money, which is yet another country from your playground and from the country where you physically sleep at night.

If you can divide your life into compartments you will be on the road to a long and stressfree life. For the lowest profile of them all live outside the USA and the European Union, in a country which is not a member of the OECD nor eager to spring currency restrictions or other silly controls on its populace. Poland and Hungary could well be attractive as part-time holiday homes for those banking in silence elsewhere.

LESSON 4:

One of the simplest but most important and effective methods used to avoid complications with the tax man is simply to drop out of your country's banking system. This is not as hard as you might think. The world is rich on opportunities. If a tourist can live in your country for a shorter or longer period of time, without having any banking in your country, then so can you. Simply use the same methods a tourist would. If you are willing you can stop the tax bureaucrats dead in the tracks. By dropping out of your country's banking system, there are no more paper trails or audit trails for the tax department or any other government investigative agency to snoop. They will have a harder time spying or prying into your personal affairs. Because they are essentially concerned with gathering money, and because time is money, they usually can't be bothered with going abroad to look for your money. Unless you are a big cat that warrants some kind of special attention, the government will usually move on to easier targets right away.

From Miami one tax adviser writes the following about tax deserters:

"In combination with dropping out of the US banking system, these citizens are using various confidential Check Cashing Services which are becoming very popular and are beginning to grow in numbers. If the IRS Revenue Agent cannot locate your banking activity and banking records, and cannot locate any paperwork on your activities, the IRS Agent will, in all likelihood, ignore you and go on to the next unsuspecting taxpayer to collect taxes. And by not having a US Bank checking account you have escaped the Federal Reserve System and US Banking Law."

***A NOTE OF CAUTION**: When opening accounts abroad you may not have to travel. But if you can, do so anyway always giving thought to who stamps your passport and what your passport will tell about your travels later on. In many cases traveling is not necessary. You can open an account in a foreign country through that bank's branch right at home. An Argentinian wanting a Gibraltar account simply walks into the Buenos Aires office of ABN-Amro, then asks them to help him finalize the paperwork with the ABN-Amro branch in Gibraltar. One client opened an account at the BCCI because the banker was a friend. He filled out the account opening forms of the Miami BCCI in Panama, then the manager sent the documents via the bank mail to Miami. It authorized his account, they gave him his number and he started operating from wherever he happened to be. Anybody can do the same thing. If a Swiss bank has a branch in the Caymans, for instance, you open an account right from Switzerland and ask a favor from a friendly banker. "We need to open an account in the Cayman Islands without going there. Give us the paper work and we'll sign it here." Doing this will save you time and money. It is tempting. In a few days you can open hundreds of accounts in all major banking havens of the world. Only one word of caution, doing it this way is NOT low profile. The local bank manager in your home country will know about your business. Since he is operating under local laws and banking regulations, he may even have to report the existence of a foreign account in your name. You can sound him out about this first. But never forget that the more people who know about your business, the less private it is. As the world is today you need all the privacy you can get.*

Chapter 8

HOW TO CREATE YOUR OWN BANK SECRECY

Do you know where your money is right now?

FACT: Your cash is being taken away faster than ever before. If you have it they want it. Your real estate is at risk.

FACT: Bank secrecy is today an illusion. Promises of bank secrecy lull you into a false sense of security. The nineties-style bank secrecy is more dangerous than having no secrecy at all.

FACT: You may know all the usual methods to safeguard your money. You may even use them. What you don't know is that today, more than 90 per cent of these methods have become illegal. If you cling to the old ways, prepare for the pokey. Many countries have begun to give out year-long jail sentences even to private first time offenders with no criminal connections and no desire other than to protect their own, hard-earned booty.

Fortunately, you can create your own bank secrecy, without the bank even knowing. And what they don't know they cannot tell. With new money laundering laws in place all over the world, top criminals have had to find different ways of cleaning their cash. The money laundering laws, supposedly invented to combat the bogus war on drugs, did not stop the baddies. They laughed and shrugged them off. It did, however, stop the Belgian dentist, the German lawyer, the French realtor and everybody else who used to hide a bit of their dough somewhere else. A large number of these people have learned their lesson the hard way. The rest will soon, unless they read this book and *change their tactics.*

You now need to choose your own Do-It-Yourself plan to hide your money. You *must* put it into motion all by yourself, without confiding in expensive lawyers, chatty accountants or shady consultants who will then know all your secrets.

IT'S TIME TO CHANGE YOUR TACTICS

Have you heard about the Copy-Not pen? For years civil libertarians thought that all they had to do to get bank secrecy was to buy a special faint light blue pen called the copy-not non-reproducing pen. These light blue pens when used in combination with an almost matching light blue bank check, would not normally be reproducible to the micro-filming process by the banks. This, many believed, made it impossible for the banks to keep records. If you think so, this is your wake up call. We have been using these special light blue pens for several years. We have put them to the test. We can tell you that it's time to change your tactics. In the first few years we found out that a microfilmed check when used in the combination just mentioned, did in fact work, in that no endorsement on the back of the check would appear. Of course we were delighted. But now is the time to quit. Because of the pressure by the IRS and the Federal Reserve, banks are now required to do something about this problem. First, they contacted suppliers of checks to banks customers and asked them to use a paper of any color to withstand any attempt by manufacturers of Copy-Not pens to produce non-reproducing pens. The check suppliers complied. Today, we have a slightly different texture paper with special squiggly lines that maximize the contrast between the paper stock and the blue pen ink. Secondly, banks have upgraded their microfilming equipment to more expensive, higher quality technology. As a result most banks in the US have counteracted and put the famous Copy-Not pen to rest. If you are still using it, don't. You will stand out and could be deemed a trouble maker. People will think you have something to hide. You could get singled out for investigation simply because you use a Copy-Not pen. In our privacy bible *PT 2* we advise *against* using telephone scrambling equipment for the very same reason. If somebody accidentally listens in and hears a scrambler in operation, they will think illicit business is being conducted over the phone lines. This will immediately open an investigation. In such cases it is far better to keep a low profile by not deviating in your behavior. Don't stand out like a sore thumb.

WHAT YOUR OWN GOVERNMENT DOES NOT WANT YOU TO KNOW

In the United States and most Western European nations today, your friendly banker is ordered by law to play detective. The government does not want you to know this. But like it or not bank officers are being used as unpaid government workers. Each bank has at least one employee responsible for tracking suspiciously large cash deposits. He or she is instructed to look out for small bills especially. If an account exceeds what is "normal", the bank employee must recommend that his or her boss call, not the police but the Internal Revenue Service, the nearest tax office.

IT IS CHEAP BUT IS IT LEGAL?

In countries with no company law anybody can form his own company free, without formally incorporating. He is filling a void by simply writing his own bylines. Where no Registrar of Companies exists, each man is in effect his own sovereign Registrar. Just ask the citizens of tiny islands Herm and Alderney in the Channel Islands. This is cheap and yes, it is legal. Where you can find other islands then settle and carve out a life.

We are not talking about creating your own country. This is for dreamers only. We are simply talking about filling a void.

The world has a lot of nooks and crannies where governments are not active. Sometimes governments don't regulate and register companies in a particular place. You can go ahead and fill that void privately, if no laws forbid you to do so. Or you can supply power. Start a club to issue car license plates. The thought may sound foreign to most people. They think "After all, isn't this what governments are supposed to do? How can I do this on my own?" Yet when you think about it, finding a non-regulated field on a small island somewhere can give you options that are cheap *and* legal. Don't be put off just because the concept sounds strange. If you had tried to explain the idea of a private shoe factory to people in the Soviet Union ten years ago, they would have thought it just as weird. What? A *private* shoe factory? But isn't *the government* supposed to make shoes? Dreamers, Believers, Losers, Suckers and Fools, governments are for you.

If you are not a dreamer you, too, can benefit from the methods used today only by an extremely secretive elite of the world's richest people. They have long understood that the idea of government being something holy with a monopoly on doing a lot of things is plain hogwash. One secret consists of finding places where the government will keep out of people's hair, leaving them with discretionary powers to do all the things government won't. One such place is neutral Switzerland. This version of self-rule is called local government. Each canton decides a lot of things for itself, as if it were a separate country. Within each canton, each town and village has a lot of powers to shape its own rules. And all areas that local government won't regulate are regulated by each citizen in his own private sphere. One result of this is that any Swiss or foreign resident in Switzerland can set up what amounts to his own tax-free, filing-free, outsider-free trust. Swiss law, based on old Roman law, does not have anything resembling the Anglo-Saxon concept of a trust. But at the same time it does recognize separate legal entities. Some of these companies are governed by federal law. Other organizations and associations are governed by the cantons. Yet again others are ungoverned (trusts) unless village-laws or town-laws specifically prohibit them. This never happens. On the contrary, Swiss courts have a history of accepting a trust as a separate legal entity in a large number of previous cases.

OUR SECRET ADDRESSES

Those wishing to set up anything in neutral Switzerland should start by studying tax lawyer Marshall Langer's *The Swiss Report*, published by Scope International. Marshall has lived in Switzerland for years and it shows. He knows his stuff. After you have read his report you will know whether you want to proceed with the obvious first step, opening a bank account in Switzerland. Opening a bank account there can, with a little help from your friends, be done by mail. A local contact is helpful as Switzerland has over 500 banks to choose from and they all differ in what they have to offer. Some will give you credit cards with no questions asked. Others will accept accounts with no minimum balance. Deposit US$10 and you're in business with them. From time to time we receive offers from Swiss or resident foreigners wanting to lend a hand by acting as "facilitators". Usually, they charge too much. One American resident operating in 1993 charged a US$1000 agent's fee just to help you open the account. We did not do any business with him. We use some cheap-to-feed, eager and seemingly honest people called **Office Services, Jupiterstrasse 56, CH-8032 Zürich, Switzerland, tel +41 – 1 382 0356, fax +41 – 1 382 0153**. They will let you do everything by mail, they don't ask a lot of questions, they are fast and they don't bill you a fortune. Their literature and information is free, so send for it and see what they can offer. However, it may be that, like us, you have grown a bit weary of Switzerland. Bank secrecy there now has more holes than their Emmenthalers.

CURRENCY RESTRICTIONS ARE NOT A PROBLEM

Just as small one-man or sometimes two-man firms can be found here and there willing to help you with any offshore problem, so too can you find "facilitators" well versed in evading currency restrictions.

Happily, currency restrictions are now largely a thing of the past in most countries. But if you do business in the Third World, your business can still be hampered by them. At least in the beginning, until you find out how easy all currency restrictions are to circumvent, often even legally. And thus find out how utterly senseless they are. A result of stupid politicians foolishly thinking that they can plan, centrally, such a vibrant thing as an economy.

If you find yourself faced with currency restrictions in a Third World country, your next step is easy. Ask for directions. The best people to ask are resident foreigners in business. They will know the easiest way to get money in and out. Most large cities have an American club catering not just to Americans, but to expatriates of all colors. Go there for lunch to meet new faces. The American consulate will give you the address if you ask. But apart from that, American consulates can't and won't help anybody with anything. The British are different. As a whole lot of expatriates from all countries, not just Great Britain, already know. The British consulates are by far the best and most helpful in the world. If you find yourself stuck with a question, you don't really want to go to your own country's embassy or consulate. Go instead to the local outpost of Great Britain. All UK consulates we have known have been able to act as a know-it-all tourist and expatriate information exchange. They help you with a smile. This author is not a UK citizen, yet we have had documents authenticated and received literally hours of all kinds of helpful service free, from various British consulates. You can even be frank with some of the British diplomats to an extent. They live out there so they know how silly the currency regulations are. US diplomats are stark contrasts. They are taught to never express a human emotion.

As an alternative to getting help from foreigners living locally, wealthy residents are usually knowledgeable about ways of beating their system. They, too, occasionally shuttle money out in spite of currency restrictions and regulations. If you can, talk to industrialists, top doctors, plastic surgeons, importers, large manufacturers, bankers or rich politicians. Finally, have a chat in private with *Cambio*-houses, although most of the owners unfortunately seem to be crooks. A quiet talk in private with employees of the local American Express office could perhaps produce results too. As a foreigner you usually have more options than a local. Some foreigners even make money exploiting this advantage and helping others. American Express officials may know some of the loopholes.

If you are stuck abroad and don't have the advantage of an ear on the ground, try to discuss options with the locals. One worldwide consultant specializing in getting around currency restrictions is David Ward, a specialist in company formation. He has solved riddles in most "problem" countries. Contact his firm **Ward & Co., The Old Workshop, Marygate Lane, Bootham, York YO3 7BJ, United Kingdom, tel +44 – 904 639225**.

Currency restrictions are never serious problems. There are always loopholes; sometimes legal, sometimes not so legal. Fortune 500 companies will have to stick to only the legal solutions. Sometimes this involves more effort. An interesting read on the subject, detailing creative problem solving on all continents is called *Unblocking Your Funds*. This book is sold by **The Economist Intelligence Unit, 40 Duke Street, London W1A 1DW, United Kingdom, tel +44 – 71 830 1000, ext 961 or fax +44 – 71 499 9767**. Those helping you get around currency restrictions, can also be used for other purposes. If lowering your profile is your aim have an informal chat with some of them. They have a lifetime of experience in beating the system and getting away with it.

Chapter 9

INTO THE TWILIGHT ZONE

This is the chapter where we must ask you to tuck the kids in safely or hide this book on your top shelf because the following pages are strictly off limits to minors and to bureau-rats. We will show you how to launder money. But we will show you that contrary to what most politicians utter, this can be done without breaking a single law. We don't advocate money laundering. But we do advocate that you take every step within your power to increase your financial privacy. Sometimes these steps just happen to be exactly equal to what newspapers and vote-seeking politicians call money laundering. That in itself doesn't change the fact that anonymous accounts and international transfers without paper trails are valuable tools used by every man who seriously cares about protecting his financial privacy. Yes, criminals too, use anonymous accounts. Bandits love international transfers *sans* paper trails. Does that mean that the rest of us should stop taking advantage of what the world has to offer? Just because criminals use get-away cars, doesn't automatically mean that the rest of us law abiding citizens should stop using cars. This is logic, but a logic that the bureaucrats refuse to understand. In their eyes just because criminals sometimes use foreign banks and anonymous transfers, this should be made illegal for everybody, honest citizens and taxpayers included. Some countries have passed laws making what they call money laundering a crime. It makes a great soundbite for the cameras. But as virtually any banker will tell you, it does not make much sense in the real world. So to restore common sense and rational thinking, let's take the bull by the horns and look at what exactly money laundering is? And what's so evil about it? Let's enter the shady netherworld of crooks and conmen. Let's enter The Twilight Zone.

THE MECHANICS OF A SIMPLE LAUNDRY

How do you most effectively launder dirty money? We are not allowed to tell you. But we will leak a few secrets. Because even though we would never advise any reader to break the law, we also feel very strongly that censorship has no justification among free men and women. Whether you plan on using this information or not, you do at least have a right to know. So the next few pages are written for informational purposes only.

The mere process of laundering money is not in itself a crime in all countries.

This process consists of several separate parts.

FIRST PART: The "dirty" money is made. This phase is usually the illegal phase, either because the money comes from crime or because the money is legitimate income not recorded on any tax return. It follows that no tax has been paid on this income.

SECOND PART: The money is deposited with one or more banks, usually in accounts abroad. The process ends here for some. They are happy with having the money hidden away in a foreign country waiting to be reclaimed at some later date. While the money sits idle in a foreign bank, unknown to the tax man at home, it earns interest – usually tax free. It waits for a rainy day to show up and some people are happy ending the process right here. But to others, this is where the true laundering begins.

THIRD PART: Having money sitting in a secret, foreign account forever is not much fun. At some point you want to spend part of the money. To openly circulate this cash it is necessary that the cash be laundered. This is the only way you can freely spend what used to be tainted money without fear of repercussions. Only "whitewashed" cash is cash whose origins can, at any time, should the need occur, be explained.

IS IT ILLEGAL?

You may be forgiven for thinking that money laundering, *per se,* always is a crime no matter where it is carried out. Most people are probably of this mistaken assumption. Flashy CNN reports and covers on *Time* advertising the latest batch of money launderers caught do their bit to re-inforce the stereotype of all money launderers as arch-criminals.

Fact is, fewer than 15 per cent of all the world's countries have laws making money laundering in itself a crime. Best known among these countries is, of course, the USA. American courts view laundering as an incentive for criminals to carry out more crime. Then again, American courts hold a lot of silly opinions with which more civilized countries would never comply. The latest, making gang membership a felony, smacks of such a totalitarian concept as crime-by-association. If you choose to freely join a club or an organization, in this case called a street gang, you automatically face prison time if found out. It does not matter that you yourself do nothing wrong. The association is enough to send you down for some hard time. No wonder freethinkers are deserting the United States in droves. Not even South Africa would dream of treating its blacks this way. Only Cuba, North Korea and China still have laws whereby the simple membership of an organization can land you in prison.

But let's get back to money laundering and let's state once and for all that despite popular media hype and despite the fact that some countries have passed laws to combat money laundering, in nine countries out of ten it is perfectly legal.

Outside the USA and its vassal states, most countries view money laundering realistically. They know that laundering cannot be made illegal. Because laundering is simply stringing together a number of often quite legal moves to form a finished process which in effect will have washed dirty money clean.

Through their court judgments, these countries are saying: As long as every single move you make in and by itself is legal, we can't outlaw the finished picture.

To use a motoring analogy, these countries are saying: "You are free to own and operate a car. But if you drive too fast or if you drive recklessly, you are breaking the law." Viewed in isolation, there is nothing illegal in owning a car. Yet you can easily break the law, it all depends on how the driver behaves. This makes sense, just as A is A.

With money laundering, you are in the same position. If you operate in countries where laundering is not illegal you still have to observe formalities. Otherwise you could land yourself in legal trouble and receive a sentence. Let's look more closely at each of the three parts involved in a simple money laundering operation, and then we'll look at how you can avoid tripping up . . .

YOU ONLY LAUNDER WHAT'S DIRTY

Without dirty laundry you don't go to the cleaners. First, there has to be something to clean.

Money made in the straightforward matter rarely needs cleaning. Once the money has been included on your tax return and tax has been paid on it, you seldom have a need to want to wash it white. What for? The exception, of course, is a small BUT. When you live in a country where your politicians are notoriously unstable and have proven themselves to be crooks, you are well advised to spirit even legitimate earnings abroad. Most African countries have currency restrictions outlawing the free flight of capital. When there is the added risk of confiscation or freezing by government order, smart money resides abroad. In the 1970s, the Soviet Union confiscated all bank deposits routinely, time after time. In 1990, in Brazil, government put a freeze on all savings above US$ 1000. After a long wait and several suicides, when depositors finally got access to their money it was worthless. Inflation had eroded the value of their savings. Smart money meanwhile hid abroad, behind bank secrecy. Other examples of white money washing itself black? In Scandinavian countries where wealth taxes easily take another one per cent tax out of every home- or business-owner's assets per year, prudent and responsible citizens understate the value of their assets. Without telling anyone, they put their legitimately earned, tax-paid white money away in secret bank accounts abroad. In effect, although no one has ever owned up to it, turning it black. This reverse money laundering is money laundering nevertheless and just as legal or illegal depending on your country, on local laws and on how you do it.

If your money is tainted to begin with, it is probably illegal in some way or another, which is why you want it washed.

We shall not dwell with the legitimacy of whether a given act is legal or has been made illegal in some country or other. Suffice to say that for every real crime, there is another crime which is only illegal because of unworthy, timid ignorance obstructing our progress.

If you're the one doing the washing, it's always better to be safe than sorry. Keep a low profile. Professional money launderers deal with illicit proceeds. On a more homely level, tainted money is merely the result of moonlighting or black work.

None of our readers fits in either of these two camps, so money laundering, strictly speaking, should not be necessary.

First of all, we don't write books for crooks. Secondly, no readers need to moonlight or work "black" off the books. Reading our reports, everyone can use our knowledge and the secrets of the super-rich to stitch together a life plan where tax avoidance simply isn't necessary. We show how, with a modicum of prior planning, *everybody* can escape tax *legally*. Money which is tax free legally is not tainted money, so there is no need to launder it. Unless, of course, you feel safer from heavyhanded and arbitrary government confiscation once the paper trail has been cut and your money has been transferred abroad, untraced.

TRANSFERRING TAINTED MOOLAH ABROAD

Essential to this step is the prior existence of one or more bank accounts, preferably in different countries. In recent times money launderers have preferred countries with strict bank secrecy. This wisdom is now questioned. Bank secrecy is sometimes just a dangerous illusion, because in the nineties, it is simply broken too often. Switzerland used to be a favorite with money launderers. New alternatives include virtually all tax havens to a higher or lesser degree. Almost all of them claim to offer some measure of bank secrecy, which to a large extent is just advertising babble.

The past four or five years has seen a development which has eroded bank secrecy from the inside out. This problem is obviously most worrying to those who have something to hide. The rest of us can continue sleeping sound at night. Yet, then again . . . under the pretense of wanting to catch drugs barons and international swindlers, law after silly law has been passed in country after country, and if you read between the lines, the true purpose of these laws is united – to get at Joe Taxpayer who thought he had sheltered a bit of his dough safely.

Belgian dentists who went to Luxembourg and hid a little gold left over from their fillings became victims of the new laws. So did Italian workers in Switzerland and Spanish moonlighters on Gibraltar. The true criminals weren't caught.

What happened, precisely?

This is not the forum for detailed analysis of every law, regulation and government decree directed at the private banking sector. A Florida newsletter called *Money Laundering ALERT* does a good job of digesting what the new rules mean to banks and how they affect the client on a day to day basis. If you want to swim with the sharks, get a subscription. Several less savory lawyers and financial facilitators are no doubt among the subscribers already. Broadly speaking, this is what has happened in recent years:

1: GOVERNMENT AGENTS have increased their firepower. They are now far more effective controlling the citizenry. Mail, phones, faxes and telex are all under surveillance without your knowledge. Government agents from all OECD countries use half-truths like never before to peek at how their own citizens bank in other countries.

2: INTERNATIONAL COOPERATION between governments has expanded widely. It is common now for departments to work together directly on cases and information exchange. Ten years ago, international cooperation took place between department heads or on a similarly high level. Today, low level staffers and desk bound bureaucrats simply phone each other, from country to country. Borders are being erased. This is partly a result of the OECD and its work on InterFIpol, the International Financial Police, and the USA-sponsored MLAT treaty (The Mutual Legal Assistance Treaty, a sort of I'll-rat-on-my-friends-if-you'll-rat-on-yours deal). Supercomputers hooked up to international networks by modem help the bureaucrats. So do super-faxes, a slow but very powerful special fax standard using US$25,000 machines capable of transmitting accurate signatures, fingerprints and other matter with fine details in a matter of minutes . . . to anywhere on the globe.

3: REGARDING LAWS some governments have passed new laws turning money laundering into a crime, along the lines of "aiding and abetting a criminal". This has so far not happened in a lot of countries. But the banks know which way the wind is blowing and they have turned to so-called self-regulation, putting their own house in order before government bureaucrats get the urge to do it for them. This means that

4: IN THE BANKS internal procedures for client relationships have changed. Almost everywhere today all new clients are photographed without knowing it, either on videotape or by a hidden still camera operated by a switch under the counter. In Switzerland, all banks as well as almost all law firms have installed taping equipment to record phone conversations. In the Swiss phone book, a small star next to the phone number designates that such equipment is connected. Now you know.

5: OPENING OF NEW ACCOUNTS is now more difficult because ID is always required and because the bank, depending on the country, sometimes may want to check your references or your background. Several banks, especially in Switzerland, refuse to accept American clients. If they do, they often require you to sign a special waiver just for United States citizens. In effect, you are signing away your right to bank secrecy and all other client's rights.

6: DEPOSITING MONEY is made more difficult by the fact that some banks won't accept cash any more. Offshore financial institutions with a majority of clients in other countries deal with most of their account holders by mail. You will learn that for every ten of these banks nine will not accept cash. When you open an account, your initial deposit must be a check. Bank transfers are accepted and you can clear checks through your account but still no cash, please.

How do money launderers survive the radical changes ushered in with this New World Order of the last few years?

Let's clear each obstacle one by one:

a: Low profile is not that hard to achieve once you know how. *PT 2,* is your must read. Study the summary on the back pages of this report, then order the complete text containing valuable low profile and privacy information never before seen in print. Always remember that the all-seeing, all-knowing Eye in the Sky does not exist. But always act as if it does. Be prudent and a little bit paranoid, as this will sharpen your senses and always make you keep your head down. Sometimes it may be necessary, sometimes not. Always act as if it is.

b: International exchange of information between governments is not anything you need to fear. If you remember to always keep a low profile and follow the PT principles, there won't be much information to exchange anyway. And the tidbits there will be worthless anyway and cannot harm you. Be careful where you put your fingerprints. And be careful how often you let yourself be videotaped. Your handwriting can be changed easily. Simply go back to what you learned in school, or use the left hand, even though the end result looks like you've had some sort of disease. Author Graham Greene wrote in his *A Chance for Mr Lever* that signatures are best faked by writing them upside down, thus confusing our normal idea of what a letter "should" look like. We wouldn't know if Greene is right or not. We have never had to fake a signature. Our line of business is somewhat different, fortunately.

c: Money launderers only need fear new laws if they don't know how to hide. Which is why these new laws *never* affect drug lords or big time swindlers. These shady underworld characters know how to hide and how to use fall guys, middle men and "ghosts". And they know how to keep such a low profile that no one knows their true identity or where they live. Either way, this type of launderer is a professional. He does his homework. The pros are almost never caught. Those with reason to fear the new laws are small-time tax evaders and others who never noticed how the world as they knew it all of a sudden changed.

d: You don't need to show up in your bank personally. Not even when you first open the account. Depending on country, most or all types of accounts can be opened completely by mail. No bank will ever be able to take your photograph. If for some reason you want to visit your bank to withdraw cash or place a cash deposit, then choose a branch that is not the branch keeping your account. The smaller the branch, the better. If you normally wear glasses, take them off or vice versa. A hat or a scarf will make you even prettier for the cameras. That's all you need, really. But if you enjoy dressing up, by all means indulge. It is not necessary. But all of us are eccentrics in some way or another, and if we weren't, this world would be a poorer place to live in. This one reader, whom we shall call Mr Jürgen, considers it his sport disguising himself for the benefit of bank surveillance cameras. It is a passion and a hobby. Hollywood style, he has an artificial wart stored in saline solution when he is not using it. But the wart is just a small part of his total make-up. When Mr Jürgen puts his fake wart in place, he has already spent the better part of an hour in front of his mirror and looks like a man 20 years older. His skin has a grey tone because the day before, he ate the same powder that Frederick Forsyth in *The Day of the Jackal* has his sniper ingest. His chins are hollowed, glued on the inside to his teeth with a non-toxic superglue removable after the bank-business by rinsing with a mouthful of nail varnish remover, then spitting the whole lot out. When banking, the color of Jürgen's hair is chestnut brown with a tint of grey, not blond like normally, and below the eyes are the griefs of a widow. A quick tint of charcoal gives the impression of a man with trouble sleeping. The eyes are brown where they used to be blue. Colored contact lenses take care of this little detail and are today available for a couple of hundred dollars from any optician, with or without strength. Like Tom Clancy in real life, Jürgen also uses smoke-tinted glasses when he goes banking. His clothes are a whole separate chapter but his main advice is to change your style. If you normally wear jeans, change to a suit. Or the other way around. In passport-style photographs, the difference between a turtleneck sweater and a shirt with a tie can be startling. Always wear the opposite of what you would normally wear.

In the United States, mail order advertisers in men's magazines such as *Esquire* and *Playboy* sell special shoes to men making them up to three inches taller. Normally, these elevator shoes are sold to small guys with tall girlfriends, but anybody can buy. Once you are in the bank, don't worry about your voice. Normally, only phone calls are recorded. So don't call. If you have to, use a voice changer and turn the dial to make the sound of your own voice darker or lighter. The modulation is always too electronic for most people's tastes but better than nothing. We have yet to encounter a voice changer where the so-called female voice does not make one sound like a fake Bianca Castafiore. A voice changer emits some electronic noise, so only use it on international lines where such static can easily be explained away. For more on voice changers and how related spy-gear can be used to protect your personal and financial privacy read *Winning Through Super Technology*, a hefty tome of more than 500 A4-pages. It used to be called *Spy Game*. Price: US$40. Order from **CEP, PO Box 865, Boulder, Colorado 80306, USA**.

e: The biggest hurdle to all amateur-launderers today is that banks in almost every locale demand proof of ID before they will open an account. It wasn't always like this. Less than ten years ago, most banks were happy when a new customer walked in the door. Seldom did they ask for identification.

Today, every bank wants ID, and most will photocopy it for the records, before you can give them your money. While we used to be able to flash a season-holder's ID to the New York Metropolitan (it worked in Luxembourg!), today most banks routinely expect nothing less than a passport. Depending on your attitude and where you are in the world, there are ways of talking them out of this. But generally speaking *identification is required* everywhere you open an account in person. Normally a passport is all that's needed. The bank will not ask for proof of your address but this will happen in the future. Be prepared. Have a library card with a dummy address or the address of some mail drop, so you can show the bank where you "live". Where can you still open an account in person and not have to show any ID? If you are lucky and can pass for *valuta-inländer*, some banks in Austria may just still let you open a *sparbuch*. But there are no guarantees and you could waste your trip. Other places? Places where bank tellers are not just stupid, but corrupt as well or at least willing to buy any lame story. We opened one account in Albania last year without ID. Other backward holes in Eastern Europe could prove mineable as well. Africa is a sure thing. Only problem is who wants to deposit money in Africa? A few success-stories have come out of Nigeria recently but unless you are desperate, stick to the beaten path.

Where, then, can you open an account in person and still get away with showing shabby, half-baked ID? In the villages of Switzerland, for example, banking with banks catering only to the locals. Or in smaller branches of banks in countries where foreigners do not normally open accounts and where there are no fixed procedures to follow when all of a sudden, out of the blue a tourist shows up.

ID is not needed, but a bank reference is necessary when you open an account by mail in the British Isles. The banks in Gibraltar, Isle of Man, Jersey, Guernsey etc will not enquire as to your financial status. They will simply write the bank you give as reference and seek confirmation of: a) your name, b) your address, and c) your signature. That's all. Thus, all three things have to match. Normally, you are expected to give your daily bank as your reference. We don't. We always refer to an obscure Swiss bank where we have an account established just for that one purpose. A Swiss bank is an OK reference to give, although the Swiss hardly ever confirm anything.

Sometimes the bank will want a reference from your existing bank even if you open the account in person. This is a sign of trouble, a sign that they don't believe your story. Give them the reference, then let the account lie dormant. Forget about it. If you can't give them a reference, make up some excuse and close the account before it even opens. This happened to one reader. He showed up in Andorra with a South American passport. According to the passport, he was supposed to speak Spanish. He even had a Spanish name. Nevertheless, he spoke English with the bank, forgetting that in Andorra, everybody understands Spanish in addition to Catalan, the national language.

f: The most discreet way of transferring cash to your foreign account is the personal way. Withdraw cash at home, go abroad with the notes, travel anonymously, paying cash for your ticket, go to your foreign bank, count the money, deposit it.

This way there won't be an electronic paper trail. Don't forget that all money transfers are electronic. Sensitive details of a transfer are stored in the computer memory for ten and twenty years after it took place. Even in a country with so-called bank secrecy. There is no guarantee that ten or twenty years from now, an opposition political party won't have changed the laws. What will happen if Switzerland one day joins the European Union? The last remnant of the already quite tattered Swiss bank secrecy could disappear.

If you are unhappy with travelling abroad, carrying cash, there is another private solution that will cut the paper trail. Buy a cashier's check with cash either in your home country (in Holland, for example) or in a neighboring state (say Belgium or Germany). You may have to place your order before ten in the morning, then pick up the check after lunch. Don't panic. Different folks, different strokes, and each country is different. Pay cash, then mail the cashier's check to your foreign bank, giving it instructions to clear it, change into the currency of your account with them, then deposit the proceeds in your account.

Other ways to avoid personal contact with your bank? If you bank in Luxembourg or Liechtenstein, use the money-eating ATMs, automatic tellers that actually accept cash instead of dispensing it. Such machines are ideal for 24 hour deposits and you get a receipt on the spot. If your bank does not have such a magic helper, ask about using the standard night deposit box as long as you can do so in a way that won't raise eyebrows. Ask when you open the account, then formalize everything at once.

Finally, you can have others deposit funds in your account. Couriers or clients will be happy to and this way your name is kept out of the picture. Just don't forget, theirs may not be, depending on what details they divulge when they make the deposit. Also don't forget that one person – you – can always keep a secret. Whether more people can is doubtful. Every time you let someone else (spouse, family member, client, customer, courier, anybody) know that the account exists, you run the risk of having a future leak that may come back to hurt you. We are, unfortunately, speaking from the experience of more than one reader.

Some banks don't take cash. Inquire in advance using a pen-name, or have a friend or professional adviser ask. If your bank won't accept cash, sell your cash to another bank by buying a cashier's check. High street banks in most countries routinely sell cashier's checks (banker's checks) to non-customers walking in from the street. You may have to give a name but in all the European countries we have worked with, nowhere have we been asked to show ID. To be on the safe side, don't buy an international cashier's check in a foreign currency. Buy a national one in the country's local currency, as your (foreign) bank will be able to exchange it anyway. There will be a record of the exchange later, but that shouldn't matter too much. It is more important that you don't have to show ID when you sell your cash and in return buy the cashier's check. This will keep your name out. The record later of the exchange will not have your name on it anyway. It probably won't even have the name of your (foreign) bank, since one large bank in each country often handles clearance of foreign checks for smaller banks there. In Britain most of this is done by Barclays Bank.

When buying your cashier's check put the name of your bank on it, but skip the word bank, skip the address and skip the country. If you are sending it to Julius Baer Bank of Zürich, Switzerland, simply have the issuing bank write it out to "Mr Julius Baer" or "J Baer". The bank will have a record of this but no more information to go on. Their record is worth next to nothing.

Another school of thought says, leave it blank altogether. Ask the bank to make it out to blank. Don't give the name of the recipient. The bank may find it strange and you could be lectured on the risk of anybody being able to cash a blank check. This is true, which is why as soon as you leave the bank you fill in the name of the recipient yourself. From a privacy viewpoint this option beats all. Yet we don't want some stupid, underpaid bank teller thinking "how strange", then filing a Suspicious Transaction Form. Asking for a cashier's check made out to no one is strange in itself. It is enough to prompt raised eyebrows. Unless you have some justifying story (*I am going to buy a car this afternoon, but I am wavering between two sellers, so I prefer to fill in the name myself later, once I've made my decision*) you really shouldn't play too fancy.

LAUNDERING

Most of us keeping funds in foreign banks are perfectly happy with just that. At least for the time being.

Our money has never been tainted to begin with. Our money has always been white. The only reason we are banking in Bermuda or Gibraltar, as opposed to some other countries, is because we feel the banks there are safer. We earn a healthy, tax free interest.

As an added bonus, we don't have to waste valuable time filling out silly government forms to please hungry bureaucrats.

To others it may be important that their funds or part of them re-enter circulation quickly.

Some simply withdraw the funds. This can be done by writing a check, withdrawing in person, using a piece of plastic or by interbank transfer. Withdrawing cash in person with or without the help of a piece of plastic is best in terms of low profile. A check written to a third party may be acceptable, as long as you keep in mind what the paper trail will be able to tell future snoops about your affairs.

Never transfer money between your home country bank and your foreign bank account. And never deposit checks from one bank in the account of the other.

None of what we are dealing with in this paragraph has anything to do with money laundering. Because to launder money, it is not enough simply to withdraw it from your foreign bank. That won't make it less tainted. Although, to be fair, we do concede that it is somewhat tougher to identify source once your cash has been on a planetrip around the world.

To succesfully clean tainted money, it is not enough just to have the money show up again. You also need to be able to explain where this money comes from and how it got to you. People may want to know. If you cannot tell them, and if they are the kind of people prone to abuse of power, they may go away. But they may also tag along and that is not a pleasant prospect. So you need to have a full explanation ready, just in case.

Further, if you're not yet a PT, you need to look at the tax aspects of whitewashing money. Normally, you will have to pay income tax wherever you are resident. Or at least have a legal, plausible explanation as to why you consider your gains tax free.

Once your money is white, you can spend it openly without fear of the tax department or other government agencies.

Traditionally, casinos and race tracks have been claimed as fountains of sudden wealth. To support these claims, creative non-tax payers have been known to scour betting windows of race tracks after a race, picking up the winning tickets that others discarded after cashing. Even government lotteries can be used to support your claim, as long as no record is made of winners. And you must have proof of the purchase to begin with. In Brazil last year, a crooked member of Congress, Joao Alves, was facing corruption charges. He was asked how he made the money to buy more than 50 luxury apartments, several private airplanes and generally surround himself with luxury, all on a politician's salary. "I won the state lottery", he claimed. "I won the big prize. Twenty-six times. With the help of God".

It helps if your winnings are tax free. Government lotteries usually are.

The traditional *pizzeria*, which in Italy is a corner sandwich stop, is another old-time favorite among money launderers. But you don't need to make pizzas to profit.

Any business or chain of businesses will do, as long as it is common to receive payment in cash and not issue receipts bearing the name of the customer. You can think, so we shall not state the obvious. But isn't it a funny coincidence that in more than one country, the video game arcade business has ties to organized crime? And that owners of coin operated self-service laundries seem to get in legal trouble all the time, on totally unrelated charges?

An almost complete list of ideal cash-businesses can be found in *How To Do Business Off the Books*, an American underground-press title written by someone with the unlikely name of Adam Cash. It is available from Scope International at £10 (US$20).

Other ways to launder money on a household scale?

This all depends on your local tax department in whatever country you reside. Which is why you need to opt for full PTdom: with the silver bullet, a PT simply couldn't care less what his ex-taxman thinks or not.

Those readers not yet full-blown PTs need to spend time thinking out how to hoodwink their tax department while at the same time getting away with it legally.

Sometimes, working as a sales representative for some foreign company is enough. You get a free company car, free housing and a generous expense account with a couple of foreign credit cards thrown in for good measure to see you through. All of this paid for by the foreign company. A company that you created for that purpose, running it in cooperation with a foreign lawyer or accountant; or even better, with a PT friend keen to help.

In some countries you won't be allowed to pull it off. Depending on where you reside, busy-bodies in the tax office could well get the idea that a company car carries a value and that free housing is surely an unearned benefit that you should be taxed on. Usually, however, even the most draconian gulag will let you keep some semblance of a corporate expense account without it affecting your personal tax status. So hold on to those credit cards.

A sit down with a local tax adviser is a good idea at this stage. He can tell you what is tax free and what's not. Then find a way to channel your foreign loot into what could eventually become a tax free gain to you at home. Ask a lot of questions, but let him do most of the talking. Don't tell him anything important, but use your head. Also read between the lines of this and similar reports. Not all information is fit to print, unfortunately. Sometimes, you simply have to be creative. An ugly necessity for resident taxpayers forced to support high-tax welfare states.

In several countries, minority shareholders investing in foreign companies can receive their gains tax free once they have held their shares for a minimum set period of time, often three years. Liquidating such a solvent company after the minimum holding period will bring all capital as well as earned interest and other gains home to each shareholder tax free. If the company was located in a tax haven, even better because it wouldn't even have paid local tax to begin with. Just make sure from the outset that your tax man at home agrees with your interpretation. Sometimes he will want the foreign company to have carried out some sort of real work, whatever that is, because in his screwed-up mindset, mere investment is less than noble.

If your tax man is too pig-headed, consider borrowing from your own company. Arms-length loans as opposed to shams are tax neutral. You will have use of money, often unconditionally, without ever paying a penny in tax for this privilege. If you are a resident of one of the high-tax countries where stamp-duties on loan contracts are the norm to make them legally binding and thus acceptable to a snoopy tax man, make sure the agreement is signed in a foreign jurisdiction so as to avoid having to pay what is in effect just another tax.

One hint in a somewhat similar vein (and we can't spell it out, sorry): when your company refunds your expenses, the money you receive is not taxed.

If you can't accept a loan but need to own the money outright in your own name, it will be necessary to read the small print of local laws. This is not the scope of this report. But loopholes do exist. Especially in what is called "treaty shopping": the art of combining the laws of two or three different countries, then matching their double taxation treaties to produce perfectly legal results that the bureaucrats hadn't expected when they drafted the laws and later treaties.

Treaty shopping is quite common. Top accountants don't advertise it, but they all know a trick or two. For a fee they will share their knowledge, and usually this is money well spent. Normally, we *never* advise working with lawyers, accountants or any other leeches. But if you are trapped in high-tax hell with no means of escape other than treaty shopping, we are willing to let you break our standard rule. I am a former lawyer who *hates* lawyers. Why do I hate them? Because during more than 300 years, no lawyer ever seemed to change. In the words of Sir Thomas Moore, when he described Utopia, there were " . . . no lawyers among them for they considered them as a sort of people whose profession it is to disguise matters." Right on, Sir Thomas.

For years a popular treaty shopping ploy has involved Ireland. Most of the Irish double taxation treaties used to not tax dividends in Ireland, nor in the foreign country where the recipient was resident. In other words, due to the treaty, dividends were tax free in both countries. Coupled with another aspect of the Irish treaty, whereby Irish companies would receive royalties with no withholding tax at source, such an Irish company could license a trademark to a chain of cash businesses, say pizzerias. Getting income tax free, then paying out dividends tax free. For years this ploy was the ultimate down-to-earth laundry. Some even made sure that their Irish company didn't pay tax on profits, by taking advantage of brainy Irish accountants and of the many special provisions in local Irish company tax law. You can still operate an Irish laundry this way. But many countries have become wise and will soon be amending their double taxation treaty with Ireland to put a stop to this. Some have already done so. They feel that taxpayers are abusing the system. Isn't it funny, there is a blatant example of how governments set up rules for everybody to follow, then change these rules as soon as it looks like somebody may just be winning the game without having to cheat.

The world is rich on double taxation treaties and many of them are pure virgin fields just waiting to be mined. And speaking of mines, one former member of the European Parliament, KR Petersen, made a lot of money with a block of shares in a strange and somewhat unknown Australian goldmine. More than ten years ago, when he was just starting out on the path of legitimate business, this holding made it possible for him to magically beckon capital every time the need arose. Goldmines are handy in this way and are only surpassed by money that grows on trees. Even though gold as such does not grow on trees, it can be found in a mine, especially a secret mine on the other side of the world, every time there is a pressing need.

During your quest into the wide world of deal-making you will need contacts and the odd helper or two. A shortlist: dealers in gold, precious and semi-precious stones, mining people, leasing experts, factoring folks, experts in accounts receivables and other sorts of financing.

WAS THAT A UFO WE JUST SAW . . . ?

Facing banks that require ID before they will serve you, you are forced to hand over your one and only identity. That is, if you only have one. Many of our readers today have two passports, some have even more. And contrary to what the press always tries to tell you, getting a second passport can be done quite legally. *The Passport Report* gives you all the information you need, including some words on how to execute a legal name change prior to getting your second passport. Eventually, after hard work and effort, you can have all the passports you want. But the legal route is often difficult if you need to acquire a citizenship in another country. This may take years of residence there or a heavy investment, sometimes both. *The Passport Report* does show loopholes. Yet normally, either way, it is not a breeze getting a second passport.

There is, as shady types already know, an easier way. Stolen blanks are often sold by criminals to other criminals. Lost or false passports abound, too. All are illegal, so you are well advised to avoid either of these solutions like the tax man himself.

Is there an easy way to get passports legally? There is.

Those in the know can now obtain suitcases full of passports. All of them legal to use and carry, and all available for petty cash! They are fake but authorities know it, and thus they are legal. Choose any name and any picture to assemble your own identity. Three passports in the world are 100 per cent counterfeit, yet still 100 per cent legal to carry and use. All of them can be had for very little money. And you can order as many as you want. You cannot order blanks. But you don't need to show any ID when ordering. Anybody from anywhere in the world can order without hindrance. No one will lift an eyebrow if you order several passports with the same photograph but different names. Everything can be done by mail order, so you never need to travel or show up anywhere in person. The finished passports are not returned to you as registered mail, so you will not have to sign for anything anywhere. When receiving them simply sign on the dotted line in the passport where your signature is expected to go.

Don't hop on an international plane with your new "passport". You may like the thought of travelling incognito under a different name. If so, travel by bus, train or by boat. Don't become an "unidentified flying object". The airlines won't let you! Officials will check your passport, and if they see a passport they don't know, they will at least look for a visa to your destination. Since you won't have any they will not let you on the plane. That could mean a wasted ticket or they could summon higher-up officials and you may have some explaining to do. This won't land you in legal trouble, since a toy passport or camouflage passport is essentially just that, a harmless toy. But save yourself the hassle. Please note that none of the three passports is any good for commercial air travel.

The TEXAS passport is a souvenir passport. You can compare it to the toy police badges made of plastic and sold in children's stores worldwide. You cannot use it for crossing borders, nor is it any good in banks. Although Third World backwaters like Central Africa, Bangladesh or Albania could probably be convinced to accept it as full and valid ID. Then again, they would probably accept an old tea bag with the right story.

The CAMOUFLAGE passport is better. FBI agents use them and so does the US Army. When an American does not want the world to know he is an American maybe for fear of kidnapping or terrorist acts he dons his camouflage passport. It is issued in the name of a now defunct country such as Ceylon or British Honduras, now called Sri Lanka and Belize, respectively. The camouflage passport can be used for banking almost everywhere, provided you look the part and come up with the right story plus assuming that your bank teller is not *too* educated. But you should not cross borders with it.

The third passport is the most professional of the lot. The WSA passport, or WORLD SERVICE AUTHORITY passport, is a United Nations style passport usually reserved for refugees and stateless persons. But charitable donors will receive one for each contribution, issued in any name. It is even better for banking than the camouflage passport and you can cross many borders with it too. For proof of this, the World Service Authority sells an inexpensive paperback book (US$15) entitled *Samples of Visas in the World Service Authority (WSA) Passport.*

This book, World Government Document #315P, has 140 pages full of photocopies of entry stamps and entry/exit visas from almost every country in the world. Although only a couple of nations recognize the WSA passport as a legal, valid, fully official document, most countries will still let you enter on it. The book shows that this is indeed possible and also gives you hints and tips on how to be succesful in obtaining the visas. Even the most unfree nation on earth, the hermetically sealed United States, has issued B1-B2 unlimited entries visitors' visas to holders of the WSA passports. So when ordering your WSA Passport, be sure to fork over the extra US$15 and get the book as well.

Just as with the coveted Camouflage passports, middlemen also peddle WSA passports at outrageous prices. But why pay more than base? We will show you the direct way to WSA, thus guaranteeing that you do not pay a dime more than you have to.

In this section we will examine all three passports and show you how to get them. We will look at how to get supporting ID. Most persons carry more than a passport. So should your *alter ego*. A lot of this is available by mail.

Lastly we will show you where to go to build a background for your new persona, maybe even give him a job, references, a tax history, the lot.

THE TEXAS PASSPORT

Developed as a joke and party gimmick this toy still looks impressive. It is a bound blue book with raised gold lettering and your photo inside. To an extent it resembles the old US passport. Border guards in Afghanistan could probably be fooled by it, but most bank tellers in the western world will have seen a US passport and will know that Texas is not an independent nation yet.

Therefore, we are hard pressed to find any practical use for it other than for fun or for playing games with thick officials.

The Texas passport is cheap and it can't hurt having one. In Europe, order with name, address, US$20 cash (including postage and packing) and just one single passport type photo from: **Five Continents Inc, PO Box 608039, Orlando, Florida 32860-8039, USA. Fax +1 407 339 0895**.

A few weeks later you will receive your new passport in the name chosen.

Use it for registering in those South American flea-bag hotels where the receptionist insists on keeping your passport in the pigeonhole overnight. In case of theft, and that is often the case, either staged or real you only lose a US$20-outlay not your real passport.

From time to time, souvenir passports and commemorative passports can be had for fees usually similar to the price of the Texas document. Two years ago, a Norwegian company advertisement in the old Robert Maxwell newspaper *The European* was selling a royal blue EEC Passport with stars of the 12 member nations. The irony is that Norway does not even belong to the European Union. We have seen Disneyland passports and various promotional passports from clothing stores, oil companies and others vying for customer loyalty. Some are free. All are worthless.

THE CAMOUFLAGE PASSPORT

This clever little document is well established. It has sold thousands and has been featured in *Time* Magazine and various other magazines and newspapers. Government forces buy and use these passports. So do criminals. But most are issued to ordinary citizens and travellers like you and me.

The camouflage passport along with supplemental ID including drivers license is sold by Scope International Ltd as an invaluable service to all registered report buyers.

The price of the package in your own name or any name you choose is just a few hundred pounds sterling. The supplier states:

> *We sincerely hope that you will never have to use your Camouflage Passport. But if there are incidents, we'd like to hear about it. Your handling of the situation could be of great benefit to further clients.*

Your camouflage passport already has a used look. It is half full of bogus entry and exit stamps, all beautifully done up from such non-existing ports of entry as Aukland and various suburbs of Rio de Janeiro .

If you return your passport every year or so you can get updates. This won't cost you a penny, except for a self-addressed envelope and approximately US$25 to cover the cost of the courier service.

You get a full history of "your" nation as well, including demographics, political situation, geographics and climatic situation. Entertaining and well thought out. Memorize it, so you can always tell foreigners about "your" land, its population, its national anthem, its income, its education system and so on and so forth.

Our agent hints that you might consider, particularly if you are using a different name, getting business cards etc in your "camouflage" name. Credit cards may also have different names if the number is the same.

When you order your camouflage documents, you cannot choose the country. This is done at the discretion of the issuer. The list of their available countries is kept secret. But if you order two or more passports, you can ask that they be from the same countries, if that's what you want, or you can tell our agent that they have to be from different countries. For more information or to order immediately, please phone and ask to speak to Richard or Stewart. Call now **+44 705 631751** or **0705 631751** if you are within Britain. Then mail your order off with your funds enclosed and four different passport type photos per passport. One for the passport, the others for your drivers license and identity card. With the order you devise your own:

- Name
- ID-number (at least six digits)
- A street number (five digits or less) for your fictitious camouflage country address
- Sex, height, eye color, date of birth and identifying marks (if any)
- Name of wife or husband (if any)
- Name of child/children (if any)
- Country of residence ie where you claim to live now (a real country, include street address if possible)
- Finally, let our agent know which areas of the world you plan to use your camouflage passport in most, then tell them the name and address you want the finished package mailed to. These last details will not appear in written form anywhere in the actual document itself.

And their advice? Know and develop your personal history, particularly if it's fictitious. This should be true for the individual as well as for the entire family. Remember names, dates, etc. Go over information as you begin your trips.

Apart from checking in at hotels, camouflage passports have been used for banking, even in quite a number of First World countries. Do not attempt to cross borders with it. You could try the World Service Authority document instead, or better yet, use the passport of the citizenship you were born with. For air travel on passenger planes internationally, *always* use your real passport, not any of those described in this report. When checking in, ground staff are now obliged to make sure that you will not be refused entry to the country of your destination. If they don't the carrier can be fined thousands of dollars. And as there are no certainties ever when it comes to the borderline passports we focus on in this report, you are best advised not to use them when boarding an international flight. Use your real passport.

THE WORLD SERVICE AUTHORITY PASSPORT

The United Nations, the Vatican and the Red Cross have the right to issue "own name" passports to refugees and stateless persons. So docs the World Service Authority of Washington DC, USA. The WSA, legally registered since 1954, is a global human rights authority that has no official connection with any national government. It is a private charitable organization adhering to the United Nations' "Universal Declaration of Human Rights", especially articles 13(2), 15(2), 21(3), 28 and 30. These are the basis of all WSA Documents, especially the World Passport.

Unlike the Red Cross, the United Nations and the Vatican, WSA is prepared to issue complimentary passports to all donors. If you give money to their cause you are rewarded with a specially issued ID card, a passport and a host of written material.

A US$50 donation gets you a crappy looking cardboard passport. Avoid it. It will do you more harm than good.

Instead, invest US$250 in the WSA. Then you are given the special donor's passport, a very impressive looking thing that easily classifies as one of the most beautiful passports in the world. The donor's edition is leatherbound, goldblocked, colorprinted and with a full 40-plus pages and translations in all major languages including Japanese, Russian and Arabic.

You also get the ID card, the book and all the instructions plus other written material.

The deluxe model, the donor's passport is super for banking everywhere and even relatively OK for crossing borders.

For more information and the form to fill out, write **World Service Authority, World Office, Suite 1106 – Continental Building, 1012 14th Street NW, Washington, DC 20005, USA, tel +1 202 - 638 2662, fax +1 202 – 638 0638** or **World Service Authority, 8th World District, Hills Nakano #208, 1-1-12 Nogata, Nakano-ku, Tokyo 165, Japan**. Also read *The Passport Report,* where we go into greater detail covering the uses and the abuses of the World Service Authority passport. More than one fraudster and con-man has used the WSA passport to extract money from innocent dupes in the past. We cover several of these cases in *The Passport Report,* complete with the list of warning signals showing you how to spot a scam. There is also a full and updated chapter on Camouflage Passports. The latest revised edition is out now.

SUPPORTING ID BY MAIL

Most people carry more than just a passport. So should your *alter ego.*

A valuable book that may help you procure various forms of half-baked ID is called *ID By Mail.* It is compiled by Barry Reid, author of the Paper Trip books on alternate identities, and published by his Eden Press. Order from **Scope International Ltd, Forestside House, Forestside, Rowlands Castle, Hants PO9 6EE, tel 0705 631751 fax 0705 631322.** See the PT Booklist for more titles and all prices.

The WSA passport can be had with a WSA Identity card as well.

And the Camouflage passport already comes with three pieces of supporting ID, a residence permit, a membership card and drivers license.

A free, instantly-issued credit card-like piece of plastic can be had by anybody, in any name, just by joining the Delta Frequent Flyer Program. You don't have to have ever been a Delta Airlines customer. In fact you don't even have to want to travel ever, and joining is free. Simply write to them with your name and address at **Oakfield Court, Consort Way, Horley, Surrey, United Kingdom, tel 0800 414767, fax 0293 773325**, stating you would like to join. You do have to tell them your company name also. But this won't be checked, so go ahead and indulge in your wildest dreams. Tell them anything, except Delta Airlines, of course. When we joined we claimed to be with the United Nations. So our credit card ID lists not just our name, but UN as well. Do you have more than one name? No problem. Delta will let you join its program again and again. Each time issuing a very official looking ID without any semblance of background check. What more can a PT ask for? Maybe another piece of plastic from another organization backing up the claim from Delta Airlines? No problem. The so-called Complimentary Card is free as well and very official looking. State name and company name, which will be embossed on the credit card ID, then write **Executive Service, via V. Monti 8, I-20123 Milano, Italy, tel +39 2 481 94271**. This organization rents out furnished offices and secretarial services on a short term basis to foreign business people visiting Italy. Their ID card is a mere gimmick designed to get you on their mailing list, but it's a two-way street, so by all means get it.

HOW TO BUILD A PAST

Although it will not be necessary in the majority of cases, you may still want to create a fictitious past. Talk to Wilf Benjamin from Three R's Ltd in Canada. He can help you with banking. He does remailing and then he has two other services which he describes as REFERENCE SERVICE. *Your fantasies can really come true here. Imagine if you put on your resumé that you have been a financial consultant making US$150,000 a year and a phone call is made or a letter written and your claim is verified by someone 1000 miles away. Fee: US$5 per inquiry. US$100 unlimited for three months.*

Some other mail drops will do the same, especially if you instruct them to do so beforehand. His other service is listed as DISINFORMATION SERVICE. *If you want some parties to believe that you are here when you are really somewhere else then we provide a 'gone out to lunch' or 'away from his desk' or 'he is in Europe on company business' answering service. Fees: US$25 per month.*

For signing up or more information, get in touch with Wilf Benjamin at **Three R's Educational Ltd (RRR), Box 242, Station M, Toronto, Canada M6S 4T3, tel +1 416 848 8102 / +1 416 847 8135/9 / + 1 416 856 6237.**

For more on creating an instant past, consult Wayne Yeager's book *Status for Sale*. The book is full to the brim with little-known addresses, including that of Antidote Press below, and comes complete with a 1994/95-update. It costs US$20. Mention WG Hill and postage will be free. Order from the publishers: **Charter Publications, PO Box 85, Salvisa, KY 40372, USA.**

Next, you want to read the recommended and outrageous underground manuscript *Job Reference Kit, 1994 Edition*. This book comes complete with not only company letterheads, but also blank 1992 W2 tax forms for you to fool around with at your leisure, making it possible for you to create an instant tax history without paying Uncle Sam for the privilege. The manuscript is written by Auto Genous and sold by Antidote Press of California. Other reports by the same company include *Underground Car Dealer* and *Underground Businesses*.

When thinking up a personal history for yourself consider some of these ideas. How long did you live there? Do you still have family there? What kind of house did you live in? When did you leave? Why did you leave? Do you go back very often? Who do you see there? You may want to acquire a few snapshots to keep in your wallet. Most people travel with a couple of photographs. It does not matter if it is of someone else's family, house and dog. Only you know. If you do not shoot your mouth off it will stay that way.

THE BLACK ART OF GHOSTING

Ghosting always means you assuming to be someone else, creating a new identity from scratch by inventing a fictitious name and if necessary, getting ID. Always dream up your own pen name or other artist's monicker. Never step into the shoes of an existing physical person. This could land you in legal trouble.

When it comes to banking, the black art of ghosting takes on two distinctly different appearances:

1) You bank purely by mail, with the bank only knowing your ghost name and your maildrop address; or
2) You bank in person using a banking passport with a misleading identity. When we first heard about the concept of a "banking passport", we were shocked. We were almost disgusted. Later we learned how the world works. We also learned of a few real life cases where banking passports saved the life of political refugees. As a result, we are now staunch defenders of the banking passport and the use of it to keep your assets in your possession always. For several pages of detailed banking passport how-to information, read the new and latest edition of our *Passport Report*, available from Scope International Ltd.

You have two ways of ghosting, by mail or in person. Banking by mail is the safest and the one most people feel comfortable with. Ghosting in person is not all that tough either. In fact being a little devious can be fun, especially since you know that you are not cheating anybody, nor defrauding nor swindling, and that the bank does not mind your little escapade. You can of course mix the two options above. Some people do. Some even have a whole closet full of ghosts with bank accounts to match. This is limited only by your imagination, your time and the fact that you should probably not have too many of your own ghosts operating in the same country at the same time. One per country is a manageable limit.

Banks will let you ghost if you tell them what you are up to. The corrupt campaign manager of Brazil's impeached ex-president, Fernando Collor de Mello, stole millions of dollars, then fled the country after his pal's fall from office. His name was Paulo César Farias. Before he ran away he had been in New York where Citibank helped him open a ghost account under the totally fictitious name of John Burnett. When the whole affair got untangled, some newspapers in Mr Farias's home country ran pictures of the signature card, signed by one of the bank's VPs of operations. Laconically, it reads "John Burnett (Special Name)". In Citibank, "Special Name" is internal code for a ghost account.

Banks will let you ghost but banks will also want to know your true identity. A serious ghost *does not have* a true identity. Because banks will sell you out at the first whiff of trouble. PC Farias is just one case in point. If you are a big fish in your local pond, our advice is: give up the ghost. Don't do it. If your career and thus your future earnings depend to a great extent on your public profile, who you are, your reputation etc etc you should not jeopardize it. The risk of ruining your career through sudden exposure of your ghost is simply too great. You never know what muck-raking journalists can get up to in the future. Information gathering technology systems are becoming more advanced. We can't know what database-seeking tools a journalist will have ten or fifteen years from now. He can set out on a trip down some future Information Highway, then return with a lot of ugly looking garbage for his front page. Public figures, performers, diplomats, hot shots of any kind, forget about ghosting or, at the very least, have someone else ghost for you. And only if you trust that someone and then still only with sharing information on a need-to-know basis, and never in writing.

For the rest of us, ghosting especially by mail is more attractive. Before you start your program, think of what excuses you can come up with if your cleaning lady finds a credit card in another name or if your wife discovers bank statements written not to you, but to a fictitious name and another address. My favorite standby is: "G Host is an old friend from college. He is on a two year trekking trip in Nepal and I am managing his financial affairs on his behalf while he is gone." You may even get the tax man to buy it. But then again, tax men have heard of ghosts before. In the worst case scenario, they will open a criminal case for tax evasion against you. During the case, one of their claims will be that you are the ghost. If you deny it, their stancc will be something like "Fine, in that case, we will ask the authorities to hold you in custody while waiting for the real Mr G Host to step forward." If you don't want to rot in a jail cell waiting for this to happen, your only unattractive alternative is to retract your previous denials. This is all heavy duty stuff, so please give some thought as to how far you want to carry your ghosting. And think of all this *before* you start your program.

Ghosting is a good thing. If we didn't feel this way we would not have written anything about it in this book. Out of a random sample of 100 PTs each banking partially with the help of a ghost, 98 or 99 will have happy experiences. Having said that we are not blind to the potential negatives of ghosting. To pull it off with no risk of anything backfiring you need to adhere strictly to the low profile principles described in this report and expanded upon in *PT 2*. If bad luck gets in your way, a tax case or even a passport tangle could be next. How? If, for some reason, your picture runs in the paper, for instance. Some bank clerk somewhere sees it and recognizes you. But he does not recognize your name. In his records you have been using a different name. He then checks with the signature card and finds a photocopy in the files of the passport you used to open the account. Eager to do his civic duty and earn his brownie points he phones up the newspaper. A journalist soon arrives at the bank to compare notes, then leaves with a copy of "your" passport. The next day, your picture is in the paper again, this time next to a photostat of the banking passport you used to open your by now uncovered ghost account. No, we are not trying to scare you. We are merely trying to wake you up to the fact that this is the real world and life can be tough. Not everything works out the way you want it to, despite the best of intentions. By all means go ahead and be a ghost. Ninety-nine per cent end up Happy Ghosts forever. In your quest for utter privacy and eternal tax freedom do not blind yourself to the potential pot holes.

Chapter 10

THE BEAUTY OF BACK-TO-BACK LOANS

Lynden Oscar Pindling, the black former Prime Minister of the Bahamas, lives mainly on loans. Most of these come from foreigners seeking favors. Records show that the Prime Minister and his wife had received nearly US$17 million in gifts and loans from foreigners over a period of 12 years, starting in 1977. The difference between loans and gifts seems to be unclear. Pindling keeps scant financial records and although he does, on some loans, keep up interest payments, most lenders never expect to be repaid. All loans were unsecured with no documentation and no provision for the payment of interest. Today, Sir Lynden, who was knighted by Queen Elizabeth in 1983, lives in Lakeview, a property described as something between a villa and a palace. The mortgage payment is US$4500 a month. On top of this the former Bahamas Prime Minister has interest payments on bank loans ranging from US$7000 to US$8000 a month. Since his annual salary was a relatively modest US$100,000 he has to obtain new loans to keep his head above water. For him, however, loans are not hard to get. He was Prime Minister of the Bahamas, chronicled the following way by the Miami Herald in its article "A Nation for Sale": *You can buy an airstrip, or an island. You can buy citizenship. You can buy protection. You can buy justice. And should your drug cargo get seized by police, you can even buy it back.*

For those of us with less influence to peddle, loans are harder to come by. But back-to-back loans, borrowing against your own funds on deposit somewhere else, are always sure things. Besides, they are cheap to come by. Instead of paying a full interest, you normally pay a "spread" to the bank or financial institution putting the loan together. The spread is the difference between the highest deposit interest rate and the lowest rate at which the bank lends to its most solid customers.

PTs can stop reading right here. They won't have a need for back-to-back loans, unless they are engaged in business somewhere and pay taxes. Or unless they are in a special situation, where they for some reason eg bankruptcy, alimony or some other court intrusion entirely cannot show that they are earning a lot of money. Those who don't pay taxes normally don't need to shield income. Taxpayers of all types, personal and corporate, read on. Back-to-back loans are for you.

Back-to-back loans are one of the most preferred ways tax evaders get their money back into the country while at the same time avoiding having to pay tax on it. Black money earned from moonlighting or selling goods in the informal economy can make a stop-over in the foreign bank account of an offshore corporation, then come back to you as loans granted not by the corporation, but by the bank itself or by one of its correspondent banks in your home country.

The price for all of this is low. Of US$100,000 untaxed money sent abroad, US$99,000 would come back to you as a loan. Of US$10,000 paid in interest, US$9900 would be made on interest from the security held offshore. The US$9900 would be tax free while the US$10,000 would be tax deductible, in a normal case. So even though it looks like a back-to-back loan costs you something in the neighborhood of one per cent, you could find yourself making money on the deal in the form of a tax deductible expense. The loser is your government, since you won't be paying what they think is your fair share of tax. As a result, back-to-back loans are a gray area of finance. They shouldn't be advertised too loudly.

Back-to-back loans are used not just to bring money back from offshore or to borrow money for personal or business reasons. Because you are, like Prime Minister Pindling, living off loans you have no personal property that can be seized or attached in court proceedings. You are on safer grounds from creditors, ex-wives, bankruptcy, foreclosure, IRS liens and other ills of the world.

Because you are setting up your own loan, you can pretty well dictate the terms. Don't make them too outlandish. An exotic blend could draw attention to you. Yet loans come in all shapes and sizes and if you can keep everything at arms-length, arrangements of the loan can be almost anything. One facilitator of such loans writes that:

A. *The loan can be a 1 year, 5 year, 20 year or 50 year loan.*

B. *The interest rate can be 8 per cent, 12 per cent, 20 per cent, etc.*

C. *Interest can be paid at the end of the first year only, at the end of the fifth year only or at the end of the twentieth year. And all the capital can fall due at any time selected. The system is very flexible.*

D. *The monthly payments can be US$100 or US$300 or US$1000 or US$10,000. It is possible not to have any payments at all during the first year or the second year or all principal and interest can be paid in a balloon payment at the end of the loan.*

The point is you decide exactly what you want. Terms, conditions, length of the loan, interest rate, amounts of payments to be, etc . . .

Later, in the same material, the facilitator writes: *Hundreds of examples can work for you. All you have to do is simply let your imagination run with ideas. What can be accomplished is limited only by your imagination.* This paragraph is preceeded by one stating that *when the Friendly Loan Company receives your first US$375 monthly interest payment, the Friendly Loan Company can send it back to you each month so that you can make all of the remaining 59 monthly payments with the same first original payment.* While this certainly sounds tempting, a PT-in-waiting would be more cautious, always working at arms-length and in a way that can stand up to scrutiny.

You are best off organizing back-to-back loans directly with a bank. This lends substance and credibility to the arrangement. You also lessen the risk of something going wrong, for example crooks absconding with your half of the "back" before lending it "back" to you. Working with a bank you will have to do a bit of leg-work. What you are asking for is a personal loan which is secured by funds on a blocked deposit. That the funds belong to a company, albeit a company you control, directly or indirectly is no obstacle. You will get the loan as a personal loan or any way you want it, regardless. Putting the loan package together is not too complicated, but don't expect the bank to have a standard product ready. You need to tell them what you want and how you want it done. You also need to negotiate fees individually. In an ideal setup your offshore company has money on deposit earning a tax free interest rate. This money secures your loan. If you are a tax payer, you can usually deduct interest payments made to the bank, depending on the rules of your country and what the loan looks like. Most foreign banks dealing with the private international community are familiar with back-to-back loans, but tailormade solutions don't exist. The bank will be sympathetic and will listen. It will want to help you. After all, you are offering it yet another chance to make a buck. Just don't skirt over the details or assume that all can be arranged with just one phone call. It can't. You have to play an active part in giving yourself the loan. This will involve some meetings and should at least involve one trip. No standard packages exist.

Try to keep as little in writing as you can. At least concerning the mechanics behind the deal. Work only with banks in foreign jurisdictions, use the PT Five Flag theory to the hilt. For even more added secrecy, have someone else visit the bank to set everything up. At best, the bank doesn't even know you . . . except as a third party who obtained a loan. Your resident agent acting as a director for your offshore company may be that "someone else" willing to visit the bank and put everything together. If you yourself assume that role, it may be wise if you are not at the same time also the borrower. Have a third party borrow the funds, then lend them to you or someone in your circle of influence.

This may all seem a bit technical, but it is just like learning how to swim. Go ahead and get your feet wet. If you find yourself on unfamiliar turf, you may want to contact a couple of consultants, private firms specializing in back-to-back loans and similar tax related solutions. We are not recommending anybody here, so holding on to your money is your own responsibility. We don't want to see you lose it. Having said that, we haven't had any adverse reports from one company arranging discreet back-to-back financing using offshore banks in several different countries: **Global Consulting Group S.A., P.O. Box 945, Suite 922, Centro Colon 1007, San Jose, Costa Rica.** Global deals almost exclusively with Americans. From Global, order their US$15 CLP program, a 12 page brochure detailing how back-to-back loans work when you structure them through the Global Consulting Group. CLP stands for Client Loan Program. Biased towards Americans and dealing with American tax law, the CLP text shows how individuals and companies get a tax deductible itemized expense while at the same time repatriating money from offshore back to the on-shore side, without any income tax consequences. This, using nastier words, is borderline money laundering. But only in the eyes of over-anxious prosecutors is money laundering in and by itself a crime. Who gets hurt by a back-to-back loan? Nobody. So where's the crime?

Global describes its Client Loan Program as *specifically designed to give the individual a legal tax deductible itemized interest expense deduction against his personal income or in the case of a business, an operating or overhead interest expense deduction against all business income.* It is also recommended and highly informative. At US$15 and another US$5 later on for CLP II, a package of contractual documents needed to proceed with the actual loan itself it is a steal. If this is something you have an interest in, go ahead and order it. Global's text is the best we have seen in the business. Read it, even if you want to organize the loan yourself without the help of Global, which takes ten per cent of all interest payments for its trouble. Is this expensive? The spread that your bank charges could easily be a full per cent, sometimes more. And with interest rates at today's low levels, this equals more than what Global charges you. On top of that, most banks have fixed charges for granting loans and other charges for securing them. Global charges you only the ten per cent. You will probably find they are the lowest priced game in town. Don't be obsessed with just saving money. Peace of mind, secrecy and security is far more important than saving a buck here or there. Our advice is work with whomever you feel most comfortable with.

You don't need to have your own offshore company to set up back-to-back loans. Service companies such as Global will readily lend you theirs. But even if you go it alone, as we think you should, dealing directly with the bank, an offshore company is not essential. What really matters is that you have funds in an account abroad and that you can tie these funds down to serve as security deposit for your loan. That the funds are held in a company name is an added benefit. It will give you some measure of secrecy if the bank ever decides to lift its own secrecy and sell you out.

Eventually, you will have to pay back the loans. Or will you? Start by working with long term loans, 20 to 30 year terms. If you can secure them by real estate, you have the added benefit of your house being "no go" to greedy creditors. There is already a first mortgage on it . . . yours! As an aside, it must be said here that US taxpayers taking advantage of back-to-back loans have to secure them by personally owned real estate if they expect to get the interest rate deduction. One of the latest changes to the IRS code is the removal of the interest deduction for the Individual on everything except his personal real estate. Using a real estate secured back-to-back loan to pay for your new car, a vacation or college tuition is a great way of keeping your interest payments deductable.

With 20 or 30 year loans, the time for paying back is a long way down the road. When that time comes you can always adopt the attitude of all western governments. They are heavily in the red. Instead of repaying the national debt they simply borrow more. You can do the same.

Back-to-back loans are flexible, and 20-30 years from now you will no doubt have made enough to grant yourself another loan. The keyword here is roll-over financing. Don't worry too much about the long term. Tax rules change. Problems disappear. And like the politicians are fond of always reminding themselves, in the long run we are all dead. So go ahead, borrow more. Roll over finance will keep you happily in hock forever. Your friendly bank or loan company will always be pleased to lend you more, even if you are not the former Prime Minister of the Bahamas. The question then becomes, at what point does it stop?

Chapter 11

AROUND THE WORLD IN FIVE EASY STEPS

If you are not already familiar with the "five flags" theory of PT, read the summary in the back pages of this report, then read the two volumes of the PT Bible. Part one deals with the theory, part two with the practice, offering hands-on, how-to solutions for privacy seekers and lesson after lesson in low profile.

This report deals with banking, only one of the five flags necessary in a complete PT plan. Another, the controversial and highly informative *Sex Havens*, deals with the playgrounds. Yet others deal with tax havens and the perfect official residence.

A TAX HAVEN WITHIN A TAX HAVEN

As a sex haven style playground, the United Arab Emirates (UAE) does not have much going for it. Not only are the local womenfolk unavailable, you also risk capital punishment if you pursue them in any vigorous way. Just looking at a girl can get you in trouble with lesser educated enforcers of Islam in this Arab nation so rich on oil but poor on civil liberties.

Despite its failure to attract scores of pleasure seeking tourists, the United Arab Emirates is attracting money. During the last couple of years, this gulf state has quietly been placing itself on the map of offshore advisers and tax planners worldwide. As part of a government strategy to shift away from sole reliance on oil proceeds, the Jebel Ali Free Zone has been created. Here, anything goes. Even whisky and women, the worst of all things western have been let in. Why? Because the Jebel Ali was set up to attract not local money and companies, but foreign ones. It has worked.

We can best describe Jebel Ali as a tax haven within a tax haven. Although long a low tax area for businesses and a no tax place for residents, the United Arab Emirates failed to attract foreign investment. Part of the reason was local politics, which in that region of the world is religion and the ruling families all rolled into one. A larger part was too many laws on the books.

With the Jebel Ali government planners set out to create a UAE-style tax haven, but with even fewer laws. In the Jebel Ali free zone, foreigners can do what they want as long as they stick to what they do ie foreign companies and residents cannot change horses midstream and move into areas of businesses other than those for which each individual entry was originally approved.

The absence of laws, government control, tax and currency restrictions all adds up to a good thing. Even better, at least for the time being, is the fact that Jebel Ali is a well kept secret. Doing business with this super liberal tax haven will not get you noticed overseas in the way that relations with more shady money larks would. Transfers from the USA to places like the Turks & Caicos or the Bahamas are under close surveillance. Several federal agencies scrutinize them all, independent of one another. We know of no such operations against businesses dealing with the Jebel Ali or with the United Arab Emirates in general.

Do we have to spell out what this means? Smart folks have been moving their smart money through the Jebel Ali Free Zone recently. The place has never been tainted by scandals. Only in 1993 did a few small voices suggest that the Jebel Ali could possibly be a money laundering center.

"Could possibly" is putting it mildly. "Is certainly" would be more to the point. And the UAE even brag about it.

To bring even more of this sort of business to Jebel Ali, the United Arab Emirates is sponsoring full page ads in leading English-language financial and economic publications. The ads are all the same. And it is some ad! If ever one spelt it out this was it. Showing a picture of a fresh-faced, educated Franklin Jurado type money launderer going quietly about his business, nineties style with the phone and his PC, the heading reads as follows: "He hasn't paid tax since 1987. He transfers his money overseas. He's known throughout the Middle East. And the only auditor looking for him is his golf partner".

What money launderer caught up in the bumper to bumper fears of the crumbling west of today would not want such a blissful existence? These four headline sentences, coupled with the photo of a happily optimistic tax-cheat banker are aimed squarely at all money managers fed up with the way the west has made it difficult and in many cases even illegal for them to do business. Knowing this full and well, the marketing department of the Jebel Ali Free Zone made the right choice for its own slogan: "Freedom to do Business". The freedom is a complete freedom to do your own business in peace and quiet, with no laws to bar you and no regulators to make your life hell or to scare away your clients. Nearly every type of business is being welcomed with open arms, as the Jebel Ali Free Zone Authority will be more than happy to tell you. For customer service or marketing requirements, their PR department can be contacted at **PO Box 17000, Dubai, UAE, tel +971 084-56578, fax +971 084 56073, telex 47398 DPA EM.**

Complete tax freedom for residents is a matter of course. Corporations are given a minimum 15 years tax holiday. When these first 15 years run out, expect another 15 to be added on top of them. And so on *ad infinitum* until we are all dead and buried. Unlike most other places in the region, 100 per cent foreign ownership of any company is allowed. So is the free transfer of all profits to anywhere, not subject to any license, permission or even overseeing. These facts have prompted banks, financial services companies and other helpers to set up shop in Jebel Ali. Many multinationals have moved into the zone as well. They use Dubai as a marketing hub for the region's estimated 1.3 billion consumers. Doing this in a regulatory-free environment and with no taxes to pay whatsoever adds to the pleasure and attractiveness of Dubai. Side by side with multinationals such as the Cali cartels are found US stable names such as Nike, IBM and Philip Morris. Whatever their business, they all appreciate the freedom to do business, as the marketing slogan correctly puts it. And in Jebel Ali, let there be no doubt about it, the authorities are clearly saying: "Come on in, folks. Make yourself comfortable. We're open for business!"

The United Arab Emirates earns its money on oil and oil royalties, so they are not too busy collecting taxes. The world's largest man-made harbor is in Dubai, housing the Jebel Ali zone. Several international names have built factories and handling centers for import/export. Besides those already named, you'll find Reebok, Citizen, Caltex, Airwell, Star Energy, Aiwa, Mitsubishi, Sony, Black & Decker, York, Schlumberger, McDermott, Shell and Air Products.

From a statistical point of view there are plenty of customers in the area. The region surrounding the Persian Gulf is home to more than a billion people. Right now, few of these folks buy Reebok shoes, watches from Citizen, cars from Mitsubishi or air conditioners from York or Airwell. This could change.

In the large free trade area, you will find small western villages where alcohol and nightlife is available. You can play tennis and golf with other expats. You can live and work there. If you are not keen on travelling, it is possible to live your entire life inside one of the western compounds.

The government of Dubai allows 100 per cent foreign ownership of local companies as well as no exchange controls and they do not interfere with inward clearance or exportation of capital. Of course there is no limitation on exportation of surplus and what is even better, there are no taxes at all! The government is willing to guarantee that this will last at least another 15 years.

For those living in the area, note that no personal income tax exists, nor capital tax, nor VAT. Local labor is cheap and you won't have to pay import duties on anything you bring in. Export duties don't exist either. As they say: "We're open for business!"

WHERE THE SMART MONEY GOES

Smart money wanting to save on its total global tax bill stays away from all the usual tax havens. It goes where no tax man would ever dream of raising his red flag alarm. They go to places that on the face of it are high tax countries, but where special deals and concessions, often unknown to foreign countries, can make life a lot sweeter than a first glance would lead to belive.

In the European Union alone, four such countries are France, Greece, Ireland and the Netherlands. None are low-tax countries, yet all four have sweeteners to soften the tax bill. In some cases doing away with tax entirely if you fit their criteria.

FRANCE

France is far from being a tax haven. When it comes to personal taxation, the country has the most complicated statutes in all of Europe. Having said that, in the rural parts of southern France it is still possible to negotiate flat rate taxes with the local tax office. Foreigners who have done so report that the effective tax rate works out at between 20 to 25 centimes to the franc. If you are burdened with heavy payments to the system, France is not normally recommended as the country to escape to, unless you escape in the still of the night, PT-style, and stay off computers.

Because of the complexity of French tax law there are loopholes you can exploit to receive what in effect is a ten year tax holiday. You need to establish some sort of manufacturing or production. Then you need to locate your setup in a designated enterprise zone. These zones are fortunately choice locations on the sunny Côte d'Azur, the Riviera of Southern France where the sun is shining. Ireland, with similar enterprise zones and tax holidays offers only endless rain.

Setting up in a French enterprise zone may even turn out to be a money-spinner. Under job-creation schemes and programs, you can get EU money to pay for training and hiring staff. You don't want to venture into the thicket of EU law, Brussels-sprouts and Strassbourg-regulations? Fear not. This jungle is navigated free of charge by business offices in the French enterprise zones. Their consultant works free and will take care of all the practicalities so you won't get a headache from messing with the silly paper tigers of the EU. All you have to do is sign on the dotted line, then sit back and wait for the check.

Several biggish firms are already established in the enterprise zones of southern France. Yves Rocher, Coca Cola, Hobie-Cat, Beaufor-Ipsen, Matra, Thomson, Oreca, Noral and many others and lots of smaller ventures too.

Get more information from the commercial attaché at any French Embassy or from **Provence Industrialisation, 185 Avenue de l'Infanterie de Marine, F – 83000 Toulon, France, tel +33 9403 0066, fax +33 – 9403 0075**.

GREECE

Greece, like France, is certainly no balmy oasis for tax-adverse PTs. Yet it also has its redeeming features that the smart money is using. If you fit into one of the Greek pigeon-holes, Greece could well become a base or at least a link in your international strategy.

The country is a member of the European Union (although that is hard to believe at times). No red flags are raised anywhere when you receive payments from Greece or transfer funds to Greece. The reason is of course that you pay taxes in Greece. Quite a few taxes, in fact. But Greece has exemptions which are there for the same purpose, to attract foreign capital.

In the Greek tax code, offshore companies are Greek companies which have been established to run business in other countries. They get tax exemption under law no. 89/67 and law 378/68. As if this wasn't enough, the laws 2687/53 and 4171/61 can grant tax holidays to manufacturing industries attracted to Greece. And using European development funds, the whole hulabaloo can be paid for with other people's money.

The law no. 89/67 regarding Greek offshore companies has attracted some 2500 firms, mainly industrial companies, shipping companies and companies trading worldwide with Greece as their base.

In order to get special tax treatment ie tax freedom these companies are not allowed to do business in Greece, only abroad. In return they are exempt from all taxes, VAT included. At the same time they are allowed to import all their office equipment, furniture, office machines and other assets without paying customs, VAT or import duties of any kind.

To establish a company under law 89/67 you have to file an application with the Greek Ministry of Coordination. With the application you have to enclose a virtual mountain of silly red-tape documentation which has to be translated into Greek by the Foreign Ministry in Greece. You also have to enclose a bank guarantee of US$50,000. This proves to the Greeks that you're not a loafer.

When you form the company, you will be asked to sign a form stating that the money you'll be using to run your company is not earned in Greece but will be imported. You need to spend around US$50,000 a year on rent, salaries and other expenditures. If you spend a lot less, you may see your permission to run a company under law no. 89/67 withdrawn by the Greek Ministry of Coordination. The way around this is to give yourself a salary hike.

The Greek offshore companies, which need not be offshore but can be run from downtown Athens, fly right in the face of Brussels harmonization. But that's the way the Greeks do business, only acknowledging EU membership if and when it suits them.

IRELAND

Since the Republic of Ireland joined the EU it has earned very well on the membership indeed. Southern Ireland with a per capita income roughly that of Spain is still Britain's poor cousin. The Irish are trying to change that, partly by vying for foreigners with a mass of easy-going tax legislation. Foremost, Ireland wants to attract what they call "hi-tec/low polluting" industry to the island, especially to the western part, a poor and underdeveloped region where it rains a lot and where the main pastime of the locals is to stay indoors and get drunk.

The area around the old Shannon Airport is one such development zone. Before airlines started using Boeing 747s for transatlantic flights they had to refuel for the long journey. Usually, they did so in Shannon, Europe's westernmost airport. When the need for refueling disappeared, Shannon sank into a ghost-existence. Unemployment there has been chronically high ever since. Government planners have arrived and later left with their bag of tricks to kickstart new development. One scheme offering tax exemption for exporting companies based in Shannon was all the rage in the seventies. It failed miserably. It has been replaced by a new package. Using the Shannon rules, manufacturing companies pay between zero and ten per cent in company tax. In most cases your actual tax bill comes to 4.5 per cent of net profits, according to local accountants knowledgeable about the application of the rules.

The word "manufacturing" is defined in extremely liberal and broad terms. So the virtual tax exemption can also be used by software firms, PR companies and anybody who assembles anything, even if the bits assembled were actually produced outside Ireland. What seems to count most to the Irish is the fact that you will be bringing work to a country with a lot of youngsters and great unemployment.

For a resident company with assets in the country Ireland is only a tax haven to the extent that you are producing goods of some kind.

If you are doing that, Ireland can be one of the best havens in the world. The country is both a member of the EU, well known everywhere, and party to a long list of double taxation treaties.

Personal tax freedom is available too. If you are a writer, artist, painter, poet or some other creative type, you can still take advantage of the traditional Irish tax exemption if you choose to settle down permanently in the country. Many famous scribes have retired to Irish country cottages. Here they are living a life in complete tax freedom, harvesting royalties from all over the world and not paying a dime in tax.

If you don't know how to string two words together but if you'd still like to use Ireland as a tax free vehicle, look into the possibility of using exempt-companies in either the Shannon area or the Customs Dock House of Dublin. The latter is a sort of onshore "offshore" zone for financial service companies dealing abroad. By housing your company in the Customs Dock House you are free from Irish rules and regulations, and free from Irish taxes too. All with the OK of the Irish authorities. They encourage you to come. Using EU coercion money, since Ireland is a recipient of development funds, they will even pay your start-up costs. Leading Dublin accountants Peat Marwick, Arthur Andersen & Co, Price Waterhouse all have free literature on the incentives. Contact their libraries for more details.

Located in the Customs Dock House, housed within an existing company servicing your operations, you can set up a company with nil running expenses and no offices, yet with "judgment proofing" and the advantage that you are operating an EU-company from a preferred location, Dublin. And not paying any tax at all, whatsoever.

There is no doubting the fact that the possibilities are there for some creative tax thinking involving Eire's 27,126 square kilometers. The country's almost four million inhabitants are sort of well educated. Most of them are young. They are said to be service minded, hard working and eager to work with the rest of the world. The phones work very well. Something we can't say for Greece or lesser tax havens. And the mail will only take a couple of days to reach the rest of Europe. There are daily flights to Dublin from all European capitals.

For foreign investors willing to invest in Ireland, note that you can get state guaranteed investment loans at around three per cent per annum, as long as you can come up with matching funds yourself. A total package would seldom involve less than £1m, of which your part equals half.

THE NETHERLANDS

Holland is no rosy tax haven either. The country has the silliest welfare system of all EU countries, with more people on fake disablement payments than anywhere else. For years Holland has had the doubtful honor of vying with Denmark and Sweden for first place in the list of countries with the hardest, highest personal tax rate.

Yet Holland, curiously, has laws whereby multinationals can get what amounts to almost a tax holiday by consolidating their international operations and running the show from a base there. Dutch holding companies are now more popular than ever, paying next to nothing for the privilege of utilizing the Dutch network of double-taxation treaties to recoup profits tax free from other countries.

A case in point is the Swedish clothing giant Hennes & Mauritz. For many years the group held its various international companies under the umbrella of a Danish holding company. By doing so, it could take advantage of what in Denmark was called an "international exemption" while at the same time writing off inventories under depreciation rules far more lenient than those in home-country Sweden.

However, Hennes & Mauritz have moved their international base to Holland. H&M is now centered around a Dutch NV, same as a joint-stock company which is even more favorable seen from a taxation point of view. A huge number of other multinationals have done the same.

If you are receiving royalties from trademarks or patents, Holland could be a good place to set up shop. Financing companies or Luxembourg-style holding companies are also candidates for lenient Dutch tax treatment.

The Dutch tax authorities are surprisingly cooperative. Unlike pig-headed bureaucrats in most other countries, it seems that when you talk to the Dutch, they listen. They are almost kind, which is quite an experience when you come from countries where official smiles and friendliness inevitably are a cover for something very nasty coming up around the bend later on. In Holland you can on relatively short notice get a firm advance ruling on the possible tax liability of a planned disposition. This advance ruling is real. It will stick in court. But it does not hedge, like other countries' advance tax rulings, by always stating "Yes, you have to pay tax" in borderline cases or other instances of doubt. In Holland you can even strike a deal beforehand with the tax man ie agree on how much your future tax bill should be. This makes it easier for international finance companies and leasing companies or recipients of royalties to budget the tax and in this way calculate expenses involved in the offers which are given or collections you cash in. A reader who used to work in Holland reports that a case of his was discussed directly with the Dutch Ministry of Finance. Later, we learned that this was not exceptional. It often happens.

Bank secrecy in Holland is a myth. It doesn't exist since it is only limited by the professional secrecy of the banks concerning a client relationship. Numbered accounts do not exist and to open an account you have to prove your identity. If the account is for a legal person, all corporate papers have to be shown too. The two main Dutch company types are the BV and the NV, similar to Germany's GmbH and AG. From a fiscal point of view, there is no difference between the two types, but while NV can both issue shares on names as well as bearer papers, the BV can only issue shares registered on names.

Founding a company in Holland takes approximately 12 weeks. If you don't have time to wait, find a lawyer who will sell you an empty shell company.

Curiously, in Holland, locally registered companies do not have to have any administration, any office or any management in Holland if they don't want to. Some multinationals with Dutch NVs as their hub have NO PRESENCE whatsoever in the country. This does not exempt them from the theoretical Dutch tax liability. But in borderline cases where interpretation of double-taxation treaties are involved, this fact can move the power of actual taxation to another country.

Holland is primarily used in international tax planning due to a large number of quite reasonable double taxation agreements. With some of them, you can still use Holland as a stepping-stone for funnelling money out to the virtually tax free Dutch Antilles. The Dutch Antilles do not have independent double taxation agreements. But in some cases the Antilles are included in the Dutch treaties. For years, playing a shell-game involving three countries with the loot ending up on the Dutch Antilles, has been a favorite pastime among taxplanners worldwide. Sadly, most tax gatherers have now become wise to this. As a result, they have revised their double taxation treaties with the Netherlands. Today, several of the treaties specifically exclude the Dutch Antilles. If this is your game, don't let some misinformed adviser mislead you with an old or outdated text. Get the latest double taxation treaty between Holland and the country you are going to work with, then see what it says about the Dutch Antilles. You could be on to a good thing. Or you could be about to venture in where angels fear to tread.

The Dutch Antilles consists of six islands, geographically divided into two groups. Aruba, Bonaire and Curacao located about 50 km from the coast of Venezuela, and St. Maarten, Saba and St. Eustatius located around 50 km East of Puerto Rico.

Aruba broke loose and declared its independence as a sovereign country on 1st January, 1986, but in real terms the island is still a part of the Dutch Antilles.

The Dutch Antilles is home to around a quarter of a million people, most of whom live in Curacao and Aruba. These two islands have become the financial and trading centers of their area. Lots of foreign banks have setups on Aruba or Curacao, in the capital Willemstad.

The official language is Dutch and as monetary standard they have their own guilden, NA-G (Netherland Antilles Guilden). The Dutch Antilles were made part of the Dutch kingdom by a 1954 law and since then, political life has been uneventful. Ever since the close of the Second World War, local government and business have worked hard to establish an attractive climate for international business. The Dutch Antilles practically invented the concept of tax haven in the Caribbean. Although many neighbors now offer more advantages, the Dutch Antilles had a headstart and as a result, a lot of banks and private offshore companies call these islands their home.

More than 25,000 companies are registered on the Dutch Antilles, not all of them small. Several multinationals, from Shell to Unilever, have operations there. All company names end with NV. This stands for *Naamloze Vennootshappen* and is Dutch for joint stock company. Companies with Curacao as their home can use the free port area, ideal for production companies. The Dutch Antilles freeport competes mostly with Colón in Panama and with the Bahamas. In Curacao, free port companies only pay two per cent tax of surplus earned by export – inclusive re-export. This percentage tax, the state guarantees, won't rise before June 1999 at the earliest.

Other taxes? All companies have to file an annual statement together with a filing fee.

Companies owned by non-resident foreigners are not subject to currency restrictions. They do have to pay tax, but tax is low. Corporate taxes start at 2.4 per cent of the first 100,000 NA-Guilden profits, then 3 per cent of the rest. These percentages apply if your income is derived from investments, from holding companies, from real estate and trade of real estate and intangible assets such as for example patents and trade marks or copyrights. If you made your money in insurance, you pay double percentages: 4.8 per cent on the first 100,000 NA-G, then 6 per cent on the rest. And if you became rich in shipping or air traffic, brace yourself. Your tax rate is 7.73 per cent, then 9.66 per cent on everything over NA-G 100,000. Local tax law states that these percentages cannot be increased at any date earlier than 30 June 1999.

Around 30 banks are resident on the Dutch Antilles, among them Banque de Nova Scotia, Barclays, Bank America and the internationally minded Dutch ABN Amro bank. These banks are traditionally strong in the Euro-dollar market, but they don't shy away from simple deposit-taking. There is no tax on interest. Neither are profits paid from a Dutch Antilles company to persons abroad taxed in any way.

As a place to live and do business, the Dutch Antilles is not half bad. We visited not long ago. The prices, like all Caribbean islands, are a bit on the high side. But you don't pay anything for the wide sandy beaches, the palm trees, the sunshine and the quality of an almost tax free life.

You can make money there, too. Unlike islands that purely cater to tourism, the Dutch Antilles is populous enough to have industry. They want more, and local government has done its bit to attract foreign factories. This has partly been done by extending the harbors in such a way that shipping today is a big industry combined with import/export and a great deal of re-export. Re-export, as in Hong Kong, seems to be a nice little earner for the resident foreigners.

Scores of expatriates work a few hours a day with documents which are changed. They also over-invoice from companies located on the Antilles. This is not strenuous work. You can make thousands just from an hour or two a day, like some Americans are doing as you read this. The rest of the day they sit in the sun. Or go to the beach with a book and a cooler full of beer.

Some operate as resident agents and directors for Dutch Antilles NVs, since it is a requirement that all companies have at least one director who is a resident of one of the islands. This director can be a legal person, too. In other words, another Dutch Antilles NV established for the purpose.

Other foreigners operate company-mills, forming Dutch Antilles NVs. It takes four weeks and then they sell them readymade through classified ads in international publications. Shares can be either on name in which case at least 20 per cent of capital must be paid-up on incorporation, or bearer with the requirement that all of the nominal capital is fully paid. There is no minimum capital requirement. You can freely divide shares into classes and you can also freely choose what currency to denomiate the shares in.

The Dutch Antilles and Curacao in particular would not be a bad place to put down roots. Due to the Dutch influence life is civilized and very European. At the same time, you can bask in sun and live tax free.

Everything works, unlike many other Caribbean island-paradises. The mail gets delivered. The phones work. The islands have the most efficient infrastructure of the region. Flights are plentiful, with several direct inter-continental connections.

Due to the Antilles being gradually excluded from the Dutch double taxation treaties, the locals have been negotiating their own instead. Currently, treaties are in place with Holland, the USA, UK, Norway and of all places Surinam.

Chapter 12

ENCOUNTERS ALONG THE MONEY TRAIL

Depending on who you ask, between 50 and 100 of the 200 odd countries in the world are banking havens or tax havens, sometimes both. Where you draw the line is often hard to establish because a lot of havens are only attractive to foreigners. Locals living there, and companies doing business locally, usually pay quite hefty rates of tax. Some of the banking havens offering banking secrecy, supposedly, to foreigners also forget all about the secrecy pledge when it comes to protecting the interests of the local depositor.

A commonly heard figure is that the world is home to around 80 tax or banking havens. Of these, less than a fifth are true tax and banking havens in all aspects. But this is changing. Even countries normally thought of as high-tax, red-tape bureaucracies hold secrets that few outsiders ever get to know about. Just take Japan, for instance. A little known secret is that in Japan, of all countries, you can use some on-shore "offshore banks" to sidestep the normally closed regulatory red-tape. In a brave quest to win some of Japan's deposits back from Asian banking havens, notably Hong Kong, the Japanese passed some laws in the 1980s and eased others. That has resulted in offshore banks located in downtown Tokyo. These banks cannot serve Japanese, only foreigners and foreign subsidiaries of Japanese firms. Because they are outside the main Japanese banking system for all practical purposes, they are exempt from almost all banking regulations. Yet because no offshore authority exists either, there are no laws substituting those that the offshore banks have been made exempt from. In other words, a complete and utter void. A lawless world of banking where you are free to do everything you want. Right in the middle of buttoned up Tokyo. "The Wild East" of the money business has long been Hong Kong with its influential stock exchange and its no questions asked gold market. All eyes are on Hong Kong and what will happen in 1997. After 100 years as a British Crown Colony, the capitalist outpost will return to China. Although sort of a communist country, yet in many ways with far more freedom to do business than our own western-style democracies, China has promised to keep the capitalist trappings of Hong Kong in place for at least another 50 years. Six million Hong Kong Chinese are hoping they can believe the leaders of Red China. Quite a few of Hong Kong's inhabitants run trading companies, shipping firms and import/export operations. A lot of these setups are mere re-invoicing, where all the staff do is take pad receipts before re-exporting goods to high tax markets. Hong Kong, a tax haven, has an estimated 10,000 fully legal re-invoicing operations. Most of them are housed in closet sized "offices" in huge office hotels. Because of a chronic housing shortage, some of these closets-cum-offices double as bedrooms at night. The most widespread perk of working in Hong Kong.

Hong Kong, where English and Chinese are spoken, has no currency restrictions. A number of international banks, including some Swiss, are represented in Hong Kong. All signs are that they will stay on after the 1997 handover. These banks let you operate numbered acounts and, as a special Hong Kong innovation, something called the "Hong Kong Chop Account" and hailed by some to be the ultimate in bank secrecy. With a chop account, your name does not appear anywhere nor will you ever have to put your signature on a single check or document. Instead, all transactions are done with a small seal or stamp identifying the account holder by a number of quite complex Chinese signs. The stamp serves as a signature on checks. "Bearer checks", you could call them, since the bearer of the check book and the little "chop" is the person who without any restrictions can pass out checks as long as funds in the account cover them. The Hong Kong currency is the local Hong Kong dollar (HK$), and since the country doesn't have a central bank, three large private banks are issuing their own Hong Kong money, from 10 dollar notes to 1000 dollar notes. For more information on this very different method of banking contact Robert Sterling through Scope International.

In the future, everything can happen in Hong Kong. The colony could die, like Shanghai. Or with a little luck, it could become one of the new banking havens in the millenium. Which is why, despite its past successes, we felt it right to include Hong Kong in this chapter. Old HK may still have a lot of spunk left. And should things go wrong, Hong Kong Chinese have a two year escape valve in nearby Macau.

The Portuguese colony of Macau, some 40 miles from Hong Kong, consists of the Macau peninsula and two small islands, Taipa og Coloane. Taxation is based on the territorial principle: all earnings stemming from abroad are not taxed. Income made at home is taxed at between 3 per cent and 11 per cent for individuals, with companies paying 2 per cent to 15 per cent. These low rates result from gambling. Two-fifths of Macau's budget is financed by profits from the casinos, the big draw for visiting Hong Kong Chinese and other tourists.

In 1999, two years after the British handover of Hong Kong, Portugal will hand over Macau to the Chinese. They won't close the casinos.

Many countries are ready, eager and willing to take over as financial centers if Hong Kong fails.

Brunei is one. This tiny Muslim sultanate on Borneo's northeastern shore got rich in the oil business. For individuals living there Brunei is a pure tax haven. Personal income tax does not exist. Companies, however, pay 30 per cent of profits. If more than half of all profits are derived from abroad, such a company would be better off locating itself in Bahrain, where it can apply for exempt status and total tax freedom. Like Brunei, Bahrain is a tiny miniature-version of a country. The 300,000 population consists of Muslims. They don't let Islamic banking practices stop them from attracting foreign capital. With a law passed in the eighties, so-called OBU banks could locate in Bahrain and get total tax freedom. OBU stands for Offshore Banking Units. So far, some 80 banks have opened subsidiaries or branches in Bahrain using the OBU laws. This is an impressive number. Bahrain is a major financial center with a lot to offer adventurous privacy seekers. This new banking haven has, for the time being escaped the hawkish eye of US regulators. If they can keep it that way, maybe they can carry on the mantle if Hong Kong fails.

GIBRALTAR IS THE SUNSPOT OF THE SHADY DEAL

Gibraltar, the British colony on the south coast of Spain, wants to be the Hong Kong of Europe. And if Hong Kong ceases to be the Hong Kong we know today, once the Communist takeover of 1997 is complete, Gibraltar wouldn't mind filling the void. That is what Prime Minister Joseph Bossano and his government of nine people have decided. The sleepy colonial style houses in the narrow streets will be replaced by skyscrapers and finance towers proudly overlooking Africa and the European continent.

Gibraltar is not an island, although many people think so. It is a peninsula connected to the Iberian peninsula with a wide and flat sandy stretch of land. The city state of Gibraltar (often called "The Rock") is located on the rock. The wide flat sandy bit is home to the airport, built during World War II and the lifeline of Gibraltar during the more than 20 years of Spanish blockade, which until 1985 prevented people and goods from entering directly.

Gibraltar is located on the northern shore of the Strait of Gibraltar between Spain and the African continent and from the many view points it is possible to see Tangier. Before Spain joined the European Community, today the European Union, it laid claim to Gibraltar. But the Gibraltarians held a referendum and decided they would rather stay with the British. As a result, tea and scones, fish and chips, even "bangers" are all to be found in Gibraltar. Some other staples of British life, fog and the endless downpour are not. Bang in thc best sunspot of the southern Mediterranean, Gibraltar is probably the most strikingly beautiful of all European tax havens. Here, you can bank in the morning, set up an offshore company or trust during lunch, then have a picnic on the rugged side of the rock, where wild monkeys play.

The climate is first class. Shady deals are welcomed. The banks ask few questions, as some 500,000 account holders know. More than half of them are expatriates living in nearby Spain. Gibraltar is only one hour by car away from the large expat-colonies of Marbella, Mijas and Fuengirola. Foreigners descend on Gibraltar daily, not just because of its secret banking, but also to shop. Gibraltar, with no VAT and next to no import duties has some of Europe's lowest prices for Japanese made electronics.

Food, on the other hand, is expensive. The locals drive across the Spanish border to the nearest hyper-mercado to do their shopping. Life for them is not as pleasant as for the no-taxed offshore companies and banks living in a tax free environment. Personal full time residents pay income taxes at standard levels up to 40 per cent!

Gibraltar has seen a building boom in recent years, most of it on reclaimed seabed, expanding the tiny six sq km territory of the colony. So far, most of the new residences and offices still stand empty. Everybody is waiting for "Hong Kong" to arrive.

Meanwhile, life in Gibraltar is gearing up to compete with the best of the European tax havens. UCITS investment funds licensed to carry on business throughout Europe can now be incorporated in Gibraltar. So can all sorts of banks and plain vanilla offshore corporations, subject only to an annual license fee in lieu of taxes. Many yachts worldwide call Gibraltar home. Through registration in the Gibraltar Ship Registry, they carry the British ensign while at the same time benefiting from what amounts to a flag of convenience, exempting them from more onerous rules, taxes, regulations and what have you.

Unlike its main tax haven competitors, Jersey, Guernsey and the Isle of Man, Gibraltar is a member of the EU under an opt-in with the UK. As a "dependent territory", Gibraltar has to follow all EU regulations except one. The EU can never order Gibraltar to comply with VAT and similar tax rules. Benefits from the EU are enjoyed just as if Gibraltar was a full and independent member country. The main advantage of this is access to the European markets. Since Gibraltar has no industry to call its own, this really only matters to Gibraltar-based importers. Taking advantage of Gibraltar's VAT-void, they can re-export to the EU and make a bundle in the process. Shipping companies are thick on the ground. With double taxation treaties in force, any creative importer/exporter can make money while he sleeps. Here's how. Speculate in Gibraltar's EU membership (and free access to all European markets), then take advantage of the customs-free and VAT free status. Dealing only with abroad, profits can be retained tax free. All of this is not just legal, it is encouraged by top government ministers! Prime Minister Joseph Bossano says: "We can buy sugar at world market prices ie cheaper than you can in most other countries."

Bossano also has a balanced view on money laundering. He says: "Most of us are against the laundering of money stemming from violence, drugs and other crimes. This is obvious and well known. But rules intended to stop this kind of whitewashing, by turning the act itself into a crime, will undoubtedly hit everyone else but the criminals. The drug cartels will not let a couple of EU directives stop them. They will just find other ways to achieve their goal. And if they cannot do it peacefully, like today through EU banks, they will do so with violence and terrorism."

A more direct way of saying no to the Brussels dictate on money laundering has probably never been heard from a politician. But Bossano is right, you know who will be hit by those rules, innocent ones.

Gibraltar is a good place to do business from. Unemployment stands at an invisible two per cent. Inflation is lower than four. Economic growth does not seem to have stopped. Under new rules, foreigners coming to live in Gibraltar can now negotiate a flat rate personal tax on an individual basis. Corporate profits are either exempt from tax or, if you choose to operate under a different section of the local legislation, taxed at a very reasonable two per cent. For this two per cent, the government actually gives back some value – hospitals, schools, an honest legal system, a local English language radio and TV, effective policing, even, compared to nearby Spain, clean streets. For more on Gibraltar, read our *Andorra/Gibraltar Report*, a two-in-one set comparing the tax havens bordering Spain. Please see summary at the end of this book. To reserve your original registered report, complete the order form and return to Scope International Ltd with your remittance.

THE NEW BANKING HAVENS

Although everyone from pundit to professional hypes the Global Village, the new world order and the One-World government, truth is every year more and more *new* countries are being created, not the other way around.

Some of these new lands are desperate for money. As a result, they go out of their way to lure depositors from richer nations. One such budding banking haven is the Baltic Republic of Estonia. It has a nice convertible currency. Banks are free to do as they wish and all sorts of money is welcomed there with no questions asked, because the banks are new and just want to compete. The country itself is young, so a whole lot of contradictory rules and regulations are not (yet) in place, although Nordic neighbors are doing their bit to mess things up. The Swedes, especially, are actively sending delegation after delegation of bureaucrats to advise.

Another up and comer could be the Maldive islands, with a little luck. The Maldives, an independent republic in the Indian Ocean, south of Sri Lanka, consists of between 1200 and 2000 coral reef islands. The exact number depends on whether you count at high tide!

The Maldives has made most of its foreign currency from tourism. This could change now, with the government eagerly trying to make its country look the part of a 1990s style tax haven.

In the Republic of China, as Taiwan insists on calling itself, foreigners can get special tax concessions if they bring manufacturing industries to the island. This is part of a government job creation scheme. New banks will be treated with a hands-off approach and next to nonexistent tax rates by the Taiwanese authorities.

Likewise in Singapore. A heavy presence of foreign banks has made Singapore an Asian banking haven. In Europe, some mini-scandals erupted when it was discovered that European banks used their subsidiaries in Singapore to carry out transactions not legal in Europe. In Singapore, whatever a bank wants to do, it can. Almost everything is legal. Yet as a tax haven, Singapore can't compete. Hong Kong has, so far, had more to offer. But for light manufacturing industries or firms in high technology willing to relocate to Singapore, and thus bring jobs and, it is hoped, prosperity, the city/state is willing to offer tax holidays. Some of Singapore's more recent initiatives have been modelled on Ireland's.

Malaysia, the former British colony, uses a roundabout version of the principle of territoriality as the basis for taxation. As long as your profits are derived from abroad, you are income tax free, but only when you keep your profits abroad and don't repatriate to Malaysia. Most foreigners living and working in Malaysia pay some 15 per cent in tax. If this sounds like too much, Malaysia has developed the latest addition to the international list of tax havens, its own little pearl, a newcomer called Labuan.

Labuan is the latest Asian banking haven. It is hard at work trying to attract foreign banks. They won't have to pay taxes and they will be free not just from currency restrictions, but from all other government rules and regulations too, the Malaysian authorities promise. This sounds more like hype than reality. In the real world, banking supervisors always want to meddle. In a few years we will know how Labuan's bid for banking haven stardom has fared. The timid will wait and in the meantime stick to established, well known European banking havens. For pioneers, Labuan is open for business.

Keep your eye on Grenada, too. Grenada, the independent island state that got its fifteen minutes of fame when it was invaded by the United States some ten years ago, is located north of Trinidad and south of St. Vincent in the Caribbean. When Grenada got its independence in 1974, the government claimed that income tax would be abolished. This has still not happened, but we are waiting. In 1986 company tax was reduced to ten per cent, all income from abroad was made tax free and even more reforms were promised. Stay tuned. Maybe Grenada will be the next new hot thing . . .

More possible surprises in the Caribbean? Perhaps. We will have to wait and see, but don't discount the dark horse, Jamaica. South of Cuba you will find Jamaica, well known for rum, reggae and rastafari. Even though few people are aware of it, Jamaica is a corporate tax haven just like many of the other islands in the Caribbean. Jamaica has been so ever since 1971 when by law it was made possible for foreigners to buy a special kind of corporation called IFCs (International Finance Companies). Their tax burden is a lenient 2.5 per cent on net profits, as long as two requirements are fulfilled: 1. A maximum 5 per cent of the shares can be owned by a Jamaican or a resident foreigner; 2. All trade should either take place outside Jamaica or strictly with tourists/foreigners in Jamaica. If trading with locals, full corporate tax must be paid.

Even though the conditions for attracting foreign investors to Jamaica seem to be fulfilled, success for Jamaica as a tax haven has long been awaited. There are several reasons why. The communications are rotten. Telephones don't work and mail goes missing all the time. The real Jamaica is a complete contrast to the happy rum commercials which is partly why people stay away. Jamaica is a poor and overpopulated island, where the daily life consists of crime and slum. Beaches with palm trees do exist but many of them are polluted. The few nice and clean ones belong to a handful of rich foreigners protected by surveillance cameras and armed guards.

Bank secrecy does not exist in Jamaica. And even though there are no currency restrictions, corrupt local bureaucrats invent red-tape on the spot to get "oil". Thus, they make it very difficult for even a creative businessman to ply any sort of decent trade. Honest resident agents to operate your offshore company and take care of day to day dealings can be hard to find. When doing business, you are beset by incompetent hangers-on everywhere you go. Badly educated officials are a true pain in the behind, a real burden to everybody who has ever tried to do anything in Jamaica besides soaking in some sun on the beach. And even that can be a pain.

On the other side of the world, another would-be investment haven is Jordan. By passing various pieces of what were supposed to be accommodating legislation, the Jordanian authorities have several times tried to attract investment funds. It was thought that with a base in Jordan, these funds could then invest happily worldwide, paying out profits tax free to investors in different countries, especially in the Arab world. Although none of this was ever spelled out of course.

The response has been nil. Neither banks nor other foreign financial institutions ever came to Jordan to set up tent. Some odd-ball tax advisers with their own drum to beat may advertise Jordan as the Next Big Thing in tax havens. So far, based on all indications, this is simply not true. If you are an Arab, you can launder money through Jordan, but that is about it. For the time being, the country offers nothing else. Keep an eye on Jordan. The situation could change fast. But until you have proof of this don't invest.

What will happen when Liberia, which has been independent since 1847, finally digs itself out of the rubble? Once Africa's freest country and its premier tax haven, Liberia has suffered from a long and bloody civil war. Its famous ship registry, offering flags of convenience in stiff competition with Panama, holed up in Switzerland during the war. Although shooting has calmed somewhat, Liberia's Registrar of Companies along with the Ship Registry still operate out of Switzerland. If you want to register a company in Liberia, there is no point in going to Monrovia, the capital there. All offices are closed. Go to Switzerland. This is where the files are kept and where the Liberian government will be happy to take your money, then register your Liberian company or a ship under the Liberian flag. Founding a company takes two days. English is the official language of the country. With no central bank to call its own, Liberia uses US dollars. There are no currency controls or restrictions of any kind whatsoever. Liberia has what must be the most lax corporation laws in the world. In short, you are free to do everything you wish, as long as you state a willingness not to break the laws of Liberia. The laws of Liberia, like the corporate laws, are next to nonexistent. And as long as more than 75 per cent of all shares are owned by foreigners, a Liberian company does not pay tax, nor does it file any returns anywhere. There are no requirements that annual meetings are kept and no requirements as to the number of directors, shareholders or where they live. You are free to do everything you wish. As for your company name, you can call it whatever. If you want it to end with "Ltd", you can do so. Liberia is home to a million people and is totally relaxed. Its registry simply couldn't care less about petty details. A welcome change from some other havens. If Liberia is able to repair its act and beef up infrastructure, this African pearl could easily become a hot tax haven in the coming years.

The problem with new would-be havens is they are not yet stable enough for you to want to sink all your assets into them. Our only assured prediction for the future is things change. So in a changing world why not turn to Old Solid & Stable, the granddaddy of silent banking havens, the country with the holey cheese, Switzerland?

BANKING ON SWITZERLAND?

Driving north from Italy you enter the Swiss canton of Ticino, Italian-speaking Switzerland with lake Lugano and Lugano as its largest city. Here you will find Campione d'Italia, the unknown tax haven that beats Monaco for quality of life. Ticino, the southern enclave of Switzerland, borders Italy and has traditionally served as a money haven for Italians. This small canton has one bank for every 500 citizens.

Switzerland is loved by many of us as a very agreeable place to spend a weekend or a short holiday. Of all the world's lands, this may be the most pristine, orderly and outright antiseptic. Advice from an expert: When you go to Switzerland as a tourist, enjoy crystal-clear lakes, high snow-peaked mountains, and green sparkling valleys alive with flowers; just don't ask any questions about money-laundering.

Why not?

To most people's astonishment, Switzerland is not a free country. Beneath the idyllic surface lies a police state, the like of which few would imagine this side of the KGB-controlled Soviet Union. *Habeas corpus* does not exist in Switzerland as one reader found out the hard way in 1992. The same reader reports: "The police can hold you incommunicado for as long as they want to. There is no law barring them and the only way to get some air is to have your consulate or embassy lobby on your behalf. This was no easy task because it was the US embassy who had me put in the Swiss pokey to begin with." Another warning: a foreigner will, without exceptions, get lost in the bureaucratic shuffle. To avoid bureaucracy anywhere is difficult. It is next to impossible in Switzerland.

BIG BROTHER IN THE LAND OF HEIDI

"Scandal: Big Brother in the Land of Heidi". This was how the Swiss media dubbed the 1989 discovery that the police in Switzerland have compiled more than 900,000 secret files on the activities of what they termed "suspect" Swiss citizens. All information had been obtained through illegal surveillance.

Foreign governments were frequently making use of the archives. The United States Drug Enforcement Administration (DEA) had their Swiss based agents copy thousands of files. The DEA showed an eager interest in American citizens residing in Switzerland with ties to

Americans in Switzerland and Americans in the US. No one knows where the DEA photostats of these files are today. The Swiss media managed to prove that not only had the DEA used the files, the CIA had done so as well. Together, the DEA and the CIA had used their involvement in Swiss domestic affairs to bring down Switzerland's first female Justice Minister, Elizabeth Kopp. Her husband was framed in what the authorities claimed was a money laundering scandal. Around the same time, the DEA arranged stings inside Switzerland, using US agents. Among other things, these extra-jurisdictional affairs uncovered and led to the closure of a drug laboratory inside Switzerland. The American federal agents were behaving as if Switzerland was not a sovereign country. They were, in effect, writing their own laws with no regards for Swiss sovereignty and no care in the world for Swiss law, Swiss courts or Swiss feelings.

Despite their excellence and technical efficiency, for many years the Swiss internal spies were using old fashioned bugging gear for illegal entry into your personal privacy. Their telephone taps were of the out-dated analogue type where you can actually hear the surveillance. If you have ever been in Switzerland for any period of time, made a phone call, then wondered about strange clickings on the phone, you now know who was behind it. You would have been right to become nervous. Mysterious static, courtesy of DEA and the Swiss, upset many a traveler and foreign resident, prompting them to ask "What's wrong with the phone?", then abruptly ending the conversation.

In the past year, Switzerland has switched to digitally recorded surveillance done at the central switching computer. You now have no way of finding out whether you are being recorded. The best protection is to never say anything of value on the phone. Best to be safe rather than sorry.

THE KOPP AFFAIR

A curious mix of Swiss greens and socialists cooperating with American agents from the CIA and the DEA ended in Elizabeth Kopp, former Swiss Minister of Justice and President-elect, being forced out of politics. Her husband, Hans Kopp, was involved in money laundering, or so it was claimed. To date, no one has ever pressed money laundering charges against Elizabeth nor Hans Kopp. And no one ever will. The facts behind the case clearly show that both are innocent. The real crime of Hans Kopp lies in being a free spirit in a country where narrowmindedness is valued more than visions and creativity. He is a champion of liberty and of press freedom. But the Swiss papers have hounded him for years, writing about his freetrading antics. He has frequently been a go-between for tax evaders, currency traders, gold dealers and the banks. He has often established totally legal Swiss shell-companies to accommodate his business partners. Further, Hans Kopp is a visionary, a man ahead of his time. One of his more unusual schemes involved the hybridization by genetic engineering methods of a new agricultural product, the "Tomoffel," a cross between a tomato and a potato (*kartoffel*, in German).

Hans Kopp, who is a lawyer by profession, usually offered to sit on the boards of the companies he helped set up. When Mohamed Shakarchi, the Lebanese owner of the aptly named Shakarchi Trading Company, approached Hans Kopp to sit on his board, Kopp was already on the Board of Directors of at least 30 other companies. Kopp served as a titular vice president only and had nothing to do with daily operations.

As bad luck would have it, Mohamed was singled out for one of the arbitrary USA money laundering investigations. He was a swarthy Lebanese and then on top of this was dealing with not just Arabs, but Turks as well, which probably had a bit to do with it. Shakarchi does business in Europe, the Middle East, Africa and North America, but not in South or Central America, as a commodity trader specializing in gold and currency exchange. According to the police in Berne, Switzerland, Shakarchi recycled gold in connection with the Iran-Contra affair. Yet he makes sure that nothing of what he ever does is illegal. In November 1988, when the "Lebanon Connection" story broke in Zürich's *Tages Anzeiger* paper, Mohamed Shakarchi's bank, Crédit Suisse immediately froze all Shakarchi accounts. Mohamed Shakarchi called the bank to ask why his money had been blocked. The bank replied that "The recent publicity made it a necessary precaution."

As it turned out Shakarchi was exonerated. His company had done nothing wrong and received a clean bill of health. Hans Kopp got off scot free, too. He had even less to do with the whole trumped-up mess. A fictitious case invented by over-zealous government investigators, bureaucrats and fast reporters. Before the case, Mohamed Shakarchi boasted that his company had the most sophisticated currency exchange and commodity trading operations in Switzerland. His offices occupied two floors of a highly secure building in the business district near Zürich's airport. Before the Kopp affair, Shakarchi employed 22 people and grossed a revenue of SF8 billion or more per year. Ultimately, the publicity generated by the Kopp affair proved bad for business. He had to fire many of his staff and his profits evaporated. Life had become so unpleasant for his family that he sent his wife and their two kids out of the country to live in an undisclosed location. Shakarchi is a battered man. He survived the media's negative publicity. This is more than can be said about Elizabeth Kopp. She was forced to resign, simply for having a husband who sat on the board of a company while it was being investigated for alleged money laundering. It didn't matter that the Shakarchi Trading Company later got a clean bill of health, by that time Elizabeth Kopp's political career was already in tatters. Hans Kopp was a finished name. None of them ever did anything wrong. Yet they were victimized by local prosecutors, by the liberal press, by American agents and by anti-capitalists of every stripe and color. In the end, the Kopp affair turned out to be nothing. At most a storm in a tea-cup. But it did wreck several lives, even though no one was convicted. If Mohamed Shakarchi had never been investigated for money laundering, most political observers in Switzerland believe that Elizabeth Kopp today would have been that country's president. That she didn't make it is testimony to the power of US federal agents, even in a foreign country as independent, neutral and stable as Switzerland.

When going to Switzerland, arm yourself with Marshall Langer's *The Swiss Report* available from Scope. Marshall Langer is an eminent United States attorney and recognized authority in the tax haven field. He has lived for several years in the French speaking part of Switzerland.

Dr Langer shares our view that although Switzerland is a good place to spend some time, it is not the banking haven it was. Many of the scare-stories we have read about in the paper are just that. They are often planted to deter others from stashing a little moolah away for a rainy day in a land where no one knows. Yet there is no denying the fact that Switzerland has changed.

Chapter 13

WHERE THERE'S A WILL THERE'S A WAY

How do PTs die? Or to put it more precisely, what happens to their money when they die? It would be a rare but happy case to find a PT father having a PT son. Assume instead that when a non-filer and Previous Taxpayer dies, his heirs are all tangled in red-tape and deep in the claws of Tax Man. They will have to pay all sorts of crazy estate duties to inherit the money. Our PT may not like it. He lived his life in freedom, not paying voluntarily to the blood suckers. Yet there is nothing he can do, he is dead.

If you plan ahead, you can make sure this situation doesn't happen when you die. Do you know what it will otherwise cost you? For most of us, dying in a way approved by the government carries a million-dollar price tag. If you doubt it, run your own personal asset figures through a "Jewish piano", then watch the display light up and the calculatorstrip print out figures with a lot of zeros after them. This should show you. But luckily, you can avoid paying a penny to the leeches and bloodsuckers. If your money is in a tax free and bureaucracy free zone, you can make sure it stays there, even after you leave it. If you don't want all of it to go to your heirs, just plan accordingly. Your heirs won't complain. They will thank you for having had the foresight. Like most people, you will have written a will. You shouldn't include all your worldly goods in it, only those that the world already knows about. A will can literally come back to haunt you. If you wrote it early, you will probably be making changes to it. Its existence will be semi-public knowledge. In a court case with you as the defendant your will can become Exibit A, a revealing document listing your assets and your intentions. Think about this. If you are a Privacy Tycoon, you will keep certain secrets even out of your will.

At the same time you want your heirs to get what's due to them. But you don't know when you will go. The Portuguese, long masters of cheating their own government, came up with a *jeitinho* long ago. Literally translated, *jeitinho* means a little way. In Portugal, there are lots and lots of "little ways" around seemingly unsurmountable problems. A sort of secret will can be set up to deal with this situation. Since you won't have the power of any courts to enforce it, it really does not need to be a lot more than a letter, perhaps with some already made Powers-of-Attorney enclosed.

Here is how to do it.

Find a lawyer somewhere, preferably in a country where you are not known nor have any other dealings. This can be your PT flag number six, your last. Tell the lawyer that you want to leave an envelope in safekeeping at his offices, sealed with an embossed glob of wax. Tell him that it should be mailed to a specific address in the event that you do not establish any sort of contact with the law office before 31 December in any given year. This set up is to run indefinitely, which is to say that as long as the lawyer hears from you in any given calendar year, he is to keep the envelope in his possession and not send it out. Only in the event that his office receives no sign of life from you in any given calendar year, is the envelope to be sent to you. That's about it. Make sure to prepay, topping up the account every ten years or so. At present rates, 50 to 100 dollars a year should cover everything, so if you pay US$500 to US$1000 at the outset, you are covered for the near future and your foreign lawyer is kept happy.

You can have more than one envelope. Or you can leave an identical envelope with two different and unrelated law firms, in two different countries. If one lawyer moves, goes under, cheats or simply forgets to mail out the envelope, the other one will. In your letter, inform your heirs that they will probably be getting the same envelope twice. What's in the envelope? A letter from you detailing your affairs. Our letter opens like this:

Dear Steven, this will be very unsettling for you to read, but there is no way I can prevent you from feeling like you've been hit by a bombshell, especially not in your present circumstances. My intentions are good, and when the shock subsides I hope that you will realize that the following was intended as a gesture of good will, not of cruelty.

This letter has been arranged by me to be sent to you if an attorney, James F Karls of Park Avenue, New York, NY in the USA has not received any signs of life from me by 31 December in any given year.

I have only used this law firm to keep this letter for you on my behalf, and for nothing else. Please do not torture yourself by calling them to ask if they have other letters for you. They don't.

What then follows are instructions on how to take over the running of some personal investments, advice on low profile, fatherly recommendations of a few good books to read, then my own thoughts on how to make the money grow tax free in the future.

Along with the letter, the envelope includes a Power of Attorney. This is not needed for all accounts. One account, for instance, already has Steven as a co-signer, able to sign individually. Until he gets my letter, he won't know it. But when I opened it by mail I had him sign a form, covered by another piece of paper. He didn't know what he signed, but it was a signature card for a new account. That account holds a six figure sterling amount and it is, for all purposes, his to do with what he wants when I am gone. He does not need to show up at the bank with a Death Certificate or even a Power of Attorney, nor does he have to go through any of the usual tiresome motions involved when a depositor dies. As soon as he wants, Steve can sign with no further ado.

Why did I not tell Steven about the account when I opened it? Because I believe in always sharing information only on a need-to-know basis. The money is mine, not his. Only when I die do I want him to have it. As long as it is my money, I believe in keeping it private. He does not need to know about it. When I am dead, he needs this information. Having me tell him in a literal *post scriptum*, with the help of a law firm holding a private letter, is the best way of keeping private affairs private. After all, who needs the government to get involved in the morbid business of death?

In mailing out your secret will, your lawyer does not need to elaborate. You should not tell him what is in it. He only needs information on a need-to-know basis, just like everybody else. That way, emotions or greed won't prevent him from doing his job. Which is simply to write your heir(s), saying something short, matter-of-factly like: "In accordance with the prior instructions given me by my client Dr William G Hill I hereby forward to you the enclosed sealed envelope left with my office for safekeeping by said client." Signed etc.

Using the *jeitinho,* you can give yourself more than lifetime protection for the fruits of your labor.

THE PROS AND CONS OF VAULT STORAGE

As the raid on Knightsbridge in London showed a few years ago, not even the most secure deposit storage facility is immune from a gangster hellbent on attacking it. Customers lost millions of pounds in valuables: money, gold, jewelry, documents, keepsakes and family heirlooms. Many did not step forward afterwards because *like the majority of those using vault storage* they had been hiding black money from the tax man. Most of them did not have insurance.

We don't use vault storage, precisely because any one neat and compact collection of valuables will always be a tempting target to any criminal. We prefer to put our wealth into mutual funds and into bank accounts where we are insured against loss not just in the case of a bank robbery stick-up but even in the case of the bank caving in once and for all.

If you want to store valuables in a strongbox somewhere safe, do so outside your own country. Use the PT principles of the Five Flags to choose a country unknown to your enemies. This should be enough protection in itself from the risk of unfair attachments in bogus court cases.

Some offshore advisers operate vault storage, usually in cooperation with local banks. This is designed to give the client a safe haven outside the jurisdiction of his country. You can usually get them to send you more information on how to store valuables, letters, coins and other personal items in a safe deposit box with complete privacy. The newer services all seem to be located in Eastern Europe. They are said to be owned by the Russian mafia. We visited one in 1993 with a local business associate and part time philosopher, David Kaplan from Vilnius. If this vault was anything to go by, the operators will go out of their way to please the customer. When we entered, two words and a nod made the manager turn off the surveillance camera, giving us total privacy. In Switzerland, the service cameras will run and run and run and not a thousand words or nods will get them turned off. If you choose to use vault storage, be it in Switzerland, Costa Rica, Panama or the new services in Eastern Europe, make sure your valuables are well guarded at all times. Do not use services with less than 24 hour electronic guard and police protection services.

We do have a contact for anonymous safe deposit boxes. If you get in touch with Dr Reinhard Stern through Scope International he will be able to assist you. Or you could talk to one of your silent banks. Some banks offer a safekeeping service. If yours doesn't, you can always have a trusted lawyer keep a few extra envelopes in his safe. A few select friends may be willing to help. Whatever you decide to do, share information only on a need to know basis, as always.

SOME USEFUL FORMS

All Powers of Attorney should conform to local rules in whatever country they are to use. It may be that they cannot be written in English. Sometimes, they will have to be very specific, but more often than not a wide ranging General POA is accepted. Usually, it must be notarized. Where you are a foreigner in a strange land, your signature can only be notarized by your consulate there. Check first. If your heirs have trouble getting at your money later simply because a power of attorney does not conform to local norms, it will be too late for you to remedy this problem.

Apart from powers of attorney, two forms that you can use in all of your own dealings are the "Survivorship" and the "Joint Rights" forms, as reproduced here. They are copyright free.

JOINT RIGHTS

The below listed individual(s) are to have equal rights, control and authority on any and all certificates of deposits, cash, or assets listed in my name. These individuals may sign, cash, renew or perform any other act deemed necessary in the maintenance of assets listed in my name.

Name: ______________________________

Relationship: ______________________________

Address: ______________________________

City and state: ______________________________

Country: ______________________________

Telephone no: ______________________________

Signature: ______________________________

The signature on this line is a true likeness of the signature of the party whose name and address is listed above.

Name: ______________________________

Relationship: ______________________________

Address: ______________________________

City and state: ______________________________

Country: ______________________________

Telephone no: ______________________________

Signature: ______________________________

The signature on this line is a true likeness of the signature of the party whose name and address is listed above.

Statement of depositor / owner:

I, (full name), submit this form and request that it be accepted and followed accordingly.

Date: ________ / ________ / ________

Name: ______________________________

Address: ______________________________

City and state: ______________________________

Country: ______________________________

Telephone no: ______________________________

Signature: ______________________________

Signatures confirmed by -

Notary public: ______________________________

(name and address)

Signature: ______________________________

Date of expiry of commission: ________ / ________ / ________

Date certified: ________ / ________ / ________

(Seal)

SURVIVORSHIP

The below listed Individuals are to have Only Survivorship Rights in case of my Death. In such case, a True Copy of my Death Certificate, verified by a Notary Public, will be provided. Further, the full and complete name and address of the Doctor who issued the Death Certificate shall be provided along with the full and complete name and address of the Notary Public who certified said Death Certificate as being True and Authentic.

Date: ________/________/________ Signature: ______________________________

Beneficiaries -

Name: ____

Relationship: ____

Percentage: ( ) %

Address: ____

City and state: ____

Country: ____

Telephone no.: ____

Signature: ____

The signature is the true signature of the above named beneficiary.

Name: ____

Relationship: ____

Percentage: ( ) %

Address: ____

City and state: ____

Country: ____

Telephone no: ____

Signature: ____

The signature is the true signature of the above named beneficiary.

Name: ____

Relationship: ____

Percentage: ( ) %

Address: ____

City and state: ____

Country: ____

Telephone no: ____

Signature: ____

The signature is the true signature of the above named beneficiary.

PART 3
ANONYMOUS BANKING

Chapter 14

SECURED CREDIT CARDS

A few years ago only a handful of Russians carried plastic. Today, Moscow banks are fighting to see who can issue the most plastic. In a frontier atmosphere where the pioneering spirit reigns supreme, few laws exist. And of the few that do exist, even fewer are taken seriously. Russian banking is, at least for the time being, a free for all. Gung-ho private commercial institutions like the Stolichny Bank started the trend in 1993 with the first homespun Russian multi-currency credit cards and multi-currency STB cards accepted in hundreds of Moscow shops. They issue them even to foreigners. To become a client, all you have to do is write the bank's main branch at **113095, Piatnitskaya St, 70, Moscow, Russia tel +7 095 233 5892, (fax same number)**.

Another option. Bank with Sberbank, the largest bank in the world if you measure by number of branches. Sberbank has 44,000 branches! Their new Credo Card is a VISA card which is accepted worldwide and the cheapest in the world. To get it, you pay a symbolic 500 roubles. Anyone is eligible. As long as you deposit a minimum 100,000 roubles in your Sberbank account, you will be given the VISA card. Using 1994 exchange rates, 100,000 roubles roughly equals some £40 Sterling or US$60. To recoup some of its losses, Sberbank charges a fee on each purchase. But this surcharge is only a modest 0.2 per cent. The Credo Card is a VISA debit card. Sberbank will introduce real credit cards in a deal with MasterCard International.

In Russia all cards are issued without credit checks. This is good news for foreigners with a bad credit record. They have had to use US secured credit cards. But don't give those cards up yet, even those of us with A-Sterling clean credit reports have used secured credit cards to lower our financial profile. The advantage is that when you apply for them, you don't have to surrender any sensitive financial data. By playing your cards right, getting a secured credit card or two will make your purchases untraceable . . .

What is a Secured Credit Card? A secured credit card can be a debit card or a credit card, usually tied up to some of the popular international issuers such as VISA or MasterCard.

It does not differ from the ordinary cards of other bank customers. No one can physically tell the difference. Only by examining the records of the issuer will the fact be revealed that this card *was only issued because someone put up security-collateral.*

To get a secured credit card you will need to give the bank a monetary guarantee that they will not lose money on having issued you with the card. This is done by you depositing a sum equal to or larger than your credit limit. If you get a card with £2000 credit, you will need to deposit at least £2000 with the bank to calm their fears that they may, in the future, experience a loss on your account. Some banks require more. It is common for secured credit cards to get only an 80 per cent credit line on the amount of money deposited. Only being able to spend up to 80 per cent of your own money is unattractive. Most clients tend to be those who need a credit card, but are unable to get it elsewhere. They may be foreigners with no local credit history or they may be locals with a bad credit history. Whatever the reason, their very existence and need for credit cards have created a niche industry, especially in America. In addition to the card, a processing fee of up to US$600 (1994) may be asked for prior to the issuing of the card. But prices differ, and we have seen fees as low as US$100 (1993) in some instances.

One book that goes into a lot more detail is the almost 200 page *Credit*-book, available by mail order from publishers **CEP Inc, Post Box 865, Boulder, Colorado 80306, USA.** Be sure to ask for their very interesting catalog of other titles too.

PROVIDERS OF SECURED CREDIT CARDS

Since the concept of a secured credit card is uniquely American, and since credit cards are originally a feature of American society, most providers of this service are to be found within the United States of America.

The banks involved are usually only willing to deal with Americans or with residents of the USA. They do not, however, ask for proof of residence status, a visa, a green card or anything else of the sort. Though in some cases, you will have to provide a Social Security number. But anybody can get an American Social Security number. Ask an American resident to help you if you do not formally live in America. Be sure to have an American address lined up before. A mail forwarding service will do. They may even want to help you get the Social Security number if you find that it will be needed sometime down the road.

How to find a mail drop? Any large daily paper will have information listed in the "Business Services" classified section. For a more in-depth view of available service, you can also order the comprehensive *Directory of US Mail Drops*, by Michael Hoy, available from **Scope International Ltd, Forestside House, Forestside, Rowlands Castle, Hants PO9 6EE, UK, fax +44 705 631322.**

One service particularly recommended by the author is the Orlando Mail Drop, Inc., a company which has been in business since 1981. They will help you obtain your secured credit cards and may even keep you informed of new opportunities, if you ask them. Their address is **Orlando Mail Drop, Inc, PO Box 608039, Orlando, FL 32860-8039, USA** with their physical street address being at **2425 Brengle Avenue #28, Orlando, FL 32808, USA.**

The Orlando Mail Drop is now obliged to get you to fill out a so-called 1583 form from the US Post Office, regarding your identity. This is not as bad as it sounds. If you are seeking low profile, and if you are a foreigner there are ways around this requirement. Have a chat with the Orlando Mail Drop. They have helped people before. Call them at **+1 407 339 1441** or **fax +1 407 339 0895**. They will service your mail requirements for US$100 per year, with a surcharge for foreign subscribers as more time, work and cost is involved. In the UK, a reliable maildrop outfit is The Leyton Office.

For the latest information on secured credit cards available within the USA, do have their staff check the classified of the latest Sunday papers or of supermarket tabloids such as the *National Enquirer* (also available in Europe, imported) for details of new deals. We have often seen classified ads for secured credit cards in the *National Enquirer*. Also in mercenary sheets such as *Gung Ho* and the *Soldier of Fortune*. You may want to purchase these magazines yourself as part of your research.

To get hold of newspapers from areas you are not visiting, and newspapers that are not on sale elsewhere, contact Multinewspapers, a California firm. They will send you a sample or a subscription to almost any newspaper in the world, from Albania to Zimbabwe. The price for these papers is rarely over US$5 (or US$10 to other countries), and they always send the most current issue available. **Multinewspapers, Box DE, Dana Point, CA 92629, USA**.

Direct providers of secured credit cards in America, for Americans or for residents, include: **Jim Straw, 301 Plymouth Drive NE, Dalton, GA 30721-9983, USA** and the gold-card provider **CSC, 5430 Lynx Lane, Columbia, MD 21044, USA**.

Specific programs operated by banks that we know to be trustworthy and provide a fair, price-efficient service, are **New Era Bank, Secured Card Program, PO Box 1369, Somerset, NJ 08875, USA, tel +1 908 937 4600** and **Key Federal Savings Bank, Secured Card Program, PO Box 6057, Havre De Grace, MD 21078-9978, USA, tel +1 410 939 4840**.

More information is free of charge to anyone contacting either of the two banks. We do not get any commission, nor are we in any way connected to the two establishments. But we recommend them nevertheless because they have some very reasonable entry levels for first-time users of secured credit cards.

Here is how it works. You deposit US$300 to US$500 into an interest bearing savings account. That account is your collateral and your credit limit. You can then get a VISA or MasterCard and make purchases with it up to your limit.

You may also contact Bank Holders of America and ask for its directory regarding Secured Credit Cards. It lists around 100 providers of such cards, but it is only available in the United States, to Americans or resident foreigners. The list, nevertheless, may be worth a look. It is priced at US$5 and only sent to American addresses. Order it from **Bank Holders of America**, toll free dialling from within the USA to **1-800-237 1800**.

If calling from outside the USA, using AT&T's USADirect service can put you through to any North American 1-800 number from almost any country in the world, although at the normal international USADirect tariffs. Customers need only dial the USADirect access code for the country they are in and ask the operator to dial the desired service. A list of access numbers can be found in every daily issue of newspapers International Herald Tribune and USA Today.

For more information on USA issued secured credit cards, order a written transcript of the "Your Money" (w/ Stuart Varney) program from TV news broadcaster CNN International. Ask for the Sunday 25 April 1993 issue a transcript of which can be had for US$5 from: **Journal Graphics, 1535 Grant Street, Denver, Colorado 80203, USA, tel 303 831 9000**.

SOME WARNINGS

The first warning regards your choice of country. America is just about the worst jurisdiction in the world to do banking in. And it doesn't matter whether you're local or a foreigner. Laws and reporting requirements change all the time. When you bank in the USA, the scales are tilted against you. In a lot of cases, not even your bank knows what the latest rules out of Washington or IRS Headquarters say. Besides, your bank is not legally obliged to keep you abreast of all new changes. That's your job. If you slip up and forget to file some silly little form you didn't even know existed, you could be guilty of not just a misdeameanor. Yes, incredible as it may sound, some "failure to file" crimes have actually been made felonies in the land of the free! A felony carries jail time. In other words, you could find yourself facing time behind bars simply for having ventured into the promised land of the United States, wanting a credit card and putting up the required security. An operation that in 99 cases out of 100 is perfectly straightforward, above-the-board and of course totally legal. No wonder that over the past two decades, as bureaucrazy and petty decrees have taken off like never before in the United States, the prison population of that country has soared. More than 450 people per 100,000 are in jail. The highest proportion in *the world*. This figure is more than double such repressive regimes as Cuba, North Korea, China – or, for that matter, the Soviet Union in the mid-1980s. You may argue that some of these nations are prisons in themselves. So let's look at France, a relatively free country with its fair share of meddling bureaucrats busy prying into other people's lives. In France, the comparative 1994 figure of people in jail is 81 per 100,000. Clearly, there is a serious danger in banking with an American financial institution.

Our second warning has to do with the safety of your money. Try to avoid middlemen.

In a business where complete strangers ask you to send them thousands of dollars in the mail, there are bound to be some crooks. Part of the scope of these pages is to expose dishonest business practices. In earlier private correspondence, we must have revealed more than 20 such scams. Most of them, unfortunately, after someone got burned and reported back to us, to friends or to the papers. In two of the most recent cases we were able to intervene and recover part of the money, mainly by threatening on behalf of our reader to take the matter further. To our knowledge only one fraudster is active in this field. No one has been able to put him behind bars. He changes his name and his company name about every second or third month. He even hops from country to country with a fondness for warmer climates in the American hemisphere.

He operated first in Honduras as Hunter B Andrews, then in Costa Rica during 1992, then early in 1993, he started from two mail drops in Florida, calling himself Tyson Walker. He was still in Florida as of 1994, but had to move his address and change his bank account. His most recent company name and address is **Global Financial Services, Inc, PO Box 025292, SB0017, Miami, FL 33102-5292, USA** with his delivery address at **Star Box, SB0017 5161 N.W. 74th Avenue, Miami, FL 33166, USA**. The fax number of his mail service is **+1 305 471 6197** and the name he used last was that of "Mr A. Barr, Vice-President of Marketing". His new bankers are Banco Metropolitano, but to disguise where the money – your money – goes, his *modus operandi* is to always route the funds through another bank. In this latest instance, the bank is the South Biscayne Boulevard (Miami) branch of the Bank of America who unknowingly helps him.

Why this latest change of address? We know why. But to his mailing list, he claimed that "We had a bad storm in Miami a few months ago", thus forcing the company to "relocate to a new office". If you encounter future companies with grand names, offering to secure credit cards and asking for one to two thousand dollars minimum, be wary if they are located in sunny climates. We do not know the true name of the fraudster. But we know that he has so far eluded authorities, partly by selecting mostly European victims, partly by always keeping his own whereabouts unknown and always refusing to meet anybody in person.

We suggest you exercise caution in dealings with Maverick International Ltd, a Canadian firm, because you will get your credit card, but you may have to wait quite a long time and you are likely to incur further expenses along the way. This, at least, has been our own experience. Maverick International Ltd, owned by grandsounding Mega-Wealth International Ltd, Group Enterprise, promises to get you more or less everything you want. And they can get it. But they will get it from someone else, acting only as middlemen, and if their price list is out of date, you will be the one to fork over the extra cash.

Having said this, their charges are fair. Their services for one year are US$240 paid in cash, checks or money orders. Before sending any money, though, contact them first and get their "Specialty Service Combine", a two page brochure outlining what they can do for you. **Maverick International, 108 Russell St North, Suite 369, Madoc, Ontario, Canada K0K 2K0, tel/fax +1 613 473 5460.**

OTHER CARDS AVAILABLE

The most common cards issued in a secured credit card scheme are VISA cards and MasterCards, often with the Gold card option, or VISA premier option available as an extra if a higher amount is deposited as collateral.

We know, however, of one program that will let you have an American Express Gold Card in a way that works like a secured credit card program, but is more simple and far more flexible.

You will have to start by opening an offshore bank account with Tyndall Bank on the Isle of Man. To do so, you can go there in person but will have to show valid ID, a passport, to open the account. Or you can open the account by mail, in which case no ID is needed. To verify that you are who you claim you are, the bank will ask you for a current bankers' reference. If you give out details of your current bankers, they will in turn be contacted by Tyndall Bank of the Isle of Man to ask if they can provide a satisfactory reference. They will also be asked to verify your name, your address, your signature and that all of the above is correct. If you do not want Tyndall to contact your current bankers, of if you currently have no bankers able to give a pleasing reference, there are still a couple of avenues open for you to take to reach your objective. One is using an Austrian bank as your reference, referring to an account number in a name corresponding to the one given to Tyndall Bank but opened without any sort of ID. Not all Austrian banks will give you such a reference however. It depends on the bank, the branch, and the manager of the day.

The other route is to obtain a fictitious but nevertheless solid reference from a helpful bank manager, or to create your own references.

Tyndall offers various types of accounts. One is the highly flexible Multicurrency account. Beware of their charges. They are on par with those of Swiss banks. To get the American Express Gold Card, it doesn't matter which type of account you open with Tyndall Bank. But you do have to open an account. So choose any one. The bank will send you full information of all their products, current interest rates and all charges if you ask them. They will also send you account opening forms so you can start the process immediately.

"Attention New Accounts", **Tyndall Bank International Limited, PO Box 62, Tyndall House, Kensington Road, Douglas, Isle of Man, UK, tel +44 624 629201, fax +44 624 620200**.

Once the account is opened you will receive a check book. You should then deposit further funds. To be on the safe side, we suggest that you deposit not less than US$15,000/ £10,000. You can safely do this. Tyndall is a large, established bank protected by the Isle of Man deposit protection scheme, similar to the British. Tyndall is UK-owned.

Your deposit will earn above market-rate interest and will not be locked in. With your check book, and later with your American Express Gold Card, you can spend your money or withdraw the entire amount. But your assets should at least be in the account while the bank processes your application for the American Express Gold Card. This is step number two. Once your account is up and running, with funds in it, you ask the bank for a Gold Card application. If you have the required funds in the account, your application will be accepted and in about three weeks time an American Express Gold Card will be sent to you in the mail – ordinary mail, that is, not registered. So you don't even have to sign for it! Your PIN code will be sent a few days later. You are now free to use your card and to withdraw your minimum £10,000 deposit in part or in full. The card is a credit card, but not a secured credit card. Your application will be declined if you have insufficient funds in your Tyndall account when applying for the American Express Gold Card. This is available in two versions. A US dollar-version and a sterling-version. The latter comes with a built-in £1500 overdraft-facility for future occasions when your Tyndall account may be in the red.

In France, the Carte Bleu with a VISA function or MasterCard function thrown in for good measure is widely available. Here's how:

1. Get yourself a French address. This is a must. But Paris mailing services will help you for 200 to 300 francs a month. Some charge more, especially those advertising internationally. Do not use them. Since you will have to go to France anyway, because the accounts cannot be opened by mail, simply look at any free advertising paper for "Domicilation". Then call the companies in there.
2. Once you have your address, choose a major French bank or banks to open an account with. In our experience, best results can be had from smaller branches of BNP, Credit Lyonnais and Credit Agricole. Ask to see the manager. Most of them will speak English if you don't speak French. Be polite and well-dressed. Tell him that you would like to open a French account since you plan to spend quite a bit of time in France in the months to come.
3. The account will be opened within minutes. Deposit 5000 to 10,000 francs. Interest rates are quite low. But when opening the account, you will be asked if you want a check book or a debit card. Go for the lot. The debit card will be a Carte Bleu (CB) and always comes with either a VISA or a MasterCard option. Only if you are in the black book of the French Bankers Association, a registry of check or card abusers, will you be confined to only the Carte Bleu, without Visa or MasterCard.
4. Your check book and card can be collected in normally less than 15 working days from your account keeping branch. Only in very special cases will they be mailed to you. You are now free to withdraw your money as you see fit. Theoretically, this should stop you from using the card or the check book further. In reality, however, the banks will allow unauthorized overdrafts, as they earn a lot of money off this. If you are prepared to pay, note that you can safely use 10,000 to 15,000 francs before your card will be cancelled. You will have to pay up within a month or your account will be closed for good. If you pay up, you may start all over again, getting back into the red.
5. If you don't spend like wildfire and don't allow the balance in your account to fall below zero, the computers of your bank will consider you a model client. In France, they are programmed to sell all sorts of things to clients who behave well and don't get into trouble. This is how you can build up a credit history.
6. Consider that our own account had been lying dormant for three months with just 4000 francs in it. The computer wrote us a personal letter, inviting us to apply for a loan. "Just tick the box", it said. "And we will credit your account with the amount requested". Various boxes went all the way up to 100,000 francs. We didn't respond, so four weeks

later, the same computer from the same bank (Credit Lyonnais) asked us if it could please finance a new car for us. "Buy the car of your dreams", it wrote us, "and let us pay for it". The bank even offered to fork over money for the first year's insurance and the transfer fee needed for French license plates. Thus in effect lending out more than 100 per cent of the value of the new car. To put this true tale into perspective, consider the fact that we had personally been in the bank only twice. Once to open the account, then later to pick up the VISA card and the check book. The bank knew next to nothing about us. The address was a mail box and we had given no references whatsoever. BNP and Credit Agricole are reported to be even more lenient in granting consumer loans, even as late as August 1993.

Similar stories to that of France can be found in Denmark, Portugal and the UK. In mainland UK, you may find it hard to be allowed to open an account. But once you have it, cards are easy to get.

In Denmark and Portugal, anybody can open any type of account in seconds, not minutes. With a deposit of US$500 or a lot less in the case of Portugal, you can get the Danish VISA-Dankort, or the Portuguese VISA-Multibanco card. The Danish VISA can be sent to any address, even abroad. The latter will have to be picked up in person. None of the banks require that you have an address within their countries, as they service the world. We know. We have tried. Your author has a large collection of plastic from around the world, with PIN codes and statements crossing borders from north to south, from east to west. You can do the same. Very easily.

Chapter 15

ANONYMOUS PLASTIC

In a stable western country, a small and democratic member nation of the European Union, a number of banks, all of them solid and some of them state-owned are willing to issue plastic to all comers, nationals as well as foreigners, with a minimum of fuss and bureaucracy. Cards are readily given to all who deposit a minimum of around US$70/£45.

The cards are tied into several international payment systems, thus permitting their usage in other countries as well for payments and cash withdrawals from Automatic Teller Machines (ATMs) or cash boxes, holed into walls throughout Europe.

You will be given your card on the spot, instantly. It is totally anonymous, with no name on it to identify you and with only a blank space on the spot below the magnetic identifier. This blank space is for you to write your signature, or any signature for that matter. You will not be required to write a name on the card while in the bank but can do this at any time later at your leisure.

The fiscal paradise is Portugal, located next to Spain in Europe's south western corner. Apart from being the sunniest and cheapest of all EU member states, Portugal is also a favorite European holiday destination and a country with relatively low tax rates.

After a period of state control and strict currency regulations, Portugal has gradually eased its legislative regime since membership of the European Community started in 1986. Portugal has its own offshore tax haven, Madeira, with a free for all economic policy. The government has a *laissez-faire* attitude to all matters of finance, probably most typified by the fact that rules against insider trading are not yet implemented and that the country has nothing even remotely close to America's SEC.

All currency controls are lifted in Portugal. Other regulations regarding deposits and transfers have been abolished. The author of this report holds bank accounts in a total of 12 countries. Nowhere has he encountered less hassle and bureaucracy when opening an account than in Portugal. It used to be cumbersome bordering on impossible, but today anyone can open any type of account in almost any bank by just filling out one simple, unobtrusive little form.

If you open a normal deposit account, you will be given a so-called *Multibanco* card, a debit card to a national network of currently 2250 cash dispensers. Apart from being able to withdraw cash from the machines, this card can also be used in more than 95 per cent of all stores and restaurants throughout Portugal. Mail order companies accept the *Multibanco* as valid payment, as do the majority of *las putas*, the girls of the night. Motorists use it to buy gas, settle garage bills and even to pay on toll roads. Your *Multibanco* card is also accepted by most pay phones throughout Portugal, automatically debiting the cost of your call from your bank account that very minute. The *Multibanco* system is one of the most advanced electronic payment systems in the world, surpassing even Singapore in this regard. Your card is the key to this system. You can pay almost everything everywhere in Portugal. And with it and the thousands of cash dispenser machines all over the country, you can obtain on-the-spot statements, review your account, pay bills, change your PIN code and do lots of other things. The Portuguese are serious about this electronic banking. This one system covers the entire country and its banks. There are no competing systems and you can use your card in all banks, everywhere. Most banks are now installing 24 hour banking centers, complete lounges with a huge host of machines and a toll free telephone on the spot as well for those needing human guidance. More than 100 of these centers are already in operation, with the BPI bank being the forerunner. Due to their futuristic appearance, some have won international design prizes. For a look at the most impressive center, visit Lisbon's Rossio Square. The door opens automatically when you run your plastic card through the magnetic reader there.

This chapter will tell you more about the *Multibanco* card and will show you the ways in which you may go about obtaining one.

All *Multibancos* are debit cards. A credit facility can be built into some, doubling as VISA or MasterCards. The card will then perform as a VISA or MasterCard when abroad, but as a *Multibanco* when used in Portugal. Due to VISA's and MasterCard's strict international regulations, it cannot then be anonymous. If you want a plain piece of plastic with nothing on it but the account number, you will have to settle for the basic *Multibanco.* You will have to go to only some of the banks, as others insist on imprinting your name on the card. We have found one bank willing to issue cards with no name on them at all. We have been told that another two banks will operate in the same way, giving you totally Anonymous Plastic and letting you sign a signature, any signature, on the back later.

This is not a credit card. You are not allowed to dip into the red. In theory, it is not possible for your balance to fall below zero. Everywhere you use your card inside Portugal, you will be online. An unauthorized overdraft will not be accepted. If used abroad, some of the other systems' ATMs can be tricked because they are only updated with the *Multibanco* network once daily. In this way, you may run up what amounts to roughly a £200 overdraft. We fail to see why you would want to do this, though. It would be quite daft as your bank views their card as a "failsafe" debit card only, and would raise more than a few eyebrows when seeing someone circumvent their set up to earn himself a negative balance. You run the risk of having your card cancelled and your bank account closed, all for a mere £200. If you try to repeat the process the following day by attempting to withdraw a further £200 or equivalent, depending on the country, you will be refused as the ATM in question will then have been updated. This will prevent you getting more cash out.

Our recommendation is: run a tight ship. Be glad that you are one of the few beings in this world with a blank piece of plastic. This is a privilege to savor. Do not ruin your chance by misusing the card. You may find that when you try to get another one, the possibility does not exist anymore. Changes in the banking world of late have tended towards more control, more registration and tighter checks on identification. All future plastic is likely to come with your checked and doublechecked name all over it. No longer will you be able to slip by in the cracks of the system, although existing account holders would naturally keep their cards.

Can you keep this card forever?

In theory, yes. Because this is a debit card, not a credit card. Credit cards and some debit cards with future possibilities for credit facilities or overdrafts are time limited. Normally, they expire within one to two years from issue. Look at your own cards right now! You will see that they will all have to be replaced within a year, maybe two. They are worthless after expiry. But why the hassle? Because banks like to know who you are, where you are and what you are doing with "their" cards. They feel safe by knowing that in less than a year, or maybe two years time, they can refuse further cards to you. They may do this at the drop of a hat. They do not even have to explain themselves or give you any reason why they cancel your cards.

The Anonymous Plastic is different. It doesn't expire! There are no annual charges and no renewing to take care of. It lasts forever, or as long as you care to keep it. If you do not inform your bank of future address changes, this has no bearing on the status of your card whatsoever. No matter where you are in the world, and whether the bank knows about this or not, your card stays the same and stays as good and valid as ever. When you look at the face of the plastic, you will note that not only is your name conspicuous by its absence, there is also no expiry date. The face of the card is adorned *only* by a number and by the name of the issuing bank. Nothing else.

THE DIFFERENT WAYS YOU CAN USE YOUR CARD

In Portugal, as we have stated, you can use the *Multibanco* for almost everything. You will be hard pressed to find a Portuguese not carrying at least one *Multibanco* card. Even school kids are lured into the banks as customers, with special Junior *Multibancos* offering a slightly higher rate of interest for young savers and bold graphics in radiant neon glow-in-the-dark colors.

The use of your card is more limited abroad. You can only use it for withdrawing cash. You can also deposit cash, although this must be done by wire transfer or by mailing a check to your bank branch in Portugal asking them to deposit the funds in your account.

The various networks accepting Portuguese *Multibanco cards* as of 1993, apart from the MB or Multibanco system, are:

4B in Spain
SEMP in Spain
Crédit Andorra in Andorra
LINK in England

Also accepted everywhere you see the "edc" and the "Maestro" signs.

These networks in total offer some 9000 ATMs where you can get up to £200 daily or equivalent in local currency. In Portugal, the normal maximum withdrawal on a standard-type anonymous card is currently 40,000 escudos (approx £175).

When withdrawing cash abroad from any of the above machines, it is important to go to a machine belonging to one of the networks named above. Some other machines accepting cards from the networks, but not part of the networks, may not accept the distant cousin *Multibanco.*

In the UK, LINK machines are common with Abbey National outlets, for instance. Other building societies accept LINK cash cards in their ATMs, although these are not LINK machines as such. For a LINK user this makes no difference, but for a *Multibanco* user it is necessary to distinguish between the LINK network (having an acceptance agreement with *Multibanco* in Portugal) and other British networks accepting LINK (but not necessarily in turn accepting *Multibanco*).

The list of international networks accepting *Multibanco* will grow this year. Bankers BPA informs us that negotiations are currently being finalized doubling the number of countries where *Multibanco* can be used to get cash. Ask your bank when they give you the card. And ask them for an updated list at various intervals. They will be happy to supply all news free of charge.

To get cash from any of the machines accepting *Multibanco,* whether it be in Portugal or in other countries, you will not need to identify yourself. Nor will the machine know who you are, as the card does not carry a name, only a number.

Slide your anonymous plastic into the machine, then follow instructions exactly as they appear on the screen. Your only identification consists of entering a four digit Personal Identification Number (PIN) giving you authorized access to withdrawals. No matter what country you are in, you will then have to wait a maximum of only 30 seconds before getting the cash you requested. You are only allowed to withdraw whatever is already in your account unless an overdraft facility has been arranged in advance.

HOW TO OBTAIN THE CARD

All Portuguese commercial banks issue *Multibanco* cards. Not all, however, are apt at dealing with foreigners.

Here are some of the larger banks that you should consider. Banco Portugues Atlantico, Banco Totta & Acores, Banco Borges & Irmao, Credito Predial Portugues, Caixa Geral do Deposito, Banco Espirito Santo.

A very go-getting bank is the privately owned Banco Comercial Português, currently Portugal's most profitable bank. This is an all-male affair. No women are employed here at all.

Stay clear of the Portuguese branches of foreign banks, such as Barclays, BNP, Credit Lyonnais, etc. Their procedure follows that of their owners. This procedure does not include the issuing of anonymous plastic.

Of the banks on the above list, the most recommended is BPA, Banco Portugues Atlantico. It has recently been privatized and used the event as an occasion to not only spruce up logos and branches, but also to install a new advanced computer system and a new level of customer friendliness.

To open an account you will normally need to show up in person.

You will not need references, nor will you need a Portuguese address. Although having both certainly does no harm. As in any bank when opening an account, look your best. You are unlikely to be asked why you want to open an account. If this happens, though, just tell them that you are going to be spending some time in Portugal and would like somewhere to have funds transferred to. Be sure to ask for all the bank's details so that foreign banks can transfer money to your account if necessary. Do not tell the bank that you are living in Portugal full-time, as they may in that case ask you for your residence card, for a fiscal number or for other Portuguese bureaucracy-issued junk which you are unlikely to have, and certainly most unlikely to ever need. It is perfectly possible for any foreign tourist to open an account anywhere in Portugal, however, so the bank will understand why you do not have any Portuguese papers. This applies not only to offshore-area Madeira, but to the mainland as well. Non-resident foreigners do not pay any kind of Portuguese taxes on their interests. It used to be that to obtain this freedom from taxes, you had to have a special foreigner account *(conta estrangeiro)* designated by ending with the number 39 and noticeable by its lack of any currency restrictions. These accounts still exist. But with currency controls gone, any foreigner can have any type of account these days. So you are as likely as not to wind up with a "39" account and it will make no difference one way or the other.

When a Portuguese opens an account, he will be asked for his ID card which Portuguese are theoretically supposed to carry at all times. This cedula-type document is known as a BI, short for *Bilhete Identidade.* The bank knows that you won't have such a card, so they will ask you for your passport.

Copying the details from your passport, they will assist you in filling out a form asking very few questions apart from name and address. Readers familiar with Latin countries will not be surprised to learn that among the five or so questions, one pertains to your parentage. State mother's and father's names, or any names for that matter . . .

You will be asked if you want a check book, always personalized in Portugal, or a *Multibanco* card, personalized in some banks, anonymous in others. Your name will only be imprinted if you insist on it. You may have both if you ask for it. Note that banks will freely give you a *Multibanco* card and will give you a check book if you are deemed suitable. Your first check book will have only five or ten checks in it and twenty-five the next time around. This is due to the fact that all banks will cover bum checks up to 5000 escudos per check. In theory making them vulnerable to a 125,000 escudos loss if you run amok with your second check book. With 145 escudos to the dollar, this all adds up.

You are unlikely to be given a VISA *Multibanco* or a Mastercard *Multibanco* even if you ask. You need to have been a customer with the bank for at least six months and have a steady monthly income arriving in your account as clockwork. This should be above the Portuguese average of US$300, preferably double that.

If opening the account in person, the bank will know your identity by virtue of having seen your passport. A very loose sort of bank secrecy exists in Portugal, equal to that of the UK or Germany. This is not impressive but better than none at all. The best element of the Portuguese bank secrecy is that there is no automatic yearly filing or reporting to tax authorities or any other government body. Not even the Portuguese statistical institute gets any figures, although it has been pressing for data on many occasions.

The bank will accept any address anywhere in the world. It will happily send monthly statements to you care of any outpost on the globe, at no charge. It makes up for this expense by offering what is in effect negative interest rates once inflation is calculated into the picture.

If you want to keep part of your funds in Portuguese escudos, do not keep them in a standard deposit account with the *Multibanco* and/or check book added for convenience. Open a time deposit. Ninety day call accounts gave back an annual compounded interest of up to 17 per cent in 1992. In 1995 you could find 12 to 14 per cent on time deposits six months upwards.

Once your account opening form is completed, sign the signature card, then make your first deposit. It used to be that only foreign currency could be deposited in the "39" foreigner accounts. The money would then be converted to escudos at the prevailing exchange rate at the time of the deposit. Today, however, you can deposit any color of money, Portuguese included. The choice is yours.

Some banks expect you to open the account with a certain minimum, varying from 10,000 to 100,000 escudos. Our recommendation, BPA, does not. You can open the account with a dollar. But if you want to walk out of there with the anonymous plastic in your pocket, you should probably deposit just a bit more. Ten thousand escudos is in order here. This is equivalent to more or less US$70 / £45 sterling. Tell the bank that you need a *Multibanco*. Each branch has a box of fresh plastic cards. Your teller will dip into the box, then hand you a card. That's it! You now have your anonymous plastic! Pocket it, sign it later. Then wait eight or ten days for the PIN code to arrive in the mail. There is no way the bank can give you the PIN code with the card. Reason being that the bank simply do not know it. For security reasons, a PIN code is only issued once a certain card is hooked up to a new account. This is done by headquarters, mailing the secret four-digit number to your address. You should note that in order for your card to work its magic, it must have been used once in a Portuguese *Multibanco* machine *not* belonging to the issuing bank. If you open the account with BPA, then use the card for the very first time in a BPA machine, it will not work. But from the second transaction onwards, everything is possible. Likewise, if you open the account with BPA, then use the card for the very first time in a foreign ATM ie outside Portugal, it will not work either.

If you are only going to be in Portugal a short while, and if you have given the bank a foreign address as your own, you can ask for the PIN code to be forwarded to your hotel instead of your home address. You could also have it sent to a lawyer, a rented PO Box, perhaps even the bank itself for you to collect eight to ten days after having opened the account.

We have done this and so can you.

HOW TO OBTAIN THE CARD WITH LITTLE OR NO ID

If you want to obtain the anonymous plastic without having to show your passport, the main rule to remember is, do not cheat or lie to the bank. This could result in your being turned down, or in the account being closed at some later stage by the bank, or maybe even in the bank or some other body pressing charges against you.

Having said that, a lot is possible quite legally for the smooth and charming talker with a story to tell. Let your imagination loose and let it drive your tongue.

Opening an account on behalf of a foreign corporation, or maybe a relative, could be your ticket. Having forgotten your documents could be another. There are no foolproof ways, but if you do not care to show a passport, a little ID could go a long way. A little bit of *any* ID is definitely better than none. In Morocco once we managed to open an account showing a UK British Rail commuter card that was three years expired. Portugal is referred to by some as the only African country in Europe. Any type of ID is said to be valid, especially these days where a lot of EU citizens come to Portugal without passports, as it is no longer necessary. Giving an address within the EU, claiming to be an EU citizen and then showing a piece of halfbaked ID from some obscure institution in an EU country or other will probably get your account opened in a jiffy and land you that coveted piece of anonymous plastic. Of the current 12 members of the European Union, only the UK, Ireland and Denmark do not have national ID card schemes. When asked for your passport, simply say that you traveled on your national ID card instead. Then show the Portuguese bank a library card, a bus or metro ID card or some other document that you can obtain elsewhere without showing formal ID. Make sure you have a foreign but still European address to go along with the card. The bank will want to mail monthly statements to you.

A valuable book that may help you procure various forms of woolly ID is called *ID By Mail*. It is compiled by Barry Reid, author of the Paper Trip books about alternate identities. Order from Scope International Ltd.

If you are willing to put up with a bit more bureaucracy and a wait for your *Multibanco* card, you can avoid a trip to Portugal. All the banks recommended in this chapter have branches outside Portugal. Most of them are in Paris where a large expatriate population of Portuguese live, but some are also in London, New York, Grand Cayman and Zürich.

The staff in these foreign branches tend not to be as slow-witted as their colleagues at home, the Portugal-based tellers. So it is unlikely that you will get away with your wilder stories or some of your homemade ID. A trip to Lisbon or Oporto is recommended. We know of at least one person who keeps accounts in several names based on do-it-yourself camouflage passports from such non-existing countries as Ceylon and the British Honduras.

One final alternative? Having a lawyer or perhaps a third party open the account will avoid you having to show any ID. You won't even have to show up. Everything can be done by mail, and if you play your card right, your "agent" will not even be aware of your true identity. The next pages cover this alternative.

HOW TO OBTAIN THE CARD BY MAIL

Portuguese banks are not used to opening personal savings/deposit accounts by mail. But they are not unfamiliar with a third party opening the account on someone else's behalf.

Lawyers (*advogados*) are known to do this for clients residing in other countries. It must be stated that the author has never personally used this route. We cannot therefore recommend any one lawyer in particular and know of none that has a specific program in place at a set price. We would be happy to receive letters detailing readers' experiences for inclusion in future updates of this report. Any hints will be received with our thanks.

If you want to contact a Portuguese lawyer, these addresses are included to get you started:

Sousa Magalhaes, Rua de Ceuta 34, 1., P-4000 Porto, Portugal

José Antonio Ramos, Av. Ress Garcia 39, 2.E, P-1000 Lisboa, Portugal

J Henriques Silva & Associados, Av. Duque de Loulé 47, 6., P-1000 Lisboa, Portugal, with offices also in the Algarve at **Largo Mig. Bombarda 3, P-8400 Lagoa, Portugal**

Finally, **Trevor Bennett** of solicitors Bennett & Co. may be of some help to you. He works mainly with Portugal and foreigners setting up in Portugal. His address is: **39 London Road, Alderley Edge, Cheshire SK9 7JT, England, tel 0625 586937, fax 0625 585362.**

In the years to come, some young and enterprising hungry hustler will head to Portugal personally. With his own documents or a banking passport, he will then make the rounds to several banks in a number of towns and cities. In each branch, he will open an account, deposit perhaps 10,000 or 20,000 escudos. For each account, he will get a debit card and a PIN code. Soon, he will have a hundred of these, maybe a lot more if he is persistent. When that happens, he will start running a classified ad internationally, selling each bank account, just like the Austrian bearer *sparbuchs* are sold legally today. Look out for such ads. You will be able to buy an account in someone else's name, change the address to your own, use an already established international debit card delivered to you complete with a PIN code that you can change at any time you wish, simply by entering the card in an ATM and following the on-screen instructions. So far, you can't buy mail order accounts this way. In the short-term future, someone will make a bit of loot off this potential money spinner. It would be a nice addition to our toolbox, fitting right in with a handful of other secret and semi-secret banking products.

Chapter 16

THE SAVINGS ACCOUNT PROGRAM

How would you like to make 13 per cent interest a year, paid in dollars, and without an inkling of a currency risk? According to "The Savings Account Program", you can. All safe and sound by buying Certificates of Deposit with interest rates ranging from 6 per cent (30 day US$ CDs) to 10 per cent (1 year US$ CDs) and 13 per cent pa (5 year US$ CDs). The scheme is operated by **Global Consulting Group SA, PO Box 945, Suite 922, Centro Colon 1007, San Jose, Costa Rica** (read more about them in our chapter on Back-to-Back loans). Working with banks in seven countries, they pay interest on maturity or at the end of each year or, for a US$24 a year service charge, on a monthly check. Sending US$10 cash or money order will buy you their 19 page prospectus. Its intro page reads:

The Savings Account Program is specifically designed to pay you interest (in US dollars) at a rate much higher than you can obtain in any US bank with safety of your investment. Another very important consideration is that this savings program will allow you to decide if you voluntarily wish to report the interest as income to the country in which you reside. Approximately 98 per cent of our clients prefer the secrecy and the confidentiality of income and do not report any interest as income, thus avoiding additional income taxes which pushes up the net yield considerably.

Let your savings pay you a monthly income check. You can receive a monthly income check, earn a very high interest rate, withdraw your principal and/or interest at any time. And . . . you can increase your monthly income check by making additional deposits to your savings account whenever you wish. New accounts can be opened for as little as $1000 US funds.

Going on, it asks:

Why should you invest some of your cash assets with us?

The answer:

1. Your deposits are 100 per cent fully guaranteed (we can't see how, but more on that later). *2. Your deposits are backed dollar for dollar . . . which makes your deposits safe, secure and sure. No US Bank today can make such a statement. 3. No IRS reporting, no bank reporting, no tax reporting, no tax withholding, no death taxes. Protects you from liens, bankruptcy, foreclosures, liability and malpractice suits as well as divorce proceedings. Your assets should always belong to you.*

And, a most interesting feature is that:

4. Interest is paid to you tax free. Income is not reported to any government. The income is secret and the IRS or any other government agency cannot a) seize your checking account or b) examine your bank statements or bank accounts to learn of your activities or to conduct an audit.
5. We will assign you a numbered account if you wish your name to be kept secret and confidential. Most clients prefer this method.

While the Savings Account Program has its merits, you must take the above paragraph for what it is. Advertising. Some of the claims are a bit on the optimistic side. No bank records are ever totally immune from seizure no matter where the bank is located. The claim of dollar by dollar backed security looks doubtful when, on the next page of the brochure, a heading is titled *Just How Does This Program Work.* It goes on to explain that: *Very simply, we issue Certificates of Deposit on our company to the Client or the Client's Corporation back to back with a bank in a democratic country recognized for its honest and reliable laws and courts.* Of banks in some seven countries listed, none have deposit protection schemes for foreign account holders. And how, by receiving a CD on what is merely a foreign limited company, are your deposits *100 per cent fully guaranteed?* Guaranteed, they may be, but only by your trust in the future performance of that particular company. If you can live with that, the Savings Account Program is for you. Read on:

By issuing a back to back certificate of deposit, this puts one more additional stumbling block between the Client, the IRS and the actual bank paying interest on the certificate of deposit. Your name is not in the bank records which gives you more protection. This would eliminate any possibility of a bank employee being bribed by the USA IRS or a government of any other country in giving out information on you personally or that of your offshore company. Secondly, we can issue a certificate of deposit payable to bearer which means that whomever holds the Certificate of Deposit owns the certificate of deposit, but no name appears on the CD. In this way no government can ever say, or know, or make a charge that the CD is actually owned by a particular person or offshore company. For example, just suppose the IRS or some government snoop found a CD payable to bearer in your home or office or safety deposit box or wherever (with or without a search warrant), then the IRS could not say it belonged to you personally or your company. Why? Simply because you just happened to have a friend in an offshore company who can attest to the true ownership of the CD which will relieve you of any problem associated with the CD being in your possession.

This interpretation of IRS procedure is somewhat optimistic. To be fair, it should rightly have been named the "Certificates of Deposit Program" or something similar.

Commenting on these company issued CDs, the company's own pitch reads as follows:

There is a lot of built-in protection in these CD's, in that we know who the true owner/client is and if it is presented for payment by any party other than the original purchaser, we will first contact and question the original party to authenticate its transfer so that the bearer can negotiate the CD in hand. However, we do recommend that the client acquire his own foreign corporation and put the CD in the name of his foreign corporation which eliminates any connection of the client with the reporting of any income.

Again, not quite true, since it depends on where you reside. Legally, Americans can't play the game this way. So why the recommendation of foreign corporations? Perhaps it has something to do with the fact that you can, while signing up for the Savings Account Program, also purchase your own offshore company for a US$6500 all inclusive fee. It is all right there on the very same order form . . .

Here is how the company asks you to send them money.

1. Postal Money Orders: Postal money orders are a good method of transferring money because a) You do not have to put your name on the money order, b) MOs are good for amounts of US$100 to say US$3000 or so. The maximum amount of a US Postal Money Order is US$700. So if you wanted to send US$3500 that means you would need to send five money orders. A word of caution. Don't buy all five money orders the same day and from the same post office and especially from the same person. You might wish to visit several post office branches and you also might ask your wife or friend to buy some MOs for you. Just use your good common sense. c) MOs don't leave any audit trail to cause you problems.

2. Bank Certified Checks: You can purchase a Bank Certified Check for amounts not to exceed US$9999.99. Why? Because there is a law that requires the bank to fill out a special government form for all single transactions of US$10,000 or more and of course you don't want to fill out any forms. So what is the solution? Suppose you want to send US$45,000 in Bank Certified Checks. All you do is simply go to five different banks where they don't know your face and buy one US$9000 certified check at each of the five different banks and that will give you US$45,000. Simple? Yes, of course. Purchases of even less than US$9000 (each purchase) would be recommended for a lower profile.

Careful now. Structuring is a felony in itself, in the United States. You are better off banking abroad, in silence, with banks in countries where such laws don't exist.

Some banks ask you for your name which they will type on the certified check but most banks don't ask. For the banks that do ask for a name, just give them a fictitious name or give them the name of someone you don't like. And should the IRS ever look through the copies of certified checks and find the name of the person you don't like, just imagine what problems he might have explaining his name on the certified checks.

3. Bank Wire Transfers: The same applies here as in 1) and 2). Remember to keep the cash transactions under the amount of US$10,000, go to a bank that does not know you, don't use your correct name as the remitter. Use a fictitious name.

4. Travelers Checks: Travelers checks can be used for small amounts of money. There is a small risk of audit trail here but it is very remote. Remember, when you purchase most kinds of travelers checks, the seller asks that you put your name on the checks in the presence of the seller.

In some instances we have known of clients who will use this method and simply put a fictitious name on the checks which leaves no trail. Why? Because no ID check is usually requested. If you are transmitting any amount of money, using any of these methods and are asked for specific ID, then simply excuse yourself and go to another location. It is not hard to do, at all.

5. Western Union: This is one of the more expensive ways to use for the transfer of currency. Because of this, we don't recommend its use. If used however, the same kind of rules apply as mentioned in the other items above.

And how might you receive money?

1. Checks: We can send the client our company check drawn on a Costa Rica bank, a Panama bank or US bank. These checks can be certified if requested. If the client has a method of being able to cash or dispose of these checks without leaving any audit trail, then this would be an easy method to use.

2. Postal Money Orders: We can send the client US Postal Money Orders. Please remember that the maximum amount of each MO is US$700. Only the cost of checks and money orders are deducted from the client's funds proceeds.

3. Travelers Checks: Checks can be sent to a client in denominations of US$20 up to US$100. Only the cost of the travelers checks will be deducted from the client's funds (proceeds).

4. Cash by Bank Wire funds: This is another easy way of transferring to a client, however, this leaves a possible 'audit trail' which means you may want to avoid this method. In some instances a client may have a personal friend with his bank who will accept a fictitious name in the transfer of funds to the bank from this end. Only the client will know the secret name and will give it to the banker friend. Great, no audit trail. If a very large amount of money is involved, perhaps several different wire transfers should be made so as not to call attention to any large wire transfers. Use your good common sense.

5. In person and courier: One easy way to receive money is to come to Costa Rica on a business trip or for a vacation. Cash of US$5000 per person can be carried either way through customs in the US and if you have a family totaling five, you can carry back US$25,000 with no reporting requirements as each person is allowed US$5000. A special courier can be used when special needs arise.

6. US Corporation: Just suppose you wanted to start a new corporation in the United States and you needed, say, US$50,000 or US$100,000 to begin operations. Let's just discuss two ways to accomplish this. a) A foreign corporation can be formed to purchase the stock of this new US corporation. Then the foreign corporation transfers the money to the US corporation. There are many advantages of a foreign corporation owning an American company. b) Or you can make a loan to fund the US corporation. The interest on the loan can be a deductible US expense and the interest will be accumulated in your offshore foreign corporation completely income tax free.

7. Loans: Make a loan with your offshore corporation. The US$5000 customs and US$10,000 cash reporting requirements do not apply in the case of loans. A loan can be in any *amount. Again, the terms, conditions and interest can be set by you. And the interest can be a deductible expense against income and received by your offshore foreign corporation tax free.*

8. Paid bills and expenses: Suppose you need a charge account paid, or perhaps you are planning a vacation to the Bahamas, or your daughter is having a wedding, or your son wants to buy a car, or you want to send someone a gift of money, or your son is going to college, etc. Are you beginning to see the possibilities? Let your imagination decide your needs. Whatever you want paid, pay it from offshore and enjoy your right to privacy.

In addition to the Savings Account Program, offering high interest rate CDs, the same company has something it calls the ''Checking Account Program''. This program, it is said, specificially designed to give the client an offshore checking account which will afford that client the secrecy, privacy and confidentiality that he needs and requires and to which he is entitled, but can't receive in his own country. There's more: *With this particular Checking Account Program there will never be an audit trail or account statement for the snooping government officials to examine and inspect.* Now: never say never, but do look into the Checking Account Program anyway. While it won't make you the same kind of money as the Saving Accounts Program promises to do, your funds look more secure. Let's look at how the program is described . . .

THE CHECKING ACCOUNT PROGRAM

As with any bank, there is certain basic information needed such as your name, address and verified identification that you are the person who actually wishes to open the checking account. If the account is to be a personal account, the account can be in your personal name or if you prefer secrecy, privacy and confidentiality, a numbered account can be assigned to you. If the account is to be a business account, the account can also be in the name of the business or a numbered account can be assigned.

Let's mention a few of the advantages of using and maintaining an offshore checking account: 1) A numbered checking account. Your name is not connected. 2) Your private life, deposit and expense activity is secret. 3) Protection from the wife, husband, family or anybody else knowing your personal banking activities. 4) Float time is extended to about 20 to 30 days. 5) The IRS will never know of your offshore account. 6) The IRS can never audit your checking account and can never cause you a civil or criminal tax problem. 7) The IRS can never access your personal deposits and check writing expenses. 8) The IRS can never lien your checking account at any time. 9) The IRS can never gain access through the bank's micro-film. There are severe secrecy laws that protect all of our clients. 10) No suits, liens, bankruptcy, judgement, divorce proceedings or any court actions can ever attach your funds.

In order to open your offshore checking account, you must make a minimum initial deposit of $2000 US funds. Secondly, our fee to open the account is $500 US funds. This is a one time charge only. So the total net remittance of at least US$2500 will be necessary to open a checking *account. When you remit US$2500 or larger if you wish, only US$500 will be deducted from your remittance as our fee and any remainder will be credited to your account.*

US$2000 is a fairly standard account opening minimum requirement. In some cases, it is even higher. US$5000 seems to be the norm for many banks. In a few cases it will be lower. One or two offshore banks have no minimum, while some require only a US$1000 minimum initial deposit. Why the initial minimum? Located offshore, banks dealing with most of their clients by mail order want to make sure that it is worth their while. Once your account is opened, however, you won't get the boot once your account drops below the minimum. You can withdraw your funds the first chance you get and your account will still be in good standard, fully operative. Opening your account in person, most banks have no requirements as to any minimum deposit. Getting a check book and a credit or debit card, they will look to your account to see if you have any funds. Only with some sort of minimum balance, US$2000, for instance, will you get the check book. For credit cards, a higher balance may be needed. Here, a minimum of US$5000 seems to be the norm. There are no strict rules. Only loose rules of thumb.

As for the US$500 fee charged by Global to set up your account, you can save yourself this money by cutting out the middleman. Go straight to source. Open your account directly with the bank of your choice and put that $500 in your own pocket. You can do that. But working through Global may not be all bad. In our view, their US$500 fee could turn out to be some of the best US$500 you have spent in a long time, because they offer some fairly expensive secretarial services, all geared at helping you beat your enemies, the investigators, by keeping a low profile. Some of the options they offer:

1. Your mail can be received at our address and held or, at your request, forwarded to you under a separate blank cover so as not to call any attention as the result of foreign bank mail.

2. With your written permission, we could open the incoming mail and remove certain information (names, numbers, addresses) and then forward that information to you by Xerox copy in an envelope (blank) that won't disclose your connection.

3. Or we could just send you a listing of opening balances, debit and credit activity and ending balances without any identifying information or references and only you would be able to identify and understand its contents.

Services: Most clients prefer to have us do all of their banking business and the necessary work and errands that go with checking activity. We would like for you to know about these services. Please let us know if you would like to use and take advantage of these services – 1. Clerical Time. We charge US$25 per hour for all work outside the office, such as going to the bank, making deposits, errands, etc. For your information each outside transaction is about one quarter of an hour which is about US$6 in cost. 2. Professional Time. We charge US$50 per hour for all work inside the office, such as reconciling your bank statement each month and other services that may be required. The average time for an account with 10 to 15 checks per month is *about 30 minutes which is about US$25 in cost. The above expenses are considerably less than any certified accountant would charge. Let's recap the services: a. We receive and reconcile your bank statement each month. b. We provide storage facilities for your bank statements. c. We provide correspondence files for checking account activity, be it from you or from the bank to us. d. We send you coded monthly statements (no ID) showing you all activity that is easy to understand. e. We provide all the envelopes and postage in sending you this information. All the services above are included in the house fee. Outside house: The average client with average checking activity takes about one to two hours outside activity per year or a cost of about US$25 to US$50 per year. In house: The average client with average checking activity takes about three hours activity per year or a cost of about US$150 per year. You would have to agree that this is a bargain in professional services in addition to the secrecy and privacy you receive.*

3. We suggest that you have your monthly bank statements mailed directly to our office for servicing. This eliminates the postman's eyes, the family eyes and even the IRS from snooping and knowing that you have a foreign checking account as well as many other advantages.

We agree. A bargain in professional services. Which is why, from the above, you may *not* want to save the US$500 by going it alone even though you can. The main risk with Global, as we see it, is that it can be closed down, as a result of some decisive government action. It has several years under its belt but it is holding up a red flag for the IRS to sting. However, the IRS cannot close it down, since it is operating out of Costa Rica. The Costa Rica government has a history of keeping neutral. The Costa Rica government also has a history of fiercely defending that little country's right to independence. They don't particularly like the high handedness of the United States' army of bureaucrats. In one recent decision, an American fugitive found a safe haven in Costa Rica. On ethical ground, the Costa Rica Supreme Court refused to honor that country's signed and ratified extradition treaty with the United States. Because, asked Costa Rica, "Why should we observe the niceties of an extradition treaty when you yourselves (the US) only adhere to treaties whenever it suits your own purpose?" Costa Rica was referring to how the United States broke its treaty with Mexico by kidnapping a Mexican doctor, then forcefully bringing him to the US to stand trial.

Your main risk with Global is that it is going too far out of its way to help you obtain your goal. Meditate a bit on this. With a run of the mill offshore bank, never helpful, you don't run the risk of suddenly finding it closed because the IRS decided to teach the directors a brutal lesson in government Gestapo tactics. We don't think this will happen with Global. But should it, we hope that others will take over and carry the torch. It is necessary to keep the flame of resistance alive, running service operations showing others how to carve out financial freedom in this unfree world. It is necessary to help like-minded PTs obtain their goals. With two or three "Globals" springing up every time the government closes one down, we can win this underground war. You may want to go into business as a fixer or facilitator. You will be doing your fellow community of Freedom Fighters a public service. And, don't forget, no one expects you to work for free. Global is making money and so will you. This is only fair. Through future editions of this report, or through ads in publications read by PTs, you can advertise your skills and willingness to help. Sadly, today, you need to operate in exile. If you don't, your career in the Resistance will be short-lived. Your government can open a multitude of bogus criminal cases against you. Working from exile, you stand a chance of doing some worthwhile deeds. Working from your home country, you risk becoming an unknown martyr. Always operate from abroad. As some Scandinavian friends can tell you, this is not always a guarantee against persecution once your government is hell-bent on shutting your voice down. Fake charges can be invented against anybody, no matter where they reside. But at least exile offers the best barrier of protection we have so far, in this imperfect world of ours.

THE IMPRESS ACCOUNT

A final helpful hand from Global Consulting Group SA of Costa Rica is what they call "The Impress Account". In short, they offer to pay anybody with their money as long as you have reimbursed them, in advance.

Using the Impress Account, your name is kept in the dark. At the same time, the paper trail is cut quite effectively. It is very important to call your attention to the fact that when you send a personal or business check, you are leaving what accountants call an audit trail. This is exactly what you don't want to do. If you leave an audit trail for the sending of money to be invested somewhere else, and then later happen to have your tax return and checking account audited by an IRS agent, this is going to raise questions that you cannot or may not want to answer. Need we say more?

The Impress Account is your alternative to be used in lieu of opening your own offshore checking account. Use theirs! They are willing to act as go betweens, fronting for you for as little as US$10. Global describes the setup this way: *To summarize briefly, an Impress Account is a checking account that is used to "pool" incoming funds and make disbursements (payments, pay bills, etc.) for clients seeking complete privacy. For example, just suppose you wanted a certain item in the US paid and you liked the advantage of a cancelled check, but didn't want to use any US banks for the many bad reasons we all know. And lets say the item expense was US$100. It could be for any amount. All you do is send us US$110 postal money order, which leaves no audit or paper trail. The money order is payable to us. Along with the money order you provide instructions as to the name of the person or business you want paid. The other information would be the mailing address and amount paid. We pay the cost of postage, envelopes and checks. Of course, there are many other ways to forward money to us. One of the most common ways is sending us checks made payable to you or your business that you do not wish to deposit to a bank in the US for obvious reasons. We can clear. We then draw a check from the Impress Account to the party you requested to be paid. The party receiving the payment may not know the nature or the purpose of the check unless you advise us to inform the payee on the* *check what the payment is for. Some clients don't want any information to go along with the check. But most clients do ask us to send along with the check a "remittance advice" which informs the receiver of the payment exactly what the purpose of the payment is for and to whom it is to be credited.*

You pay a service fee of US$20 per year for the Impress Account. Once that is paid, you can have Global write any number of checks on your behalf, paying the following all-inclusive charges (checks, postage and envelopes included). US$10 per check for all checks under US$1000. US$15 per check for all checks over US$1000. US$25 per check for all checks over US$10,000. Before the check can be written, your funds need to have cleared. With cash and money orders, there won't be a delay. With all other monetary instruments, a delay of some 30 days should be expected, Global claims.

CASHING CHECKS

American and UK residents know their bit about check cashing services. Sometimes open 24 hours, day and night, these *Cambio*-looking counters will cash your check, in effect buying it at less than face value. The difference is their profit, a sometimes healthy profit in percentage terms, especially on smaller checks.

What you may not know is that you can, especially in the US, work with some of these check cashing services by mail. This gives you the advantage of being able to keep your true identity and your home address in the dark. They will clear your checks for you, using their accounts, and they will give you cash any way you want it. But they won't know who you are.

Michael Hoy's list of US Mail Drops, available from Scope International's PT Booklist contains several addresses of check cashing services offering to clear by mail order. All of them offer mail forwarding as well. Running a business, you could have them receive your checks on the address, open your mail, process and clear your checks right away and send you a summary every week or so of business dealt with. For a PT, life on the beach can be possible. We know of one gentleman, approximately 999 years old, who works this way. With a cellular phone, he sits on the beach all day, while his mail service receives orders for brochures. They open envelopes with US$5 cash, then forward preprinted leaflets. Our hero just sits in the sun supervising by remote control. His name is Paradise Shelton. For his full story, read the new *Sex Havens* report.

Some check cashing services are organized as clubs. They want you to pay a fee for becoming a member and in return they offer a wider range of services than a basic check cashing counter. These so-called clubs claim to be able to lower your financial profile. When you cash a check, they say, they will cut the paper trail. They will then act as a semi-bank, keeping your money until you want it, then letting you have it any way you want it. There's more. In return for your membership, the service will even do a bit of extra work on your behalf if you don't want the money outright, but want it spent. The service offers to pay your rent or house payments, your electric/water/telephone bills. Make monthly payments on your car, charge accounts. Make your loan payments, children's college tuition payments. Make an investment in secret so they claim. Buy furniture, assets in your name or other names. Start up a new business and so on. For businesses, they offer to pay directly for merchandise you don't want to show up in your books and ledgers, or pay yourself or key employees under the table.

One such organization currently charges US$100 for membership plus US$10 per month, a total of US$220 for the first year. A second club charges US$280 for the first year, then US$160 for all subsequent years. The cheapest of these associations bills you US$50 for joining, then US$25 for each following year. A regular check cashing service, of course, charges you only the fee for cashing. You are not a member of anything, nor are you on their mailing list. They don't even know you. You cash your checks and that's that. They happily forget you and move on to serve the next customer in line.

So why should you want to use a club? In our opinion, you shouldn't. In addition to the annual dues, administration costs are high and the record keeping will have to be extra detailed for everything to work out according to plan. On top of annual fees you are charged a US$1 transaction fee for each check, between US$5 and US$7, depending on the club or service organization used, for each payment turn-around (directly or indirectly to you or paid to whomever you designated) plus postage and envelope costs *and* another 1.5 per cent to 2.5 per cent of the normal cash. All in all, fairly expensive. You also require detailed bookkeeping procedures to keep track of your transactions. Accounts are sent out monthly. Sometimes mistakes happen. This means you writing them back and forth, ironing out a problem that would not have occurred had you stuck to working only with a straightforward check cashing operation clearing your checks.

If you go ahead and decide to join one of the extended services, pause and give some thought to jurisdiction first. Are they located in the same country where you are? If so, avoid them. Are they located in a country where the local tax man may, at some future point, resent the fact that they are helping muddy the waters so he can't get a clear picture of who's cashing what and who's making what sums of money, declared or undeclared? If so, avoid them. US based companies have serious problems that they simply cannot overcome. This would have a direct effect on you. It could cause you problems you don't need to be confronted with. All of your business activity must be sent directly to the club, not just the clearing of incoming checks for deposit, but also written instructions for the turn-around of your money. To back up its extensive account, the club has to keep all of your instructions on file indefinitely. When another customer does something wrong, or when the tax brutes simply decide that now is the time to fold the tent, all your letters and written instructions from day one are on file. The trail leads back to you. Along with a list of all cancelled checks and financial proof of all disbursements.

Because of jurisdiction, records can be obtained through court orders and search and seizure warrants. If the tax man wants to operate in secret, it is easy for him too. He will know exactly what banks the clubs are using. Going on a fishing expedition, he will then obtain copies of the deposit slips and copies of the checks deposited front and back to determine exactly the payee and the payor. You think that you are protected by the wildly misnamed USA 1978 Financial Privacy Act? With this piece of legislation, it appears that the federal government must notify you before any record search, then give you the opportunity to challenge it. So it seems. In reality, the government routinely claims that it would hamper an investigation if the suspect were to learn anything too early. They can only claim this in criminal cases, not civil. The end result is that a lot of unimportant tax cases, which should be tried as civil cases are labelled criminal cases. Banks, savings and loans associations, and credit card companies all fall under the wording of the Financial Privacy Act. And by the way, your "private papers" as defined by the Fourth Amendments are only papers in your possession. The courts have ruled that papers held by third parties, such as banks are not protected. Foreigners finding themselves in a case where the US government is their adversary can not count on having any civil rights at all. On numerous occasions courts have ruled that the US Constitution extends only to resident Americans or legally resident aliens. Americans abroad are not even protected by it. The solution for Americans and everybody else is don't use home based banks for clearing and processing. Operate in another country. Don't rely on others for providing the secrecy you need. Create it yourself. Combine the low profile of *PT 2* with a few of the techniques for Banking in Silence, then structure your own cash flow system with a way to: 1. Receive funds anonymously clearing checks via bank accounts, yours or others, and then 2. Spend the money, or whatever else you plan on doing with it anonymously.

In many countries the tax man works hand in hand with Customs and with Postal Inspectors. Customs has the right to open all mail coming from abroad. It claims that this is simply part of normal border customs inspection. But in reality it is a clear case of Big Brother spying on his own citizens. Postal Inspectors only open letters and read the contents if they suspect something illegal going on. This suspicion rises proportionally with the number of postal inspectors. In other words, you have people who spend their entire work day just sifting through other people's personal mail. This is simply their job. When they pick out an envelope to read, it has not been preceeded by a lengthy pondering on whether that particular envelope carries something illicit inside. The way these low level bureaucrats approach their job is more like that of assembly line workers. The only difference being that instead of assembling Ford-Ts, these workers manufacture human grief. Is this only a sickness found in the developed world? Sadly, no. If anything, Third World governments are even more apprehensive about mail entering from abroad. For this reason, always route your sensitive mail through a private mail drop in a neutral country. Use a pen name; that way "your" mail is not yours, but being held for a foreign friend due to arrive. Tell your mail drop not to forward your mail in such a way that it will catch undue attention.

A few rules of thumb. Never send more than one pound (approximately 500 grams) of mail in any one envelope. If it can be avoided, don't use envelopes larger than B5 (approximately A5 or the size of a standard piece of stationary folded once). Use standard airmail. More of these dos and don'ts are listed in the special mail drop section of *PT 2*. Be careful when using overnight couriers internationally. Whereas maybe one per cent of all international airmail is being looked over, far more than half of all couriered items are actually being opened and the contents examined by customs! In some countries the figure is not 50 per cent, but 100. Even third party transit countries are snoopy. For a while, your author had dealings in Bermuda, a British crown colony. To get to and from Bermuda, flights go via the USA. Whenever we asked our secretary to DHL us something, she would do so right away, from Bermuda to wherever we happened to be staying . . . usually in Europe or in South America. A fairly typical UPS or DHL shipment would be sent from Bermuda to, say, the UK. In the normal course of the air traffic pattern, the shipment would touch down in the United States, purely a transit point. Technically, our couriered mail would never enter the United States. It would merely be reloaded the very same hour onto another plane, bound for the UK. We would get it in the UK one or two nights later. Not once, not twice, but *every time* we would find attached a sticker informing us that our mail had been opened and read by US Customs and that it had, according to the laconic text of the sticker, passed. We all know that the United States has a great interest in everything coming out of tax havens like Bermuda. But to this day, we still don't know with what legal justification the US Customs felt it could intercept and read personal mail between two foreign countries, Bermuda and the UK, in situations not involving American citizens nor any American residents. Incidentally, to our knowledge, British Customs never showed any interest in our mail. Mere paper dealing with tax law and other boring subjects.

Another route to secrecy. Have a friend buy American Express travelers checks. If he is asked to sign the top line, have him sign the lower one later, in private. If he is not required to sign, he shouldn't sign anywhere, neither when buying nor later. He should make the checks out to you and send them to you for cashing at a local American Express office. Your helpful friend abroad should retain the numbers of the travelers checks. If they are lost in transit he can simply get his money back. No one else can cash the travelers checks, whether signed or unsigned, as they are made out to you.

Chapter 17

WG HILL'S SPARBUCH SECRETS

No more secrets? Enter the Sparbuch. Over the past few years, the banking secrecy in traditional banking havens has eroded seriously. New laws in Switzerland now require that the banks be made aware of the beneficial owner of fiduciary accounts. Swiss banks increasingly have come under heavy attack from the US authorities, resulting in more than 800 court-ordered breaches of banking confidentiality laws in 1991.

Banks in the Cayman Islands, the Bahamas, Luxembourg and Liechtenstein also have come under increasing outside pressure to disclose the identity of their customers. In the event that courts refuse to order banks to disclose the identity of their customers if the alleged crime is, for example, tax evasion, authorities in several countries now routinely cook up completely bogus drug-allegations in order to break banking secrecy laws.

One haven remains though, Austria. It is officially necessary for foreign account holders to relinquish a photocopy of their passport in order to open an account in any Austrian bank, but one loophole remains: the Austrian Sparbuch. The Austrians are outdoing the Swiss in anonymous banking. They remain untainted by the claws of Big Brother.

The Sparbuch, literally "savings book" is, to all ends and purposes, a bearer passbook. Whoever is in physical possession of the book is presumed to be the owner of the account and may do with it whatever he or she wishes. A Sparbuch is a small booklet in which the account transactions are recorded as is the case with any passbook. However, being the bearer, one does not need to produce any sort of identification whatsoever when making deposits or withdrawals in the account.

Access to the account is protected by a so-called *Lösungswort* (code word). Presenting the Sparbuch and giving the *Lösungswort* at any branch of the issuing bank gives the holder automatic access to the funds in the account.

WHAT A SPARBUCH WILL DO

An Austrian Sparbuch account may be in one of only two currencies, the German D-Mark (DM) or the Austrian schilling (AS). The schilling, however, is pegged to the German D-Mark which, in turn, is a currency in the European Monetary Snake (EMS). This implies that the value of the DM (and, thus, the Austrian schilling) may only fluctuate +/- 2.5 per cent from the baseline value. In other words, the Austrian schilling is not a free-floating, highly volatile currency, unlike the US dollar.

The Austrian schilling is currently valued at around 20 schilling to one pound sterling or about 11 schilling to one US dollar.

Deposits to the account may be made in any currency after first having been converted into Austrian schilling. It should be noted that Austrian banks offer some of the best currency exchange rates available in the retail market.

Deposits may likewise be made by direct wire transfer (SWIFT) or, depending on the bank, by check, mailed directly to the issuing branch of the book.

The interest rate on a Sparbuch offering immediate access to all funds without prior notice is three to five per cent. However, this can be increased to between six and eight per cent by agreeing to give the bank 12 months notice before withdrawing funds. Interest is compounded annually.

All interest is paid gross with no withholding tax. Therefore, the real rate of interest on a 3.75 per cent Sparbuch account is, in fact, 7 per cent when compared to an account in another country that charges a 50 per cent withholding tax on all interest payments.

To make a withdrawal, one presents the book in person at any branch of the issuing bank in Austria, gives the *Lösungswort* (code word) and states the sum required. Identification is never required on making withdrawals.

One may also mail the book to the issuing bank by registered mail, enclosing the *Lösungswort* and giving instructions to the bank about transferring the funds in the account to anywhere in the world.

As far as addresses go, the bank does not need, or even want, the address of the owner of the account. The book itself is automatically updated upon presentation, even if you leave the account dormant for years.

In other words, no account statements are ever mailed to account owners. This means that there is no risk that anyone monitoring your mail, including your local taxman or even your spouse, will ever come across statements pertaining to an undeclared Sparbuch account.

WHAT A SPARBUCH WILL NOT DO

An Austrian Sparbuch is not available in any other currency than the German D-Mark or the Austrian schilling. However, as the schilling is pegged to the DM this offers a real-life rate of stability and safety which is equal to, if not better than, just about any other currency, including US dollars, Japanese yen or UK sterling.

It is not possible to make a withdrawal from a Sparbuch account without either physically presenting the book in an Austrian bank or mailing the book in (with wire-transfer instructions) and at the same time asking that the account be closed. Likewise, it is not possible to issue standing orders eg monthly transfers from a Sparbuch account. Another minus is an Austrian Sparbuch may only be opened by bona-fide Austrian residents. If you cannot prove, by showing a national ID-card, that you are a resident of Austria, the bank will refuse to open a Sparbuch account for you.

One way around this is, of course, to go for a "foreign" account. This, however, entails that you will have to show your passport. A photocopy will be taken and the account will then be made available to you only in your real name. In addition, the bank is required by law to inform the Austrian National Bank about the names, addresses and passport numbers of all foreign account holders. In other words, opening an account yourself, unless you are a resident of Austria, means that the bank will maintain a record of your real name and address along with a photocopy of your passport, and so will the Austrian National Bank. Need we remind you of Parkinson's Law "if something can go wrong, it will"?

We have gotten around this problem. So can you. How? Read on.

THE TOTALLY ANONYMOUS SPARBUCH

An Austrian Sparbuch is absolutely 100 per cent completely confidential. If this claim sounds like something you've heard before, consider this: you may have a Sparbuch account in any name you wish. You do not need to provide any sort of identification or references whatsoever. The account may be in the name of Donald Duck. Likewise, it is possible to maintain the account in the name of a company, whether offshore or conventional, without having to furnish any documentation, transcripts from the company registry etc. You may even keep the account in no name. A Sparbuch account may simply be labelled "Anonym" (anonymous), with the word *Überbringer* (bearer) stamped on it. In this way, there will be no other record of the name on the account since none has ever been given! With an anonymous account you may clear checks, money orders etc in any name through the account, merely by mailing them to the bank and asking that the anonymous account be credited with the full amount.

OUR BEST SOLUTION

These bank accounts are, now, the only truly anonymous accounts in the world. No ID, no mailing address, no bank references, not even a single professional reference is required to open these accounts. They can be issued in any name. No statements are mailed out, ever. No paper trail is created whatsoever. It is absolutely impossible to establish who opened the account. *No one* can identify who opened the account. No tax collector, no grumbling ex-wife, not even *the bank itself* can identify who owns the account.

Scope International Ltd, is your worldwide source for anonymous Sparbuchs. Working with an Austrian lawyer, Scope is able to provide you with a legally opened, Austrian Sparbuch account without knowing your real name or address, without seeing any sort of documentation from you whatsoever and without having to see a photocopy of your passport or any other sort of identification whatsoever.

How? There is one loophole in the Austrian banking laws concerning the right of local attorneys to open Sparbuch accounts for clients, without disclosing the identity of the beneficiary owner of the account. Recent rumblings in the Austrian press, however, lead us to believe that this loophole in the law will be closed. Owing to the peculiarities of the current laws, however, the new laws will not affect old accounts, since these will be registered as normal accounts and not accounts belonging to foreigners.

As previously stated, there are two forms of accounts:

1) An account in any name. You may clear any and all checks and money orders in this name through the account. State your fantasy name in the preferred language of your choice.
2) An anonymous account. You may clear any and all checks and money orders, regardless of name through an anonymous account. This is called *üeberbringer.*

Scope is able to provide you with either account. Please state whether you wish an account bearing a name (and, if so, in which language) or an anonymous account, good for clearing checks etc in any name.

We can provide Sparbuch accounts with an opening balance of 100 Austrian schillings (about £6 or US$10). This is money actually in the account by the time you receive your Sparbuch and is not a charge.

Scope's fee for providing you with an anonymous account is £250/$400. This is the fee for schilling-accounts.

In the event that you wish an account bearing a name, there is an additional fee of £25 (US$40), bringing the total to £275. Pay in cash, by check or with a money order.

Lösungswort (code word) will be supplied to you with the account. All anonymous accounts are opened with an easy-to-remember code word, usually a common, English-language word or name. Scope keeps no files of the code words on the Sparbuch accounts we deliver.

A sample order could look like this:

Date and place:
Dear Scope

I understand that you can provide Austrian bearer-type savings books "off the shelf".

I further understand that the total charge is £250 (schilling sparbuchs) *üeberbringer*, and that an Austrian schilling sparbuch with a name costs £275 each. I understand that each price includes the initial deposit as well as the fee of your Austrian lawyer.

I am enclosing £250/US$400 (cash, check or money order).

Please mail me the Sparbuch by return post, with my personal Lösungswort which I believe can be changed by myself at a later date if I so wish.

Thank you for your effort on my behalf.

I trust you will deal with this request in a confidential manner.

Regards,

If a fantasy name is needed, be sure to add the £25 surcharge to the above. Also add another £25 (US$40) if DHL courier delivery is required and note that DHL only delivers to street addresses, not to Post Office boxes. All fees alternatively can be charged to Visa/Access/MasterCard/Eurocard/American Express/Diners Club cards.

If you dawdle, the Austrian Sparbuch door may well close. You will then have wasted what is, as of now, a nowhere-else-in-the-world opportunity to bank in the assurance of complete, 100 per cent anonymity.

A WORD OF WARNING

The Austrian Sparbuch is an endangered species! How so? Consider this: over the past few months there has been an increasing, international awareness of the existence of anonymous Austrian Sparbuch accounts. This door may well close and it will be impossible for foreigners to make use of this very valuable banking instrument without furnishing all the information and identification required by banks in other countries. Until then, however, you have an option which is, in our belief, unique in the world today, opening a major bank account without furnishing any identification, references etc. We shall also point out that after getting an Austrian Sparbuch account you may use the account book as a reference for any other bank, worldwide, when opening new accounts. But nowhere will anyone be able to discover that it is actually you who is the owner of the Austrian Sparbuch account used as a reference! For more information on the future fate of the Austrian Sparbuchs, contact our friend Joseph Koppensteiner in Vienna, Austria. Dr Koppensteiner is a partner with accountants Price Waterhouse. He may be reached at **IPW/Price Waterhouse, Prinz Eugen Strasse 72, 1040 Wien, tel +43 1 501880, fax +43 1 501889**.

A well-known Viennese law firm for business purposes is: **Dr W Schuppich, Falkesrasse 6, 1010 Wien, tel +43 1 512 9882/4799.** One of the partners is also President of the Austrian Bar Association. The firm is well geared to all kinds of business, mergers and acquisitions, etc.

Another personally known firm of lawyers, highly recommended, is headed by Dr Mandred Steininger, **Florlanig 54, 1080 Wien, tel +43 1 408 0557, fax +43 1 408 05574**. Or you may want to contact Christopher Kerres, a US lawyer who speaks fluent German and passed the Austrian bar. He is well-connected in Vienna and can help with even some of the more delicate matters sometimes facing lawyers in this historic city where east meets west. Dr Christopher

Kerres, LL.M, Austrian lawyer & Attorney at Law, **New York, Singerstrasse 69, 1010 Wien, tel +43 1 512 2286.**

Our Austrian expert is Dr Stern. He offers consultations by mail and in person. The cost for a single letter answering one or two questions is £200. The fee for a personal consultation of up to four hours is £700. If you would like a consultation contact Scope International or read Dr Stern's *Austria and Leichtenstein Report*. See back of this book for details.

The following is an extract from the Austrian Foreign Exchange Act of 1 February 1983, concerning the definition of "resident" and "non-resident" (no 9-10, para. 1, section 1):

> RESIDENT: Any natural or legal person whose domicile or ordinary residence, seat or administration is in Austria; any person who at the time of or after the coming into force of the Federal Act has been or will be in Austria for more than three months; branches of foreign enterprises in Austria and domestic companies of foreigners, irrespective of whether they are legally independent or not, are considered residents, even if their administration is abroad.
>
> NON-RESIDENT: Any natural person not being a resident, or any legal person whose seat or administration is abroad; foreign branches of domestic enterprises, irrespective of whether they are legally independent or not, are considered non-resident if their administration is abroad.
>
> Note: In the case of the domicile or residence being abroad, a person has still the status of a resident, if the legal characteristics of a resident are given. VGH 7/4/1954, Zl 2639/53 (ÖJZ. 1954, p.374).
>
> When foreigners appear in Austrian banks trying to open Sparbuchs themselves, they may be faced with the extract just quoted. They may also have to sign the following
>
> CERTIFICATE
>
> I, ... , herewith certify having read and acknowledged the contents of the above extract of the Austrian Foreign Exchange Act including additional explanations. According to this provision I am to be considered
>
> A RESIDENT *) A NON-RESIDENT *)
>
> (delete if not applicable)
>
> and undertake now to inform the Bank für Arbeit und Wirtschaft of any future changes that would alter my status as a resident or non-resident.
>
> .... , ...
>
> Place and date Signature

AUSTRIAN BANKS

Austria mimics Switzerland when it comes to banking traditions. All known names and hundreds of unknowns seem to be here, including scores of Americans such as Chase Manhattan and the American Express Bank.

Among the local banks, those most stable and also able to deal with foreigners are:
Girocredit, Schubertring 5, A-1011 Wien, tel +43 1 711 9410, fax +43 1 713 7032.
Länderbank, Am Hof 2, 1010 Wien, tel 531 240.
Raiffeisen Zentral Bank, Am Stadtpark 9, 1030 Wien, tel +43 1 211 360.

QUESTIONS AND ANSWERS

If you order your Sparbuch from Scope International Ltd, England, you will get detailed instructions on how to use it and work with it on a day-to-day basis. Here, however, are some answers to questions frequently asked.

Can I Change the Name of my Sparbuch?
Your Sparbuch usually comes with a fictitious name or designation made up by the supplier. This name can be any personal or corporate name and may even be unpronounceable. The banks in question do not care as long as they are able to enter it into their computers. Once the name is chosen, it cannot be changed. To get a Sparbuch in another name, it will be necessary to go to Austria in person to open another account. The supplier can do this if given prior notice. Also note that some Sparbuchs come with no name at all. Instead they carry the designation "Anonym". Apart from this, they do not differ in any way from other Sparbuchs and they are not more nor less secret.

Can I change the Lösungswort?
The access codeword, called *Lösungswort* or *sperrwermehrke* in German, is individual to each account and is first chosen when the account is opened. As with the account name, your *Lösungswort* can be freely chosen and may be any combination of numbers and letters that the bank is able to enter in its database. Unlike the account name, you can change the *Lösungswort* at a later date should you wish to do so. We recommend that you choose a simple word which is easy to remember, as Austrian banks require the complete and fully correct *Lösungswort* in all Sparbuch-dealings. If you fail to remember the *Lösungswort,* or if you recall it incorrectly or only partially, the bank's initial attitude will be to deny you access to the account. Since we obviously know the *Lösungswort,* you may want to change it at a future date. Normally, no one will get access to the account with just the *Lösungswort* as the Sparbuch itself is needed too. But with proof of both, you can change the *Lösungswort* as often as you like.

How can I use my Austrian Sparbuch if I seldom go to Austria?
When dealing with your bank, it is important always to remember that since the Austrian Sparbuch is totally anonymous, their only way of ensuring that you are the correct owner will be to see both physical proof of ownership ie the Sparbuch itself as well as producing the correct and current *Lösungswort.* Without either, you could be the old owner or an unlawful owner, in which case the bank will deny any withdrawals. Deposits are easy (see next page). But to make

a transfer or a withdrawal, the bank wants to be satisfied that you are in a position to do so. Normally, they expect all such dealings to be in person at any branch in Austria, as listed in the Sparbuch. But with the use of the little-known *Kontrollnummer,* often hidden inside the book or on the back cover, you should be able to deal with your bank by telephone. Exceptions do apply, as you'll see from reading on . . .

What is the Kontrollnummer . . . ?
In addition to the *Lösungswort,* the account name and the account number, your Sparbuch also has a *Kontrollnummer*, or verifiable checksum chosen at random by the bank. This is found either on one of the inside pages or on the back cover. It is often a computerprinted five to nine digit number with no designation at all.

. . . And when do I use it?
When you are not able to visit your bank in person, the bank will ask you for this Kontrollnummer to check that you possess the Sparbuch in question. You may also be asked other questions, such as the balance on various dates. If you are making a substantial transfer or even closing the account, the bank may not oblige and can ask you to come to any of its branches with the Sparbuch. However, account holders living abroad are often permitted to strike a compromise in such cases, as the bank only needs to know the *Lösungswort* and see the actual Sparbuch itself. Thus, in most cases, you can probably arrange just to mail in the Sparbuch (recorded delivery) and mail the *Lösungswort,* preferably in a separate letter, to your contact at the bank. Make sure you have the right name and address and make sure that this person knows exactly what to do once the documents arrive. When the operation has been carried out, the Sparbuch will be returned to you in the mail or left with the bank for personal pickup. This is your choice, so be sure to state your preference.

How can I deposit further monies?
Anybody can deposit funds in your account: 1, In person at any branch in Austria or abroad; 2, In person with a correspondent bank abroad, for a small fee. A list of all associated banks worldwide can be obtained from your Austrian bank; 3, By mailing a check or a money order to your Austrian bank for deposit; 4, By wire or bank transfer. You may even send cash in the mail, asking your bank to deposit, although we advise against this for several reasons. It is just as easy to buy an anonymous money order/cashiers check at any local bank where you are not a customer.

What is the balance of my account?
Your balance is usually that of the last figure entered into your *aldo*-column in the sparbuch, plus any interest accrued since that date. The figure is in Austrian schillings, a currency pegged to the stable German mark. Interest rates are similar to the German mark and change along with it. In 1994, most Sparbuchs have raised rates to between 3 and 6 per cent, from the 3 to 4.5 per cent common a year or two ago. Since updating the account balance written in the Sparbuch is

only possible every time the Sparbuch is actually in a branch of the bank your current balance may differ from that stated. Interest is usually added yearly. For the latest balance, telephone your bank, which will usually oblige and give out the information if you provide all other details, including the *Lösungswort* and the special *Kontrollnummer* devised especially for such situations.

There is no limit on the maximum balance of your account. However, we feel that your balance in schillings should never go into seven figures. A million schillings are equivalent to very roughly £50,000 sterling. You can always open other accounts. Ownership of one does not, however, make it easier to open other anonymous Sparbuchs.

IT BEATS EVEN THE SPARBUCH!

It is called the Wertpapierbuch and part of it looks like a sparbuch. Yet the Wertpapierbuch is far more powerful, while being just as anonymous.

The Wertpapierbuch, denominated in Austrian schillings, combines all the benefits of the Sparbuch with the amazing concept of an anonymous brokerage account. The Wertpapierbuch translates as "stock and bond account", but what this actually means is two separate accounts. The first is a pay to bearer passbook, which receives interest, profits and dividends from the sale of securities. The second and more important account is the securities document. This numbered document is the instrument used to buy or sell any type of securities, stocks, currencies, even mutual funds. Truly your answer to ultimate banking privacy. ID will be required to be shown to the bank before you can deal in stocks and bonds however.

Scope International Ltd has Ueberbringer Wertpapierbuchs already established and ready to use. They can be sent by DHL courier (£25) or airmail (post free) to any address in the world. The price for the Wertpapierbuch is £400 sterling or US$600.

Chapter 18

WG HILL'S OWN OFFSHORE COMPANY MANUAL

How can offshore companies benefit you when you want to Bank in Silence? Some claim they are essential. They claim that without an offshore company or two, or three, or ten you can never have true bank secrecy. When you look closer at those making this claim, you usually discover that they are resident agents or that they are in some other way connected to the industry of setting up and managing offshore companies for others. Nevertheless, you can still sometimes come across the odd independent, unbiased adviser who will recommend an offshore company as a way for you to lower your profile. Others say: "Forget it, offshore companies are more trouble than they are worth. They are expensive and they can raise red flags. PTs have other and far better silver bullets." So what are you to believe?

The truth, as always, is never a case of either/or. Nothing is ever black or white. Do you need an offshore company? That depends on what you are doing, how you make your money, who you deal with and how you want your money to enter "your system" later on. Find a blank piece of paper right now. Grab a pen. Then write down your own thoughts and answers to each of these questions. Depending on the outcome, it may be that you should invest US$1000 in a basic offshore company. It could be money well spent – or it could be money thrown away.

Now comes a very important couple of thoughts that we want you to fully understand before you read on. In the past few years, money laundering laws, banking regulations and reporting requirements have had only one class of victims: Joe Taxpayer and his pals. The criminals have gone free. Crooks and con-men won't let a few government decrees stop them. Do you think Pablo Escobar wet his pants when Germany made disclosing into law two years ago? Do you think that drug barons were stopped dead in their tracks when Luxembourg required its banks to report suspicious transactions? And who got hurt when France announced that from now on, cash deposits would be subject to extra scrutiny? No matter how hard bungling government deadheads try to "stop crime", they won't ever succeed with paper. Top criminals are too smart to let Regulation 4566.A/-X87, Rule Y5666 or Decree Z000.11.p751 stop them. They simply can't be bothered.

The world today has more than 200 countries. Half of them are either banking havens or tax havens, sometimes both. Of the rest, a number count as financial centers. All countries have banks and all countries have banking regulations that differ. With more than 200 places to choose from, smart criminals can always find differences between national legislations. Like rainwater, their money will always find a way to disappear. No law to "combat crime" will stop the financial end of things, ever. Once you understand that, you also understand the real reasons why governments are passing these silly laws, because victims are nailed, every day. There is just one slight problem. None of these victims are drug kingpins or international swindlers. Instead, Joe Taxpayer, Johnny Lunchbucket, Jane Homemaker and all their well-meaning pals get caught in the system meant, or so we were told, to trap the Cali and Medíllin kings.

Government is dishing up an ugly pack of lies. *But here is the solution.* We are not criminals. We don't want to be criminals. We don't break any laws, nor do we want to break any laws. At the same time, we don't want to be the unwitting victims of laws that were never meant to affect us in the first place. Why should we accept getting into trouble because of some regulation that was originally put in place to nail a nasty narcotics trafficker? Only a stooge is dumb enough to let his government put him in the line of fire. Right. So what to do? Simple, follow the lead of the most succesful financial operators. Study how they beat the system. Observe the methods they utilize to hide their money and get away with it legally. Then copy them shamelessly. For years, the most skilled criminals have known how to keep their money hidden and free from the risk of government seizure. If they can, so can we. We are not criminals. We don't want to be criminals. But if someone is successful and legally banking in total silence, we have the right to copy his methods, then use them in our own financial affairs. The methods top criminals use to manage their money are legal. The banks don't even know the funds are tainted. Usually, three methods are used to obscure the origin of funds. Banks receive money through offshore companies, legal businesses onshore and through middlemen of all sorts. By studying how the criminals get around each and every new law and reporting requirement, you can learn how to do the same. Using their methods won't make you into a criminal. On the contrary, it will make sure that your banking goes on undetected. You are not a criminal, yet you can safely copy the way they succeed to make sure that you, yourself, never get unwittingly caught in the system either. Just because you use sophisticated banking techniques perfected by international crooks, con-men and swindlers, does not mean that you automatically are a crook, a con-man or a swindler. After all, criminals use cars, so do you; that does not make you into a criminal. Go ahead, duplicate some of the low profile techniques that the Mafia have been using for years to elude and confuse the authorities.

The mere fact that you are using certain low profile techniques that the Mafia developed succesfully won't make you a mobster. What it will do, however, is guarantee that you can bank in silence. And after all, this is your entitlement, almost a human right. When laws make it impossible to live your life openly and publicly, you will need to hide some of your more sensitive financial affairs underground. Honest citizens are babes in the woods when it comes to protecting themselves against government abuse. This is why we must learn from those who have for years and years successfully beaten the system and gotten away with it. Today, on American computer networks such as Internet and the Well, you can often come across anarchistic sayings from citizens fed up with the way the government is taking their privacy away. They advocate using some of the perfectly legal methods top criminals have used for years to protect their privacy. And they write, with the cursor blinking on the screen in cyberspace, that "If privacy is outlawed, only outlaws will have privacy."

USING OFFSHORE COMPANIES TO ELUDE AND CONFUSE

Offshore companies are dealt with at length in Adam Starchild's *Tax Haven Report*, available from Scope International Ltd (read summary at the back of this report).

Adam Starchild recommends offshore companies to keep your name out of the headlines or, for that matter, government computers. So do we. With a few exceptions, as we shall explain here.

Most preferred solutions are judgement proof setups. Usually, you judgement proof by making sure that whatever goes on offshore has no connection with you whatsoever. Most operators do this by merely shuffling the paperwork to make it look like you're in the dark. But using strawmen, false names and nominee shareholders will not stand up in court.

We suggest you consider getting other people, preferably PTs or kindred spirits, to help you. They are not in this game for the money. They are in it primarily because they like to tell off governments and tax gatherers. You will find some of these contacts in the classified ad section of the *Mouse Monitor,* the privacy newsletter from Scope International Ltd.

Don't start pretending your offshore company is a multi-million dollar outfit with scores of employees. If reality is merely a shelf company stashed away in some resident agent's file drawer, you can't claim otherwise. That would get you in trouble.

Don't, however, make the mistake that your company is somehow less legal because it does not have its own offices or its own staff. You can still use it and it will still stand up in court. Even though most offshore companies are mailbox companies in the most basic meaning of the word, they are allowed and accepted as separate entities by other countries and other countries' tax courts, not least because you don't make them out to be more than they are. And why shouldn't they be allowed? In most western nations, quite a number of companies are operating merely from a shelf in some lawyer's office or trading out of a drawer from an accountant's desk, without being deemed fiscally "non-existing" for that reason. To deem a company invalid just because it shares offices with a number of other companies and because it has a director who is also director of other companies, due to common sense and financial reasons, is pure undiluted nonsense.

Most revenue offices are probably going to smell a rat when a foreign company is owned by a trust. You have to show them that there is no rat. That whatever goes on offshore is 100 per cent legitimate. You can do this by one or more of the following:

A) The foreign company that you work with is not based in a tax haven. We suggest you consider buying your stuff from a French company, an Irish company, a German company or whatever. This company could well be a full scale legitimate trading operation dealing in imports/exports on a broad measure. This foreign company buys the wares from an offshore company ie located, for example, in Gibraltar. The offshore company owned by you or by your trust or by a third party sells at a big markup. Thus keeping the profit in Gibraltar. But the French company or Irish or whatever sells at little or no markup when it sells to you. It will have no tax liability at home because it does not make a profit. The offshore company pays no tax because it is located in a tax haven. You will not get any heat from the Revenue because you do not deal with any shady "letter box" companies offshore. You do not even deal with a company owned by a foreign trust. The only company you deal with is a trading company in an EU country. If checked out, this company is "the real McCoy", no scam, no fly-by-night setup. Naturally, the directors would all be willing for a fee to come and testify in UK Tax Court on their dealings with you. But this will not happen, simply because the Revenue *will not* smell a rat.

B) Try to avoid paper companies. Use real companies and real people wherever possible. No nominees will ever bail you out should you run afoul with your revenue man or enter the line of fire during an audit. Also, if checked out, they will appear to be just that, nominees. You do not want cardboard solutions. A real company with real people and real business, not just a company factory will convince any revenue agent that your business is legitimate, not just a scam to cheat the System out of its fair share of your earnings.

If you have an account in the Channel Island of Sark and transfer funds out to it, these funds will be considered your funds and classified as income. If you live in mainland UK, you are taxed on your worldwide income. This includes your money in the Sark account.

If no one knows about it, and if you do not report it, there is no tax payable. Theoretically this will be evasion. In which case, if all you want to do is simply cheat on your taxes, why go through all the trouble of forming offshore companies in the first place? The main reason for utilizing foreign companies is to do *legal tax avoidance,* not criminal tax evasion.

When dealing with nigh-perfect offshore setups that are as judgement proof and *real* as can be, the main problem is always "How do we get the money out to Mr John Doe ie yourself" or whomever? If the beneficiary lives in a high tax country, he will almost always be liable to be taxed on whatever money he receives no matter where he gets it. Even if he gets it all-cash and deposits it in a top-secret Sark account.

One of the simpler, yet more elegant ways of getting round this problem is the expense account method, as a lot of fringe benefits are not taxable income. But the best method is, let the money stay in the offshore company, disassociated from you. When you move away from the high tax country (UK) and become a tax free PT Bird, you can get the money. Since you are legally not a resident of a country where you are to file income tax returns, there is *no tax* to pay on any income. This is legal and will stand up to close inspection.

A FEW WISE WORDS ON GOVERNMENT SPONSORED BLACKMAIL

British readers will know that all mainland UK law firms could probably be blackmailed into supplying confidential information to the Inland Revenue. Some scandals have reached the papers. Far more have been hushed up. The way the Inland Revenue flexes its muscles would, in plainer words, be called blackmail. They get law firms to open up by way of threats of investigations of their own affairs. As a potential UK law firm client, you need to be aware of this. However, consider that 1) Law firms in the UK have a long tradition of being able to claim client privilege. This is *respected* by the British Inland Revenue and the courts. Only in very criminal cases has the Client Privilege been breached. Also 2) the Inland Revenue would attract bad press if it started using IRS style methods of investigations. This would deter the tax man from messing with my lawyers in all but very big cases. So unless you are a multi-millionaire high profile outspoken tax evader blatantly screwing the Inland Revenue left and right, we feel that the chances of the Inland Revenue risking to attract all sorts of press and parliamentary criticism to nail you are very slim indeed. We can safely say that honest formation lawyers will *not* throw in the towel voluntarily. And if the IR starts playing hardball, our preferred lawyers are pleased to tell them that all sensitive records are kept under lock and key in Gibraltar and may only be freed after a Gibraltar court order.

Many lawyers and corporate formation agents have an interest in setting up a long string of companies for each and every client. In reality, however, there is simply no need for "the string". It doesn't need to be that long. You can cut chunks of it out, thus making the whole exercise quite a bit cheaper. Think about this. Like others before you, you can come up with some suggestions that are all 100 per cent legitimate and probably more secure than the large chain of legal entities. And a whole lot cheaper.

One common question is whether the foreign company will want to attract heat from local revenue officials. Answer: seldom. But look at it this way, even if they do, what can the revenue officials do? Nothing. Nothing at all, since the company is not evading tax in any way whatsoever and since the whole operation from a legal point of view is perfectly sound.

Now, why should they want to do this?

First of all, to get money. It may surprise you to know that the largest single sector in Hong Kong is the re-invoicing service industry. HK limited companies buy goods, ship them off at a higher price and keep profits in no-tax Hong Kong. For their services, merely opening a bank account and putting the profits from the sale into that, which is owned by the company but which only you have signing power on, they retain ten per cent or some similar nominal figure. You get 90 per cent of whatever markup there is.

We would not suggest using these companies or any other company, be it in France, Ireland, Germany or wherever, that will work with you for petty cash. They are very likely to sell out on the first whiff of Inland Revenue asking questions.

Instead, our preferred solution is working with someone on a *quid pro quo* basis. You do something for me, I do something for you.

Here is how it may work:

Let us assume you have a friend who is setting up a publishing operation in, say, Germany. He lives abroad, but works through an offshore company. Because the German FISC is like the IRS, using their whims and arbitrary powers to close down what they do not like, this friend has structured his operations so that all companies involved are "collapsible" and so that he can start up again the day after with the same books, the same trading name and just a new address and a new company.

He does, however, have a problem with the trading name, as he does not want to be the proprietor of it. As a German citizen, this person's assets including the trading name can be seized by a tax court and become the property of the government using laws similar to the US Rico. Our suggestion to him was to set up an offshore trust to own the trading name. He says that if the Revenue gets mean, they can overlook the trust and grab the trading name by court order anyway. This guy can fight the court order and probably win in so far as the foreign trust is legally established and managed right. But then again, he may not win the appeal. And in any case, such a court procedure could drag on for five years or more. All the while keeping the business of my friend closed.

So we decided that the solution would be for him to find someone ie a live person of flesh and blood who is *not* a German citizen to manage the trading name, sign licensing contracts, etc. And to make the whole setup look Kosher, we'd need an EU citizen *not* domiciled in a tax haven. This person could be you, perhaps. In return, he'll help you obtain your own objectives.

This is just one suggestion for one particular case. There are many more. But you help him and he'll help you all the way to your bank, free of charge.

Once you are PT you'll probably find that one of the beauties of life is that you are free to do exactly (read that word twice) what you feel like doing. Go where you want to go. Pay the taxes you want to pay. Do as much work as you feel like.

Because this freedom is priceless once you have experienced it, we prefer to stay away from moneymaking deals if they involve anything to tie you down ie schedules to be met, fixed hours, having to be in one place, etc, etc.

The Perfect Thing (PT) is when you can do what you want, any time you want.

Another common question regarding company formations is:

"Can I leave the setting up of such a structure until I know how profitable the business is going to be?" Our answer: yes and no.

The company factories will try to tell you "No", mainly because they want to sell you something. They have no scruples and for their "free advisory services", well, it is all just a bunch of baloney, because what it comes down to, is that they want to push their wares. Money in the till matters more than giving you sound advice you can rely on.

Of course you can wait. But we must add, we would not wait.

A golden rule, ask almost anybody, especially the tax man, is that it is easy for authorities to look through or set aside a certain setup if the sole purpose for establishing it is to avoid tax.

This is sometimes called "piercing the corporate veil". It would be quite easy for a tax prosecutor to prove in court that you only established the new "chain of command", so to speak, when you found out that you would have to pay mucho tax. If, on the other hand, you can show that this was the original setup, always in use, in rain as well as in sunshine, you will have a strong defense. No court will rule in the IR's favor as long as you can prove that the setup was not solely established to avoid taxes. You will win your case. The corporate veil will not be lifted. IR will lose. Here is the good part. They know they will lose, and they will not even mount a case. They will let the whole matter rest and you can live happily ever after. The Inland Revenue will move on to greener pastures.

Stop and think twice before going to the company factories that advertise their craft a little too much in the international publications. You may not want to deal with them after all. Why not? Offshore Financial Advisers tell Mr Client that he can control yet conceal secret assets by means of trusts, holding companies, foundations and other expensive legal entities. The disadvantage of such arrangements, necessary for active businesses but not needed for mere asset management, is that not reporting such activities is illegal anyway. To make things worse, with offshore trusts,

A) Someone else knows your business. Those persons are not necessarily: 1) Discreet; 2) Honest; 3) Cheap to feed.

B) Your advisers "need" to be able to sign checks, to insulate you, they say, and control the funds. But all too often, the adviser: 1) Makes bad business decisions; 2) Makes mistakes; 3) Is not available when you need him; 4) Gets into difficulties unrelated to you or steals from you. You can't sue!

Ferdinand Marcos, when his personal financial records were splattered all over the newspapers, was charged with many crimes even though his advisers assured him that everything was legal. Moral of story: There is little or nothing one can do in business, politics or tax-avoidance that can't be turned into a criminal prosecution. The best protection may be to do whatever you are doing without witnesses or paperwork. Avoid giving information to friends and confidants. They could turn into enemies!

Chapter 19

CHOPPING YOUR TAX BILL

If you are like your author, you are one of those fortunate few who can call themselves Prior Taxpayers. We have left the clutches of Big Brother. We are Planet Trotters roaming the world seeking new experiences and pleasures while helping kindred spirits aspire to our level of liberty. It wasn't always like this. A long time ago, your author, too, slaved to keep useless bums alive. Every morning after spending an hour on the freeway in bumper to bumper rush hour traffic, I could look forward to another pleasant 12 hour work day, sweating to please the bureau-rats. If they weren't conning me, my business partner was. My employees were stealing me blind. On top of it all, I had to deal with customers who didn't pay, claiming "the general bad economic climate" as their reason for stiffing me. Upon returning home, if my wife was not out fooling around with other men, she was yelling at me for not spending enough Quality Time with her in front of the soap operas. Then, one day, an old school chum wrote me. He had retired at the age of 40, then moved to the Bahamas. He was living tax free, stress free, even wife free. This made me see the light. During the next year, in rapid succession, I lowered my all-too-high tax bill, got rid of my crooked business partner, fired my employees, got a divorce, then finally closed my business. I, too, was ready to live my life as it was meant to be lived.

I vowed never again to pay taxes, nor any other bills to rats who didn't deserve it.

You, too, can kick the tax-habit. Just say no.

Many individuals and companies suddenly realize at year's end that unless they can come up with some legitimate method to write off a large income, they will be subject to very high tax liability, and possibly higher taxes than they have cash to cover! To say the very least, this all too typical situation is annoying and frustrating.

Every time you pay any amount of income tax, that money is for all purposes wasted. You are giving away capital that you will never ever see again. Capital that could otherwise have been put to good use earning additional income for you.

Each dollar you pay in income taxes causes you to lose three ways: First, you lose the capital forever! Secondly, you lose the annual income and the capital that it could have produced forever! And thirdly, your family and your estate will lose the capital appreciation and production of that income. FOREVER!

The solution, for some, is finding a legitimate deductible expense that can be used to offset what would otherwise be taxable income. To qualify as an expense it must be justified, reasonable and related to the production or collection of income in the past, present or future. Or it must be associated with the management, conservation or maintenance of investments or property held for the production of income. The reasonableness of the fee paid depends on the expectation of the economic benefit to the individual or business which, in turn, is related to the size of the normal taxable income and/or the total estate or business assets, and the way those assets are invested to produce taxable income.

With friends abroad, you can have your cake and eat it. You can get a tax deduction without actually paying for it. Yes, you get to lower your tax bill, but at the same time you also manage to keep your money. How is this possible? Low profile is necessary. This cannot be emphasized too strongly. Low profile is the ability to keep your mouth shut and also operate in a way so that you don't give your own game away inadvertently.

Now look at a few ways you can use to beat the rodents.

IDEA LICENSING

Join the increasing number of smart entrepreneurs who use Idea Licensing, says GTC of Holland (offering representation in other countries, too, for "hungry hustlers" who are without even huge tax bills to decrease). It is a proven, solid, legal and confidential way to send pre-tax bills to your own company and collect the benefits tax-free on a confidential account or in a tax haven. You can bill your company for virtually any amount, subsequently to be made available to you where, how and when you want. The entire procedure is based upon solid contracts, is legal, foolproof and survives scrutiny by business partners and tax collectors. For more information, discreet, contact **GTC, P.O. Box 12442, NL – 1100 AK Amsterdam, Holland fax +31 – 20 6919709**.

Similar programs are operated by Irish companies and, we are told, by a UK firm.

THE ACCOUNTS RECEIVABLE PROGRAM

With 95 per cent of tax shelters now terminated because of new regulations, this program is still untouched and working successfully. For each dollar saved, it can be invested in your own company to earn more dollars, which can then be kept tax free. Because of compounding with no extraction for taxes, your money can be doubling every three to five years depending on the type of investment. With the Accounts Receivable Program, you are legally taking money from your left pocket, getting a tax deduction, then placing that very same money in your right pocket, tax free. Your costs are less than ten per cent, deductible too. This program has survived scrutiny by the IRS, probably the world's most buttoned up, hard to please tax gatherers. It is operated by Global Consulting Group (see below). After studying their US$30 ARP information, you can choose to either work with them for a fee, or go ahead yourself, managing your own homemade program.

THE CONSULTING SERVICE PROGRAM

How would you like the equivalent of a direct tax write-off of ten to one against current income? Contact **Global Consulting Group, PO Box 945, Suite 922, Centro Colon Bldg. 1007, San Jose, Costa Rica**. US$15 will give you information on how their program can reduce taxable income by as much as 55 per cent while you are, at the same time, making an additional profit from doing so. Many professional groups are looking for better ways to fund their pension plans without the necessity of defined contributions. This program allows the professionals to fund only their own pension fund in whatever amount they choose. Yet it is fully qualified as tax deductible. Signing a real contract for consulting services, you then send in the agreed payment. Since you have retained a legitimate consulting company contractually, your reasonable fee paid becomes a legitimate itemized deduction. There are finer points to consider, which we won't deal with here. Read the Consulting Service Program for all the details, then make sure you observe those details. If you don't, you could find yourself crossing that thin red line separating the legal from the illegal.

BE SMARTER THAN THE RODENTS!

Like all tax shelters throughout history, the three described above will sooner or later be questioned by some eager tax bureaucrat somewhere or other. We know of no tax shelter which did not, sooner or later, move into what the tax man personally defines as a ''Grey Zone''. All tax shelters are borderline, and if they are not, they will become so in the future.

If you are smarter than the rodents nipping away at your capital, you will make sure to keep moving. Move the target every two or three years, changing strategy. Every time you do so, close down your current operations completely. Cut the paper trails. Move into cash and leave no forwarding address. Then start up again all fresh and clean, always using new variations or an entirely new tax shelter.

With a good tax shelter, your legal deductions will stand up to any audit, even any test in tax court. Yet at the same time, you will have kept your money in your own pocket. For a deduction of US$1000, you will have paid the full US$1000. This gives you the deduction. A small service fee is deducted, usually five per cent to ten per cent. Tax shelter operators have to live too. A few days or a few weeks later, the US$900 to US$950 flows back to you, the client, in one or more various ways. It has passed through the system and undergone a transformation. This money is yours to keep. It is tax free. Yet you still retain your deduction and no one is any the wiser.

Chapter 20

PUTTING IT TOGETHER

Begin planning your future today. Not paying tax is only half of the picture. Even when you are tax free, PT style, your money is still not immune unless it is stashed where no one knows. When you bank in silence, outsiders will have no way of knowing how rich or poor you are. With no one knowing where your bank records are, they cannot be searched and examined. You will be banking in silence. And no one will be any the wiser. Outsiders, be they an angry alimony hungry ex-wife, stupid government bureaucrats, dishonest business partners or simply plain crooks, won't have the slightest inkling of your net worth. Sending private investigators in to dig up dirt won't work either, because you are banking in silence with no one knowing where and with no one able to get access to your credit card statements or your cancelled checks. The beautiful result, never will anyone be able to prove what you own, where you keep your assets, who you work with, where you spend your vacation, who your girlfriends are, what money you paid to what political causes, and so on. This is privacy. If you think the tax savings are what banking in silence is all about, you are wrong. Far more important than not paying to Big Brother's bloodsuckers is the fact that you, finally, will be the owner of your own life. No one can interfere *unless you let them.*

Your first step is to familiarize yourself with some of the big and perfectly honest, legitimate banks operating offshore. You will find that quite a lot are familiar names, usually wholly owned by the largest Canadian or British financial institutions. American banks are represented offshore too, but they are usually more cautious. They saw what happened to Edmund Safra, the Jewish owner of New York's National Republic Bank. Because the National Republic Bank had been spreading its tentacles abroad and opening subsidiary banks in some of the more go-getting tax havens, Gibraltar is just one of many, the IRS was upset. What Safra did, however, was totally legal. The IRS couldn't stop him. But they nevertheless harassed him all they could. In unrelated money laundering cases, the US authorities did everything they could to indict Edmund Safra personally. One suspect in the Kopp affair held bank accounts at Safra's bank. And solely because of this, the investigators used him in their attempt to catch Safra. As it turned out the suspect was exonerated and Safra and his bank received a clean bill of health. Nevertheless, US banks learned the lesson. They saw what could happen if you got too keen on expanding in places their own version of Big Brother didn't like. Which is why today you will find Dutch banks, Danish banks, British banks, Canadian banks, German banks, Swiss banks and many more, but only few US banks in the tax and banking havens of the world.

A good first step would be to get yourself an Austrian Sparbuch while they are still available.

Then, you will probably want to open one or two accounts with a "mail order" bank. These are not fly by night outfits. If you pick a bank located in the Isle of Man or in the Channel Islands, particularly Jersey or Guernsey, you will see that the "mail order" banks are subsidiaries of all the largest British banks. Some of them are happy to open accounts in any currency. Most of them will issue check books right away. Some will even give you a debit card (VISA) or a credit card (American Express). Where to start? Expatriate magazines are usually rich with ads. *Resident Abroad*, a colorful monthly from the Financial Times Magazines, carries the most. Pick up any issue and choose between at least 20, and just as many mutual funds and money market funds all vying for your business and all willing to serve you strictly by mail-order. Some will issue check books and credit cards at no extra charge in whatever currency you choose. *Resident Abroad* can be found at well stocked newsagents, especially where expatriates concentrate. Or a sample can be ordered from *Resident Abroad* (Subscriptions department), **Financial Times Magazines, Central House, 27 Park Street, Croydon CR0 1YD, England**. Another sure source is the international edition of *The Economist*, our own favorite weekly news magazine. In each issue, you should usually find at least two or three banks pitching their wares.

If you are like us, you will want to travel a bit. Go to some of the more scenic banking havens, where you can combine business with pleasure. Andorra is one. In our double-issue *Andorra/Gibraltar Report*, we tell you all you need to know about this gem of a tax haven. Including, of course, extensive how-to, hands-on information on the ins and outs of secret banking in Andorra. Some of this information is so obscure that not even the Andorran authorities know it! Opening accounts in Luxembourg and Liechtenstein, for instance, banks will ask you whether you want mail sent or not. Tell them no thanks, just like in Switzerland. You will have to show your passport but you won't have to give an address. Instead, since you don't want to receive mail, the bank's computer will contain just your name. As your address, a "care of" the bank with the bank's own address will appear on the screen and in your file. Thus, all statements sent to you will actually be sent to your bank, by the bank itself. It will be kept in your file until you call and instruct the bank to forward the mail. Whenever you call in person, you will be given your mail. As the Andorra report will show you, banks in Andorra go one better. They assign you a private, bank operated PO Box so you can not only receive the bank's own mailed statements, but mail from everybody else as well. Your friendly banker servicing you as a mail drop operator.

Not all banks are so accommodating. So before you start, you will have to establish a few places where you can receive mail, bank statements, etc in various names and company names. You will probably have established a cover that cannot be linked to you in any way. Either an offshore company with bearer shares for use in true and developed banking havens, where the bankers know their trade, or a camouflage type passport for use in the lesser developed countries where banks are not sophisticated and not used to serving foreigners.

Every day in the press, you can read stories about how evil you are if you decide to bank in another country than the one you're born in. Forget this goobledygook. Follow your own good common sense and stay true to your instincts. Don't buy the government propaganda and the newspapers' lies. Who is the bad guy? Everyone who won't let you live a free, peaceful life where you can do what you want as long as you don't hurt anybody else. Government employees are the most dishonest crooks of all. The case of DEA agent Darnell Garcia readily illustrates this. Just one case out of many, where federal agents have been caught with their hand in the till, stealing your money. During the 1980s, Garcia and his colleagues looted heroin, cocaine and millions of dollars. At one point, he traveled to Switzerland and deposited US$2 million in personal bank accounts. Garcia then moved the money to the Luxembourg branch of the Swiss Bank Corporation. He continued to maintain an account at Union Bank in Switzerland. Each account stuffed with at least a million dollars.

HOW THE RICH ARE DROPPING OUT OF HIGH-TAX BANKING

The assets held by banks from a string of islands in the Caribbean rival those of the entire US banking system. Of the 12 EU members, tiny Luxembourg holds the fattest deposits in its banks. Guernsey, Jersey, Gibraltar and the Isle of Man have together attracted more foreign deposits than all mainland UK banks when counted as one. These migrating billions are one sign that when the going gets tough money simply leaves. Where does the smart money go? Everywhere, as long it can be left in peace and as long as local politicians don't try to dream up ways of getting their hands on it. Follow this money and you will have found your own pathway to financial and personal freedom. All over the world, tax havens and banking havens are becoming the new money superpowers. The wise are moving away from high tax, high regulatory red tape banking and turning to little known islands where it is possible to bank in silence. If you haven't already enjoyed and experienced some of the thrills, advantages, and benefits of secrecy and confidentiality in an international setting, now is the time to take your first step. Privacy will protect, preserve and expand your capital in the world of international finance.

All over the world, millionaires and billionaires long ago learned the secrets of maintaining as well as enhancing their vast estates. How? Simply by not seeing them eroded by unnecessary taxation. Their methods are legal (and sometimes not so legal). Fortunes have been built and then preserved by using the secrets of untangling the taxation web. Few people not in the top-wealth level have been privy to these secrets. This is changing now. The powerful monopoly on financial planning still exists, but if you are fed up with having to bear an incredible burden and not seeing any relief in sight, you too, can join. Your first step is to understand that tax offices the world over are in business for one purpose and one purpose only, to grab what money they can. Absolutely positively none of Big Brother's laws, regulations, revenue rulings or tax court opinions is written to describe, list or validate tax loopholes. If you have been a sucker, intensely studying tax laws trying to find a loophole that would lower your burden, you now know that you have been taken. These laws state how to collect taxes. They are not written to tell you what you can do, only to tell you what you cannot do.

The pathway to greater financial freedom is hidden in pages written not by tax collectors but by free men who have been there before you, tried out everything step by step by themselves, then learned the hard way how to carve out some peace and quiet internationally. Very few are reluctant to share their secrets. They fear that if too many know about the hidden opportunities they will dry up. Too many will get on the boat, politicians with nothing else to do will write a new regulation or the door will simply close, all by itself.

The fortunate few are sharing valuable information and slowly building up a counter-revolutionary underground. We are fed up with everybody lying and claiming, against better knowledge, that we are the bad guys. From the bank teller, green with envy to the bureaucrat who is merely greedy, we get blamed for all the ills of this world because we have a bit of money. Keep your head down, friend. People are shooting at us. If they are not calling us tax evaders, then they claim we are money launderers. Sometimes they use even worse descriptions. The smear tactics never seem to end but fortunately they are groundless. Bald and chubby old rich guys with buck teeth always get the short end of the stick. We get called all sorts of names and everybody thinks we are some strange sort of financial criminals. Now we are fighting back. All we want is the right to carry on our own financial affairs in private, like free men amongst ourselves. The revolt of the rich has started, as futurist Alvin Toffler in 1993 rightly predicted it would. PTs can join. It's the most democratic club in the world because you don't have to do anything. You don't have to subscribe or pay any dues, and it is strictly low profile. There are no membership cards or records. Our code word is "Stone Pillow". It gets its name from the martyrs of the underground. Those who rested their heads on pillows of stone, in or out of prison. The revolutionaries of today are in much the same nearly hopeless position as the anti-Communists found themselves in under Stalin, or freethinkers found themselves in while living in the Third Reich under the Nazis. There are things they can do. A PT will always be able to blend in. At the same time, he can fight back by refusing to let governments take his "A+A", and by messing up their files with an effective campaign of "D&M". Look what happened to Stalin and Hitler. The same thing will happen, hopefully, to our own totalitarian-minded dictatorship of high handed bureaucrats. You cannot fight a knife with an atom bomb. You cannot swat mosquitoes with an axe.

I think that says it all.

CONSULTANCY NEWS

CONSULTANCY SERVICE IMPROVED AND EXPLAINED

Right from the beginning of (Hill) time there has been a full back-up consultancy service for all readers of our Special Reports.

Initially, all consultancies were run by Dr Bill Hill from his address in Hamilton, Bermuda. When Hill retired we were left with an amazing flow of requests.

Fortunately Bill left behind his team of 'little Hills' and we have managed to carry on the good work he began.

Scope, as you know, are a publishing house and found that, due to the increasing numbers of the PT circle, we were spending more and more time being PAs to our consultants than publishers of books!

THE RESULT:

All of the consultants that we previously passed information on to are still active, but have been brought under one roof. Anyone who wishes to take up their services should now write to: Interlink SA, BCM Global, 27 Old Gloucester Street, London WC1N 3XX.

Interlink SA are extremely well acquainted with all the Special Report Consultants, and will deal with your consultancy with speed and efficiency.

- **ROBERT STERLING** leads an international group of currency and banking specialists and has great experience in legal world currency movement, company formations, tax efficient structure and banking introductions.

- **ADAM STARCHILD** in addition to being the author of over a dozen books, four of which are on tax havens, has written hundreds of magazine articles for journals around the world, including the *New York Times, The San Francisco Examiner* and *Tax Planning International.* He is also one of Scope's major writers and consultants. He has been a PT consultant for over 20 years. His intelligence and knowledge of the PT philosophy is extensive. He is an expert on all matters connected with the US.

- **PETER THOMPSON** has been putting into effect PT solutions worldwide for himself and his many thousands of clients for some eighteen years. He has helped major banks, lawyers, accountants, top celebrities and a number of well known businessmen.

- **MILES CAVENDISH** is a US immigration expert. He specializes in overstayers and deportees and is a genius in interpreting the US immigration acts, and making them work for you.

- **DUNCAN MACDONALD** immigration specialist for France, Spain and Portugal.

- **MALCOLM CONSULTANTS** New Zealand and Australian immigration experts.

- **SANDRO DE ROSA** specialists for Campione and handles Italian banking and immigration affairs.

- **DR STANLEY** Brazilian immigration and passport consultant.

CONSULTANCY REQUEST FORM

Name: ....

Address: ....

....

....

....

Telephone: ....

Fax: ....

Post to: **Interlink SA**, BCM Global, 27 Old Gloucester Street, London, WC1N 3XX

I would like a written/phone/fax consultancy with ....
and I enclose £250/US $375

I would like a personal consultation with
....
and I enclose £700/US $1050

I have enclosed details of my history, my present situation and my goals.

I have also enclosed the questions that I wish you to answer.

NB: NO QUESTIONS WILL BE ANSWERED WITHOUT A FEE

Interlink SA will consider your requirements and send your letter to the ideal consultant or discuss the alternatives with you first.

OTHER REPORTS PUBLISHED by SCOPE INTERNATIONAL LTD

PT 1 – THE PERPETUAL TRAVELLER
A COHERENT PLAN FOR A STRESS-FREE, HEALTHY AND PROSPEROUS LIFE WITHOUT GOVERNMENT INTERFERENCE, TAXES OR COERCION
5th Edition
by Dr WG Hill

PT stands for Prepared Thoroughly, Perpetual Tourist, Prior Taxpayer and much, much more.
People of intelligence and wealth owe it to themselves and their descendants to have five 'flags'. No one with common sense should give all their assets or allegiance to just one flag. Why? Because no country nor any government has ever survived more than a few generations without totally annihilating itself or its own middle and upper classes. Even in that 'last bastion of capitalism', the US, people of property were thrice forced to flee the country. In 1775, one third (the entire middle and ruling class), was forced to move to Canada. These were the Tories who supported England in the Revolution. In 1865, it happened again. All large land owners (who supported the Confederacy in the Civil War) were forced to migrate to Mexico, Europe or South America. In the post 1917 period, prohibition, confiscatory taxes, compulsory military service, and suffocating government regulations once again caused wealthy Americans (and Europeans) to seek new flags. **Five million of the wealthiest and most productive Americans now live abroad**. Eighty-five percent of all liquid private wealth is already anonymously registered 'offshore'. CAN **YOU** AFFORD TO HAVE ONLY ONE FLAG? NOT IF YOUR NET WORTH IS OVER US $ 250,000.

THE FIVE FLAGS OF THE PT

Flag 1. BUSINESS BASE. These are the places where you make your money. They must be different from the place where you 'legally reside', your personal fiscal domicile. Your business base should be in a place that gives a tax holiday to your business, freedom from over-regulation, and good access to contacts, labor markets or materials needed for conducting your business. London, Tokyo, and New York are the Big Apples for Finance and Insurance. Zurich, Hong Kong, Singapore, Frankfurt and Milan are among the second-rank contenders.

Flag 2. PASSPORT AND CITIZENSHIP. These should be from a country unconcerned about its offshore citizens or what they do outside its borders. There must be no tax or military requirement for non-residents. PASSPORTS MUST BE AVAILABLE TO FOREIGNERS.

Flag 3. DOMICILE. This should be a tax haven with good communications. A place where wealthy, productive people can be creative, live, relax, prosper and enjoy themselves, preferably with bank secrecy and no threat of war or revolution. Monaco, Campione, The Channel Islands, Andorra, Bermuda, Thailand and Gibraltar are all recommended.

Flag 4. ASSET REPOSITORY. This should be a place from which assets, securities and business affairs can be managed by proxy. Requirements are: the availability of highly competent financial managers, confidential banking, no taxes on non-residents, or non-citizens. One of the best places in which to plant your fourth flag would be Liechtenstein. Other possibilities would be Austria, Luxembourg, Switzerland, New York or London.

Flag 5. PLAYGROUNDS. These are places where you would actually physically spend your time. Normally, because of legal restrictions on how long one may stay without being inducted as a taxpayer, it is necessary to have from two to four playgrounds. One might try to avoid spending more than 90 days per year in any one of them. We look for quality of life. **For 'no nukes' and good fishing:** New Zealand. **For the most interesting sex life imaginable:** Thailand, Costa Rica or the Philippines. **Superb climate:** California. **Best food:** French Riviera or Hong Kong. **Stimulating cities:** Paris, London, San Francisco. **To buy the best things at the cheapest prices:** Singapore, Hong Kong (or Denmark, for cars).

PT fully explains all Five Flags. It is a complete guide to getting the most out of life that this Earth can offer. Each individual should have at least two, but ideally three toeholds in each 'flag'. For example:

1. A BUSINESS OR SOURCE OF INCOME IN New York, London and Singapore.
2. A PASSPORT FROM Canada, Brazil, Italy and Australia.
3. A LEGAL OR FISCAL ADDRESS IN Monaco, Campione or the Channel Islands.
4. A BANK ACCOUNT OR OTHER ASSETS REGISTERED ANONYMOUSLY IN Liechtenstein trusts or foundations.
5. FRIENDS AND FUN IN Paris, Bangkok, Manila, Buenos Aires, Sydney and San Francisco.

ISBN 0 906619 24 6.

How to do it? . . . Read *PT – The Perpetual Traveller,* available from Scope International Ltd, Forestside House, Forestside, Rowlands Castle, Hampshire PO9 6EE, UK. Price – £60 UK Sterling (or equivalent) by credit card, cash, check or banker's draft. Price includes postage and packing, and please allow 6-8 weeks for surface delivery outside UK. For quicker air mail add £15 or equivalent (allow 3-4 weeks for delivery). Ordering details and order form are supplied on the last two pages of this Report.

REMEMBER: Consultations with specialists are available to all purchasers and our no nonsense money back guarantee applies to all our publications.

PT 2

THE PRACTICE: FREEDOM AND PRIVACY TACTICS FOR THE NINETIES – AND BEYOND

2nd Edition

by Dr WG Hill

Now is the time to take proper precautions, says WG Hill, father of PT and the world's leading expert on personal tax havens, in this startling book. Contrary to the popular image projected by mainstream media and most governments, your taxes are shooting up and your personal freedom is being taken away, bit by bit. Anyone with a visible pocket will become a victim. The most dangerous place on earth is wherever *you* are. But in this hands-on guide to low profile and privacy, PT-style, WG Hill shows you how to regain your lost freedom. In more than 200 fact-filled pages, he teaches you the little-known tactics and techniques of living tax free. For the first time ever in print, he gives away all his privacy secrets and shares with you unique insights on how to escape what he terms "the scam called government". This explosive volume deals with matters that no other books ever dared in a practical, hands-on manner. You will learn all the world's unknown ins and outs of getting, and keeping, a life free from problems, frustrations, harrassment, extortion, lawsuits and the implications and ramifications of all of these – the works.

DO YOU HAVE THE ESSENTIAL KNOWLEDGE FOR A FREE LIFE?
Answer these simple questions to determine if you have the information and tools necessary for a rich life in complete freedom:

* Do you know the world's six best ways to transfer cash across borders? Do you know how to triple your interest earnings and gain when currencies change?
* Do you have a collection of untraceable credit cards? Do you have foreign credit cards in a selection of names other than your own?
* Do you know the how-to of no-name bank accounts, where ID is not needed?
* Can you name the ten best low profile mail tips? Do you have a *dead drop*?
* Do you own and operate at least one PT—PC in a foreign jurisdiction?
* Will you be able to keep your money safe despite the coming world tax-squad, the new OECD treaties and the international laws already in place? Do you know all the dangers of the nineties and beyond? Are you willing to run the risk of asset stripping and long jail sentences for a "crime" you did not commit. A so-called crime invented by money-grabbing world governments?

If you answered "no" to one or more of these questions, please do not waste any time in getting *PT 2,* the all-new tome for tax exiles and perpetual travelers. In five lengthy parts, WG Hill thoroughly covers ALL privacy and low profile questions. Even those you never dared ask. From such simple things as securing your cars or using all the unknown loopholes of air travel, Hill firmly moves on to invisible ink nineties style, crossing borders *sans* passports and what he calls the Ten Privacy Tenets. This book gives you the inside facts of essential low profile gadgets and some privacy paraphernalia that would probably be illegal if your government knew that they existed!

Contents also include... True, tried and tested: WG Hill's own telephone tactics, now with a PT shortlist for phone secrecy... All about mobile phones, Super Phones, add-on gadgets for your phones... How best to transmit faxes... The art of compartmentalizing your life... Never-before-told maildrop secrets... Secure communications... Also: The secret trust, onshore or offshore? And so much more. **Stop Press.** This volume now comes complete with a bonus – WG Hill's complete guide to banking worldwide, including some secret, super-safe havens for smart money only. Plus a complete course in bearer shares and bonds.

In his introduction, Dr WG Hill writes: *This book is dedicated to showing people of intelligence how to stay FREE in every sense of the word. While you may consider yourself a "free man" (or woman), chances are that you are not. The bad news is that even if you are currently living a fairly normal and happy life, events may conspire to turn against you and wind up stealing your money, your freedom – and ultimately, your life. Today, you are a sitting duck – unless you take precautions now. The good news, on the other hand, is that there are plenty of things that you may do yourself to thwart whatever dangers are likely to pop up – in advance, and with just a modicum of effort and expense.* Are you ready for true, undiluted, unrestrained freedom in all personal and financial matters?

Do you believe that "an ounce of preparation is worth about a ton of cure"? If so *PT 2 The Practice* is for you. If you are not content just "letting things happen" then it makes perfect sense to make sure that they don't – or, if they still do, that this will not be to your extreme disadvantage.

ISBN 0 906619 40-8.

PT 2 is available from Scope International Ltd., Forestside House, Forestside, Rowlands Castle, Hampshire PO9 6EE, UK. Price – £60 UK Sterling (or equivalent) by credit card, cash, check or banker's draft. Price includes postage and packing, and please allow 6-8 weeks for surface delivery outside UK. For quicker air mail service add £15 or equivalent (allow 3-4 weeks for delivery). Ordering details and order form are supplied on the last two pages of this Report.

Right now, in his brand new first edition of the PT sequel, WG Hill gives you the low down, no-nonsense, straight facts about how to set up those seemingly elusive safeguards that may shield you in times of trouble. If you put the information in this book to practical use you will find that you, too, can keep your money, your freedom and your life. And forever be home free, PT.

REMEMBER: Personal consultations are available to all purchasers and our no nonsense money back guarantee applies to all our publications.

THE PASSPORT REPORT
HOW TO LEGALLY OBTAIN A SECOND FOREIGN PASSPORT
9th Edition
by Dr WG Hill

Why entrust your life and your freedom to any one government? Politicians regard you as an expendable national resource, but *you* do not 'belong' to any one country if you hold several passports and nationalities.

A second passport ensures mobility. Millions of individuals would be alive today if they'd had second passports before the holocaust in Germany, and repression in Argentina, Cambodia, and many other countries.

Many countries now 'sell' passports. The wording of their laws describe entrepreneurs, financial benefactors, treaty traders, and special investors in government loan paper as being welcomed new citizens. But the bottom line is the same: put up from $10,000 to $100,000 and you can obtain an almost instant passport. Other countries offer instant citizenship if your ancestors were nationals, or if you are of a certain race or religion. Thailand if you are Buddhist, Israel if you are Jewish, Lebanon if you are a displaced Moslem. Almost anyone can qualify for a free passport, and anyone with about $15,000 can have a choice of several more. *The Passport Report* closely examines the official and unofficial channels in more than 70 countries.

Citizenship can now also be thought of as a business proposition. But what countries offer more advantages? What are the net costs? Taxes, investment opportunities, travel restrictions, financial privacy, social values and retirement are only a few valid considerations closely examined in this Special Report.

A Second Passport could save your life, your money and your freedom. The key to this option is your new passport. Specifically, your 'second' passport, one which you can obtain from another country. This valuable document can open opportunities you never thought possible and provide 'back doors' that could literally save your life. The reason governments don't make it easy or publicize such options is that they are concerned with controlling and taxing their own citizens, and could regard popularization of second passport procural as a threat to 'national security'.

Most countries have well established, but little-known, procedures for issuing passports under circumstances which most observers would regard as loopholes. It is knowledge of these *exceptions* which allows intrepid individuals to obtain multiple foreign passports, and thus choose the countries most suitable for their purposes.

Put another way, *it is perfectly legal* to obtain several foreign passports so long as one knows the special rules for their issuance. It is of course legal and possible for citizens of most countries to obtain one or more passports without giving up their present citizenship, even though the widespread belief is that certain countries do not permit dual nationality. Yet approximately ten per cent of the populations of countries like South Africa and the United States of America legally hold dual nationality. How dual nationality can be obtained legally is fully explained. In many situations there is no residence requirement, and in a few places there is *never* even any need to visit.

The Passport Report is unquestionably the most detailed and comprehensive guide on this subject. Dozens of contact names and addresses of reliable passport providers and lawyers are given throughout the book.

Here is a brief overview of the contents of *The Passport Report:*

* The first step: psychological preparation.
* Those who advertise and claim to provide second passports.
* How to determine which passport suits you best.
* Over 70 countries examined in detail.
* Eliminating taxes with your second passport.
* Indirect routes ('back doors').
* Documents usable in lieu of passports.
* Should you hire a lawyer or agency?
* Instant passports and how to get them.
* Non-citizen passports; Diplomatic and service passports; Refugee passports; Provisional passports; Honorary passports.
* Dual nationality: problems and benefits.
* Actual case histories detailing exactly how individuals went about securing second passports. Most informative!

This report will open your eyes to many ideas and options you've never thought of before. More significantly, it will allow you to realistically appraise the risks of not having a second passport and assets properly placed to enable you to escape, survive and prosper. War, revolutions, political changes, personal economic reverses are all possible, if not inevitable at some time or another. Are you prepared?

The Passport Report provides referrals to reliable lawyers, passport providers and specialists for assistance, and consultancies are available to all purchasers. You will find *The Passport Report* to be an invaluable guide.

With over 375 pages packed with unique and vital information, *The Passport Report* is the most detailed and useful book of its kind. Remember our extra special guarantee applies if it does not deliver more usable and accurate information than any other report on the same subject, at any price.

The Passport Report is available from Scope International Ltd. Price £60.00. See last two pages in this report for ordering details.

ISBN 0 906619 19 X

Guarantee. If you can find a better report on the subject, we will not only refund your money but pay for the better report as well.

THINK LIKE A TYCOON
HOW TO MAKE A MILLION OR MORE IN THREE YEARS OR LESS!
THE TIMELESS CLASSIC BEST SELLER
5th Edition
by Dr WG Hill

Do you sincerely want to be rich without knocking yourself out? Do you want respect? Do you need love?

Learn the incredible secret that will bring you the *happiness only money can buy.*

You CAN become a millionaire in three years or less while, at the same time, having three times more fun out of life. Of course you are sceptical. So read on.

My name is WG Hill. I did not make my millions (like some authors) by writing books about things I have not done myself personally. Starting from scratch, without money, special skills, contacts or luck I founded eight totally unrelated part-time FUN businesses. I saw **each** of them earn me over a million Pounds **each** in three years or less.

While I was making all this money, I managed to go to an average of five parties a week, plus two or three concerts, plays or movies. **SEX!** My love life didn't suffer either – as I had more "companionship" in a year than most men have in a lifetime. What was the sex-appeal secret of a grumpy, overweight, middle-aged bald guy with crooked teeth and thick glasses? **I was doing things that appeared exciting and glamorous to women. I *was* the action and they *came* to me.** There is no aphrodisiac that comes anywhere close to the appeal of **MONEY** and **POWER!**

When thousands of people depend upon you economically, some will fawn and dote upon your every word. Some try to gain your good will with gifts, sexual favors, bribes and offers you can't refuse. *When you can refuse, you know that you have arrived.* When you can go to the best restaurants in town with your friends and order anything you fancy without considering the price, when you can travel the world free as a bird, you know that you have ARRIVED! If you can *live anywhere* in the world, have any partners and friends you want, tell off or ignore government bureaucracy, union officials, politicians and former bosses, then you know that you have found FREEDOM!

With money, everything else will fall into place. *Try it!*

Would you trade your present life for what I have just described? Then read on. Years ago I was broke, physically in bad shape and seriously in debt. Then I found concealed in a window box a dusty tattered old book. It had been hidden in the summer cottage of my close friend's father. He was a very rich and powerful man. Later on I discovered that he owed his good fortune to his own discovery of this book many years earlier. Reading the timeless volume I discovered an amazing formula that every single super-rich person seems to have used to gain wealth. It was so incredibly easy to understand that I started to apply it within twenty four hours. In six months I was a millionaire. I never had to work again.

In Chapter One I learned how to avoid mistakes that keep 94 per cent of the population just plodding along in a miserable rut – dissatisfied with everything. In Chapter Two I discovered how to "Think Like a Tycoon" – how to set and achieve goals. Chapter Three taught me how to *achieve these goals quickly* – not by moving up some corporate ladder for 30 years. I saw how to make things happen *fast* plus how to strike it very big in two or three years (at the most). Chapter Four taught me how to use credit and borrow unlimited funds (usually interest free) from bankers and investors. Another important chapter told me why all the "investments" I thought of as sound are really only for suckers.

Although the book I read was written two hundred years earlier, it was like Aladdin's Magic Lamp for me and changed my life dramatically. After two hours of reading I never earned less than a million a year for the next 30 years. Other millionaires went up and down like a yo-yo, but I just kept having more and more fun by getting richer and richer.

Now after many adventures, at the age of 49 I have retired (in great comfort I might add) to write my memoirs. Before doing so I wanted to pass on to other ambitious lads the age-old secrets that made me a millionaire at the age of 24.

I took the original timeless secrets of wealth, transformed them into modern English and added my own experiences and a bit of humor. Then I tested out the formula on my best friend, a poverty stricken but talented jazz musician. Let's call my buddy "Warren Trumpet". For years my friend had been insisting that he sincerely wanted to be very rich. I gave him the manuscript of my book. In six months he was a millionaire. In two years more he had gross annual earnings of over FOUR MILLION DOLLARS. As a jazz musician, even with a hit record, *The Girl From Ipanema,* he had never earned more than twenty thousand a year. Warren never had much of an IQ. A highschool dropout, he used to read and write like a ten year old. But that didn't stop him from using my unpublished manuscript to become one of the richest men in the world.

If he can do it, you can do it.

Truth is, I'd like to give away these secrets. If everyone used them, the world would be a richer, more productive and happy place. But I learned from the SPCA (Society for Prevention of Cruelty to Animals) that if you give away a puppy dog, that dog is more likely to be mistreated and kicked around than if you *SELL* that same dog for $100.

I want to give you respect, value and seriously apply this incredible, exciting formula. *I will not give it to you for free.* On the back page is the order form you must complete and send to Scope International now, if you want to get a copy of my sumptuously bound, gold blocked, limited edition of ***Think Like A Tycoon. How to Make a Million or More in Three Years or Less.*** (Personal registered copy, not for resale).

ISBN 0 906619 30 0

THE ALBANIA REPORT
THE MOST UNLIKELY PT-PARADISE IN THE WORLD?
1st Edition
by Dr WG Hill

It almost sounds like a fairy tale land right out of your favorite childhood storybook. A country of tall mountains and lush valleys, where free men live only by the laws they have made for themselves, where there are no taxes, no oppressive rulers, no government regulations but instead, plenty of free land for everyone. Yes, free land!

This country exists. Until just a couple of years ago, Albania was the joke of the Balkans. Today, it is without doubt the one East bloc nation with the best prospects for the future.

This latest country report from Dr WG Hill, the world's leading authority on tax havens, is based on several recent visits to Albania. He and fellow PTs are enthusiastic in their praise of this country. Now, for the first time in print, they will show you too, how you can get a foothold in what is surely a free and democratic state.

Albania is unique in being the only real European country with a tax haven status. Sure, some small states palm themselves off as tax havens. But all suffer from too many people on far too little land. The largest of them, Andorra, is so tiny that it does not even appear on most maps of Europe!

In Albania, on the other hand, the problem is the exact opposite. Too few inhabitants have far too much land and they simply don't know what to do with it. As a result, they are giving it away for free!

WG Hill shows you how to qualify for that free land giveaway. He also writes that tax freedom is not the only thing Albania has going for it. A wealth of other attractions should draw you to its beaches, its mountains and its green valleys. Is Albania poor? Very much so. Is it a place to avoid? Not on your life.

Currently, Albania is the only European country where your own private patch of beach frontage can be had at a realistic price. Where else in southern Europe, from the Atlantic shores of Portugal all on through to the isles of Greece, can you still afford to purchase a stretch of coast? Where, in Europe, are private beaches inexpensive to purchase? Nowhere, except for Albania.

Here, beachfront property is still available. Real estate developers can purchase for a few thousand dollars. The temperature is high and the sunsets are spectacular. If you are like us, just sit on your own private mile of beach and watch the country develop. If you are more adventurous, go ahead and build on it right away. No one is stopping you and building is cheap. Labor cannot be found cheaper anywhere in Europe. Even Bulgarian workers demand salaries higher than those in Albania!

This report is current right now. It presents some sensitive and hard to find information that very few other sources in the world can show you. All information is written by WG Hill and people who have tried and done everything themselves. It is written in such a way that you can do it all yourself, without needing expensive lawyers or consultants or other go-betweens. You will be the one in charge, not the lawyers nor the tax man, and you will harvest the fruit of your labors. Because in Albania, your profits are TAX FREE. The country is one huge tax haven!

When you enter, there are no currency restrictions whatsoever. You can bring in whatever currency you want, and in whatever form and amount. Same with export. Take out what you want. This applies to all nationalities, Albanian or not.

The odd foreigner who has so far ventured into Albania was surprised to find a beautiful almost tropical paradise. This is not a bleak, Balkan outpost. It is an exciting tropical-looking oasis with palm trees, cactus all over, majestic mountains and miles upon miles of sandy beaches. Albania is stunning. The girls are nice too, with a country-girl kind of feel to them even in Tirana.

Today, you can get in on the ground floor. For those who qualify, land is free. But if you want more, just bring a few hundred dollars. One thousand dollars will get you an ocean view.

In *The Albania Report,* WG Hill shows you how to invest in the country. He starts by showing you how to double your capital at no risk, simply by entering the country by car. He then proceeds by showing you how to buy land and, just as important, *where* to buy land. Free land? WG Hill explains the scheme and how it works, complete with addresses and how-to information. But real estate is not the only way to make money in Albania. Use WG Hill's secrets in a separate chapter full of special wealth builders' tips, then retire with your second million or buy hunting rights. A special chapter deals with joining the last of Albania's blue-blooded nobility. Another is entitled "A Loophole just Begging to be Exploited" – here, of course, we cannot reveal the contents. What we CAN reveal, however, is that this loophole is a proven moneymaker for a foreigner who wants to live part time or full time in Albania. US $20,000 monthly for two hours of work per day is the minimum you will make. But don't spend it all in one place – set aside £20 for rent. That is how much your seafront apartment will cost you: per month! How to live like a king for less than $100 monthly? This report is full of that information too. Retirees of all ages have gone to Eastern Europe before and live full and interesting lives for the price of a ham sandwich. Now, in Albania, the door is open. WG Hill shows the way in and all his best secrets. No other book, exists detailing all these opportunities. We urge you to reserve your personal copy today. Plus: Important warnings and scam alerts are included as well, along with addresses and an abundance of other information. And yes, some beachfront property is still available. So snap it up before it is gone! Order today using the priority order form at the back of this report.

ISBN 0 906619 45 9

THE CAMPIONE REPORT
SWITZERLAND'S SECRET SEMI-TROPICAL TAX HAVEN
4th Edition
by Dr WG Hill

WG Hill, the world's leading expert on personal tax havens predicts that Campione, a strange accident of history, anomaly of geography and climatic freak, will be one of the most fashionable tax havens of the next decade.

This report shows anyone how to become a legal resident of this soon-to-be discovered enclave of the super-rich. *Campione is a unique semi-autonomous community located entirely within Switzerland.* But as a separate country, it is **not subject to any Swiss laws, taxes or tax treaties**. Strange as it may seem, becoming a resident of Campione gives one all the advantages of being Swiss, but none of the disadvantages. No compulsory lifetime military camps, no heavy Swiss income taxes, none of the disadvantages of being (as Switzerland is) *outside* the European Union.

Campione is a part of the EU with all the benefits of passport free, visa free travel. Its citizens have the right to travel, work, engage in commerce or perform services anywhere in the EU. Best of all, Campione has "in practice" no income taxes. This Special Report shows you how to achieve these tax benefits even without acquiring residency.

Campione also is one of the few places in the EU where there is no VAT (value added tax), which seriously reduces the price of goods and services.

The Campione Report tells all the secrets, but here are some more highlights:

Campione enjoys a freak Mediterranean climate found only in the small Italian Swiss Province of Ticino, where Campione is located. Because it is on lovely Lake Lugano and considerably lower in altitude than the rest of mountainous Switzerland, its white sand beach supports a small grove of tropical palm trees. Your 'sea-view' villa in Campione will be gently caressed by balmy yet non-humid tropical breezes. However, although Campione is in a 'Banana Belt', nearby ski slopes are clearly visible. Half an hour on the local funicular railway takes you up to the powder runs!

The cost of living is less than half that of Monte Carlo, Paris, London or New York. There is no pollution, industry or crime. The mountain and lake scenery is breathtaking. The sub-Alpine climate and year-round temperature is second to none. A vibrant social and cultural life is a few minutes away in Lugano or Locarno by regular ferry boat. Take the superhighway due south from Campione and in forty-five minutes you can hear the world's best grand opera at La Scala or visit the fabulous shops of downtown Milan. There are more bankers and stockbrokers locally in Lugano and Chiasso than you can count. The area is second only to Zurich in the proliferation of financial services. All Tokyo, London and Wall Street publications are available at many stands on the day of publication. Locally you can eat in several hundred ethnic gourmet restaurants and see first run English language films in a movie palace the likes of which no longer exist in most big cities. Most of the action is in Lugano, ten minutes across the lake by 'vaporetto' bus-boat, or over the one mile long causeway by car.

Shopping, dining, night clubbing, golf, horses, tennis clubs, spectator sports, every pleasure known to man is available. Modern hospitals and internationally known clinics attract the wealthiest people of the world to the area for a variety of cures and treatments. As to morality and personal eccentricity, local Italian Swiss are easy-going and more tolerant than their German Swiss brothers fifty miles to the north.

For an inexpensive, stress-free, tax-free life, Dr Hill suggests, "Move to Campione this year. Buy property soon, before it is over-publicized and discovered." *You could probably make twenty times on your money over the next decade in this semi-autonomous town that practically pays you to live there.* Only a short drive from Italy, France, Austria, Liechtenstein and Germany, Campione is still a sleepy peaceful and unspoiled tax haven. But it appears to be heading rapidly towards becoming another Monaco. The ground floor is now. The present population of 3000 is just 10 per cent of Monaco's. Monte Carlo has 35,000 people on a similar square mile of waterfront. Campione in 1993 is like Monte Carlo in 1949, before it became 'in' and developed into a mini-Manhattan.

This Special Report gives the who, what, where, when and why. Hill feels that Campione is a great place to escape to, while it is still relatively uncongested. In five or ten years as it becomes overcrowded, it will be the place you can escape from. But your little villa would hopefully be a million dollar hotel or apartment site by then. In the meantime, you have a conveniently located European home base, you can pick up an EU passport and you can enjoy life in Campione, one of the most unusual spots on Earth.

THE MONACO REPORT

HOW TO BECOME A LEGAL RESIDENT OF TAX-FREE MONTE CARLO, MONACO

5th Edition

by Dr WG Hill

There are many places where you could live and be free of income taxes, inheritance and estate taxes and real estate taxes. But most are isolated, too cold, too hot, too Third World, or simply too dull. Monaco is the only tax haven located a short drive from several truly major cities, and at the same time in a resort area well known for its glitter and the non-stop action of major gambling casinos. It boasts fine beaches, golf and tennis clubs. This report looks at tax havens in general and compares Monaco with the runners-up: Andorra, Bermuda, Campione and Liechtenstein. It provides a simple test to see if Monaco is 'your cup of tea'. Tax havens are discussed in a way that shows how they may be used to advantage by middle class people (not just the very wealthy) fed up with high taxes and government controls. But more importantly, a new possibility is discussed: the option of being a 'Permanent Traveller', spending up to six months a year in the most enjoyable places of the world, being able to avoid taxes entirely because you are legally classified as a tourist. The report also goes into the question of how to earn a living, manage a business, handle investments, form corporations or trusts, etc.

The Monaco Report documents how, contrary to popular belief, it is possible to live in a hotel, eat regularly, and have a pleasant month in Monaco on a budget of £20 a day. But as a practical matter, a liveable apartment with a sea-view will cost about £500 a month – considerably less than half the price of similar accommodation in New York or London. And the weather is far better! There are a few problems in paradise, one of them being the French Government. But for those who read this Special Report, the effect of French fiscal measures can be completely and legally avoided by not making the mistake of transferring substantial assets to Monaco banks and fiduciaries. The moves to win the game are all in *The Monaco Report.*

The surprisingly simple legal steps to take to become a resident and obtain the coveted Monaco Identity Card are revealed. It is absolutely free, the main requirement being the ability to support yourself without taking away a Monegasque's job. There is no net worth requirement and once in Monaco, many interesting jobs and opportunities are available. Also covered are such questions as whether to buy or rent; how to buy a luxury car for less than half the usual price, and register it tax-free in Monaco; exchange controls; meeting new friends or single men and women; why Americans have a particularly good deal in Monaco; even advice on getting a good parking spot . . .

The Monaco Report is masterfully written and is designed to spare you many months of seeking answers and save you many thousands of dollars by obtaining the wrong ones!

A comprehensive appendix includes: Attorneys, stockbrokers, management, business and finance consultants, banks, medical practitioners, dentists, motor dealers and garages, supermarkets, hotels (with price ranges), restaurants, cinemas and theatres.

ISBN 0 906619 20 3.

The Monaco Report is available from Scope International Ltd., Forestside House, Forestside, Rowlands Castle, Hampshire PO9 6EE, Hampshire PO8 9JL, UK. Price – £60 UK Sterling (or equivalent) by credit card, cash, check or banker's draft. Price includes postage and packing, and please allow 6-8 weeks for surface delivery outside UK. For quicker air mail service add £15 or equivalent (allow 3-4 weeks for delivery). Ordering details and order form are supplied on the last two pages of this Report.

REMEMBER: Consultations with specialists are available to all purchasers and our no nonsense money back guarantee applies to all our publications.

Two reports in one volume – Double value for money:

THE ANDORRA AND SECRET ENCLAVES REPORT

UNDISCOVERED FISCAL PARADISES OF THE PYRENEES

&

THE GIBRALTAR REPORT

IDEAL BASE FOR YOUR OFFSHORE COMPANY?

3rd Edition

by Dr WG Hill

WG Hill, the world's leading expert on personal tax havens has found another place where real estate values should double in a very short period. It is the ultimate personal tax haven of Andorra, a medieval principality secluded from the rest of the world, yet a short drive from sparkling beaches, mountain lakes and the Mediterranean. The nearest big city is that bustling European economic powerhouse, Barcelona. Andorra is a hidden haven for the few in the know. Property is still affordable. Living costs are low. Natural beauty, powder snow in winter, miles of ski and hiking trails plus the lowest prices in Europe on a huge selection of goods makes this Mini-Switzerland the top personal tax haven in Europe. It's an important place for what it doesn't have: Andorra has never had an economic depression, nor AIDS, nor random violence, nor police intimidation. No nuclear plants are in the vicinity. Andorra has no leftist political parties. It hardly has any government at all. Of the 60,000 people that inhabit this alpine tax refuge, the number employed by the state is less than 100, or 0.4% of the population. There are no taxes whatsoever! Labor unions are strictly forbidden. There is no hint of a "socialist mentality" among the natives. The unregulated banking system is among the safest in the world. It is sound, prosperous, computerized, streamlined, discreet and very customer oriented. Some of the wealthiest people in the world prefer Andorra's low profile banks to those of secretive Switzerland.

In the all new third edition which has been revised and expanded for 1994, WG Hill reveals the secrets of two Spanish enclaves. Os and Llivia are both small, provincial towns hidden in the mountains of Andorra. In fact, they are only accessible via Andorra. These secret enclaves could be your key to tax freedom. For those interested in becoming prior-taxpayers of North European countries (Sweden, Denmark, Germany), these little spots could provide the ideal solution. As most of our readers are aware, these countries mandate that if one of their citizens moves to a tax haven, he must continue paying taxes to his country of origin. By implementing the plan spelled out in this report, you could achieve the best of both worlds, all the conveniences of a tax haven, but the fiscal address of high-tax country. Best of all, property prices are even less than those in Andorra-proper.

Dr WG Hill shows you where, how and when to buy bargain property in this unknown alpine paradise and its enclaves. Now is the time to get in, he says. The prices in Campione tripled within two years of his special report being issued. Will it be the same in Andorra? In Andorra there is no crime. There is free health care for everyone, including old age pensions. Mail is free, too! Schools are free for everyone. Most entertainment is free. Dining out in a first class restaurant before a free classical music concert is cheap. Andorra has 250 restaurants, some of Europe's best skiing and the largest number of Mercedes limousines *per capita* in the world. Its people are affluent. They do not pay any taxes at all. Andorra is cosmopolitan. More than two-thirds of all residents are wealthy, selfmade foreigners, most of whom moved to Andorra because they were fed up with government red tape and destructive bureaucracy.

Chapters include: Andorra as a Sex Haven, Shopping in Europe's Bargain Basement (where they give you a discount when you buy with credit cards), Why you should **not** form an Andorran corporation, How to get local passports, and much, much more. Andorra is located on the north eastern border of Spain, facing southern France.

On the Spanish *Costa del Sol,* on the south west coast, is Gibraltar. This sovereign British Crown Colony is fast becoming the preferred European tax haven for offshore corporations. "The Rock of Gibraltar" is the ideal place to register your tax haven company, your trust, your car, yacht or airplane. In this report, WG Hill examines in great detail the financial advantages of Gibraltar. He also considers quality of living, the real estate market, where to get the most interesting car deals in Europe and how to get the best out of life in Gibraltar. This corporate tax haven is prospering after a 25 year border embargo with Spain. In more than 20 in-depth chapters, Dr Hill covers all the secrets of this unique place where you can drive without a driving license. Where setting up a tax haven corporation "offshore" and buying Branston Pickle, British Bangers or HJ Heinz tinned soups is easy. He answers questions like: "Yachts, casinos – Is this another Monaco?", "Gibraltar, the new Hong Kong?", and "Should you get a Gibraltar Passport?" Other chapters include: Confidential Banking in Gibraltar, How to Set Up Your Own Tax Haven Corporation, Owning a Home in Next-Door Spain plus Gibraltar Secret: Why the British Army Pays Your Bills when you Live on Gibraltar.

The Andorra & Gibraltar Report, is available from Scope International Ltd., Forestside House, Forestside, Rowlands Castle, Hampshire PO9 6EE, UK. Price £60. See last two pages in this report for ordering details.

ISBN 0 906619 31 9

THE CHANNEL ISLAND REPORT
HOW TO ESTABLISH AND MAINTAIN A TAX HAVEN DOMICILE ON A CHANNEL ISLAND (UK) FOR £50 PER MONTH
2nd Edition
by Scope International

A businessman, weary of government red tape, lawsuits and domestic problems, arranged to sell his business and investments for a sizeable sum. If he could keep the proceeds he would enjoy financial security with a very comfortable income. But if he had to pay all the required taxes his economic base would be cut in half.

Being both ethical and cautious, he rejected the appeals of tax shelter promoters and schemes that sounded fraudulent. "If only there was a way to keep my hard-earned money working for me instead of seeing it taken away." So he endeavoured to determine whether establishing a tax haven domicile was a good idea for him, and how much time one actually had to spend at such a residence. His findings were:

1. IS MOVING TO A TAX HAVEN LEGAL?
   Generally, yes. Almost all countries permit the free movement of their citizens. In peacetime, most nations also permit assets to be transferred abroad. But more importantly we discovered this basic principle of international law: *A government has jurisdiction (power to control) only over those people and property within its frontiers.* Once someone removes himself and the family jewels from a particular country, for all practical purposes that jurisdiction ends. (Exceptions are deportation and extradition for serious crimes).

2. DOES IT MAKE ECONOMIC SENSE?
   For this particular client, yes indeed! We concluded that anyone who enjoyed travelling a few months a year and who was not absolutely tied down to a nine-to-five job in a high tax country should at least consider tax havens. A mere change of legal address could typically double the income of retirees. In most cases the tax savings alone could finance all travel and living expenses. Greater financial freedom and flexibility are also factors to consider.

3. HOW MUCH TIME MUST ONE SPEND AT A TAX HAVEN?
   You don't have to live there. Domicile is normally a question of personal intention, not physical presence. Thus, a person who calls a certain place 'home' can travel elsewhere for years, but his domicile will stay the same. True, some tax havens, notably Monaco, have fairly strict rules to the effect that to retain a resident's card one must actually be physically present six months a year. But many other tax havens don't issue residence cards or even keep track of their citizens. A domicile with this sort of informal approach is to be preferred. Residence is proved by such things as a mailing address, telephone listing, apartment lease, or house deed, etc.

This particular tax haven is 100 per cent English-speaking, and has far tougher bank-secrecy laws than Switzerland.

The government is perhaps the least intrusive of any nation on earth, and is a protectorate of a major power. It is politically stable, located within commuting distance of Paris and London. It is totally free of crimes of violence or fraud. Communications are excellent. This report contains all the information you will need to know about establishing your own tax haven domicile in this unique location.

ISBN 0 906619 38 6.

The Channel Island Report is available from Scope International Ltd., Forestside House, Forestside, Rowlands Castle, Hampshire PO9 6EE, UK. Price – £60 UK Sterling (or equivalent) by credit card, cash, check or banker's draft. Price includes postage and packing, and please allow 6-8 weeks for surface delivery outside UK. For quicker air mail service add £15 or equivalent (allow 3-4 weeks for delivery). Ordering details and order form are supplied on the last two pages of this Report.

REMEMBER: Consultations with specialists are available to all purchasers and our no nonsense money back guarantee applies to all our publications.

THE SWISS REPORT
by Marshall J Langer
2nd Edition for 1994

Some countries pride themselves on being 'like Switzerland', but there is only one Switzerland, the most respected small country in the world. *The Swiss Report* gives you an inside look at the country and the institutions that make it tick.

Switzerland is not exactly a tax haven but it is the world's greatest *money haven.* Chances are you already keep some of your money in Swiss banks. *The Swiss Report* takes you inside this country that is deservedly called "the world's safest place for your money."

The report describes Switzerland's banks, its world-renowned bank secrecy, and attempts by other countries to end that secrecy. It discusses the controls that limit non-residents to buying small amounts of Swiss real estate. It describes the companies typically used by investors and how you can save money by using a limited liability company instead of a corporation.

Langer considers Switzerland to be both a tax planner's dream and his nightmare. Correctly used in the way spelled out in the report it can be a base for you to earn money at a tax rate of 11 per cent or less, but it is hard to get that money out of Switzerland without paying a 35 per cent federal tax.

The report tells you how to visit Switzerland, places to visit, where to stay, how to travel around, where to eat. Would you like to stay longer? The report also tells you how to live and work in Switzerland, or retire there. Sure there are restrictions on obtaining permits to live in Switzerland. If it didn't have them, millions more would try to live and work there. Residence permits are difficult to obtain, but not impossible, and *The Swiss Report* tells you how to get them. It even discusses how you can spend up to six months each year in Switzerland as a 'Permanent Traveler' (PT), legally remaining a tourist instead of a taxpayer.

Dr WG (Bill) Hill regards Marshall Langer as his 'tax guru'. Langer is a tax lawyer and the author of several books including the standard reference work on tax havens, *Practical International Tax Planning,* published by New York's Practising Law Institute. After more than thirty years of law practice in Florida, Langer moved to Europe. He lived in Neuchatel, Switzerland for five years and still operates a company from there. Dr Hill has encouraged Langer to share his know-how about Switzerland with readers of these reports. Langer's clients have willingly paid him large fees for many of the insights he has learned as a Swiss-based international tax planner and which he now shares with you in *The Swiss Report.*

The Report answers these questons:

Is Switzerland freer than the USA or Great Britain?
Should you apply for a resident's permit or live there unofficially, as a PT?
Should you move there at all?
What's the real cost of living?
Regional variations?
How do you avoid or reduce Swiss taxes?
How can you use Swiss bank accounts and the Swiss secrecy laws to your advantage?
How safe and secret really are your financial affairs?
What are the Swiss really like?
Will you have to do military service?
How long before you can apply to be a citizen?
Where can you get a good meal?
Swiss punctuality and other peculiarities – how do they affect you?
Should you buy a home or rent?
How can you benefit from Swiss tax treaties?
Can you survive with just English?
Will Switzerland join the European common market?
Can a foreigner own a Swiss company?
How can you negotiate a flat income tax in advance?

These and many other questions are answered in *The Swiss Report.* We highly recommend it.

ISBN 0 906619 28 9

The Swiss Report is available from Scope International Ltd., Forestside House, Forestside, Rowlands Castle, Hampshire PO9 6EE, UK. Price £60 UK Sterling (or equivalent) by credit card, cash, check or banker's draft. Price includes postage and packing, and please allow 6-8 weeks for surface delivery outside UK. For quicker air mail service add £15 or equivalent (allow 3-4 weeks for delivery). Ordering details and order form are supplied on the last two pages of this Report.

REMEMBER: Our no nonsense money back guarantee applies to all our publications.

THE TAX EXILE REPORT
CITIZENSHIP, SECOND PASSPORTS AND ESCAPING CONFISCATORY TAXES
2nd Edition for 1994
Marshall J Langer

Are you fed up with paying confiscatory taxes? Are you willing to move and to do whatever else may be legally necessary to escape your present tax burden? If so, *The Tax Exile Report* is for you. This report is intended for the small minority of well-to-do individuals who are no longer willing to tolerate increasingly unfair tax systems and are prepared to **vote with their feet**.

Marshall Langer's newly revised report tells you how to overcome the **tax octopus** – eight different criteria used by the United States and other high-tax countries to tax you on your income and your capital. To avoid confiscatory taxes you must eliminate each of the eight tax tentacles, one by one. Langer's report tells you how to do it.

Langer tells you how to change your **residence** and your **domicile,** and when and how to acquire another **nationality**. He explains how to cope with **community property rules**. His report also tells you how to change the **source of your income** and the **location of your assets**. He helps you to **watch your timing** and to deal with problems caused by **family members who remain behind**.

Should you become a **perpetual tourist (PT)** or should you move to a new homeland? The report will help you make the right choice.

The Tax Exile Report deals with the special problems involved in leaving high-tax countries, including the US, Britain, Canada, Germany and the Nordic countries. Langer concentrates on demystifying the US rules and telling you how they really work. He tells you how to plan around the US **anti-expatriation rules** and the departure taxes imposed in other countries. His report devotes twenty chapters to a review of suitable destination countries, describing the benefits and pitfalls of each of them. Surprisingly these include some of the high-tax countries that others are seeking to escape. Langer explains that most high-tax countries play both ends against the middle. They constantly squeeze their captive 'customers' while seeking to attract new investment from abroad.

The depth of coverage can best be seen by reviewing the partial summary of the **table of contents** which follows.

SUITABLE PLACES FOR RESIDENCE, DOMICILE, CITIZENSHIP AND PASSPORTS
MOVING TO AMERICA (the US): Part-Time Residence Is Best, Longer Stays Are Dangerous, New Investor's Immigration Program
MOVING TO AUSTRALIA: Requirements for Business Migration, It is Difficult to Abandon Residence
MOVING TO THE BAHAMAS: Investment Promotion Program, Other Advantages Include No Taxes
MOVING TO BERMUDA: Requirements, Other Advantages Include No Taxes
MOVING TO BRITAIN (the UK): Advantages, Possible Disadvantages, Residency Rules Retained, Domicile Rules May Improve
MOVING TO CANADA: Requirements for Economic Migration, Comparing the US and Canada
MOVING TO CAYMAN: Immigration Quotas, Other Advantages Include No Taxes
MOVING TO THE CHANNEL ISLANDS (Jersey/Guernsey/Sark): Jersey Wants Only the Very Rich, Other Advantages, Possible Residence or Domicile in Sark
MOVING TO COSTA RICA: Requirements for *Pensionado* Status, No Tax on Foreign Income
MOVING TO IRELAND: Advantages
MOVING TO ISRAEL: Shipping Magnate Moves Back to Israel
MOVING TO MALTA: Other Requirements for New Residents, Other Advantages
MOVING TO MONACO: Acquiring Residence Takes Time and Money, Other Requirements, Not for French Citizens, Other Advantages
MOVING TO THE NETHERLANDS ANTILLES (the NA): Advantages for Dutch Emigrants
MOVING TO SWITZERLAND: Retire With a Lump-Sum Tax Deal, Visit as a *PT* for Almost Half of Each Year, You Can Get a Work Permit, Other Advantages
MOVING TO TURKS AND CAICOS: Residence Permits Are Available, Permanent Residence Certificate, Nationality and Belonger Status, Other Advantages Include No Taxes
MOVING TO URUGUAY: Self-Help Program, Investor Program, Other Advantages Include No Income Tax
MOVING TO OTHER EU COUNTRIES (France/Greece/Italy/Portugal/Spain): Millions of *PTs* Live Near the Mediterranean, Homes Are Owned by Offshore Companies, *PTs* Avoid Official Residence, Former Domicile Remains Unchanged
MOVING ELSEWHERE: Tiny Andorra in the Pyrenees, Anguilla – Escaping From Civilization, Antigua Has Beautiful Beaches, Barbados – a Sophisticated Caribbean Island, British Virgin Islands Offers Superb Sailing, Campione Is a Back Door to Switzerland, Isle of Man – Close to the UK, Mauritius – In the Indian Ocean, Mexico Attracts Retired Americans, Montserrat – a Pleasant Caribbean Island, Northern Marianas – a Plan to Save Taxes, Panama as a Place to Retire, Singapore Attracts Hong Kong Chinese, South Africa Has Political Problems, Sri Lanka Is Disturbed Politically, Other Possible Safe Havens
SHOULD *YOU* BECOME A TAX EXILE?
YOUR ULTIMATE ESTATE PLAN
RESOURCE LIST

Why is Marshall Langer uniquely qualified to write this Report?

He is a member of the Florida Bar, and practised law in Miami for more than 35 years. He has worked as an international tax adviser in Europe since 1985, living in Switzerland and in England. He was a partner in the law firm of Shutts & Bowen, Miami, and remains of counsel to that firm. He was also an Adjunct Professor of Law at the University of Miami for many years. In 1990, Langer received the Florida Bar Tax Section's award as **Outstanding Tax Attorney of the Year.**

Dr Langer is a graduate of the Wharton School of Finance and Commerce of the University of Pennsylvania (BS in Economics) and the University of Miami School of Law (JD *summa cum laude*). He has lectured extensively at tax institutes and seminars throughout the US and Europe, as well as in Japan, Hong King, Australia, Canada, and the Caribbean. He has written numerous articles on international taxation and books on tax and other subjects. He is the author of *The Swiss Report,* published in 1991 by Scope International. He is also the author of a leading book on tax havens and how to use them, entitled: *Practical International Tax Planning* (the third edition was published in 1985 and is updated annually). In addition, Langer is co-author (with Rufus Rhoades of Los Angeles) of a five-volume set of books on taxes and tax treaties called: *Rhoades & Langer, Income Taxation of Foreign Related Transactions* (updated four times a year).

The Tax Exile Report by Marshall J Langer is available from Scope International Ltd. Price £60 ($100). See last two pages in this report for ordering details.

Personal consultations with Dr Langer are available to all purchasers of *The Tax Exile Report.*

ISBN 906619 34 3

THE TAX HAVEN REPORT
2nd Edition
Adam Starchild

The words "tax haven" bring to mind far off corners of the planet with millionaire populations. This population, of course, spends most of its day drinking daiquiris on the beach, its funds secure in various numbered Swiss bank accounts. Not so, according to Adam Starchild (well, he doesn't refute the daiquiri bit). Tax havens need not be the exclusive refuge of the ultra-rich. People of average means need no longer be captive slaves to the State in today's modern jet-set era. In his newly revised *The Tax Haven Report,* Adam Starchild reveals these secrets of the ultra-rich so that us lesser mortals can take advantage of the many benefits tax havens have to offer.

As modern governments continue to expand and swallow human rights, deficits and taxes grow. All free-minded individuals must seek a means to protect their assets from this monster out of control. As Starchild explains, it is legally possible to pay absolutely no taxes. Your government may want you to think otherwise. The media may love to tattle about the misery of a particular celebrity "tax evader", but a very important point remains unnoticed. While "tax evasion" is illegal, "tax avoidance" is not. This distinction is crucial, and thus Starchild explains it at great length.

Starchild goes on to cover this exhausting subject from start to finish in a clear, easy to understand style. No legal jargon here. He brings over twenty years of experience to the production of this report and doesn't hop on the bandwagons for the latest "fad" tax havens. (It is not commonly known, but tax havens are just as interested in finding you as you are in finding them.) He explains everything from the basic criteria you should use when assessing a tax haven to how you can put them to work to save you that big chunk of your income whisked off each year by Big Brother.

For entrepreneurs and businessmen, he explains the ins and outs of tax haven corporations and trusts, including how they are formed, how they are controlled, where they can be located, and, most importantly, how they can seriously reduce, if not eliminate, the tax burden of your business.

Starchild explains the basics of some of the known and not-so-known tax havens of the world. He divides them into easily identifiable categories, including:

No-tax havens: The Bahamas, Bermuda, The Cayman Islands

Foreign-source-income havens: Panama, Cyprus, Malta, The Isle of Man, Jersey, Guernsey, Gibraltar, Hong Kong

Double-taxation agreement havens: The Netherlands, Austria, Luxembourg

This report also includes detailed chapters on both Liechtenstein and Switzerland. In stark contrast with most tax experts, Starchild successfully argues that Switzerland no longer has a great deal to offer as a tax haven.

This report is essential reading for anyone interested in reducing his tax burden. With over 170 pages of vital information, we are certain that you can develop a successful plan to reduce your tax burden as a result of reading this report. We are so certain that we do not even hesitate to offer it with our standard money-back guarantee. Unless you are absolutely satisfied return it within 28 days for a full refund.

About the Author: Adam Starchild has been a business consultant for nearly two decades. He is the author of over a dozen books, four of which are on tax havens, the earliest having been published in 1978. He has also written hundreds of magazine articles, for journals around the world. Amongst the many publishing his articles have been: The Christian Science Monitor, Credit & Financial Management, International Business, The New York Times, The San Francisco Examiner, Tax Angles, Tax Haven & Shelter Report, Tax Haven News *and* Tax Planning International.

His consulting clients have ranged from wealthy individuals to banks, trust companies, investment companies, book publishers, import-export companies and tour operators. Often critical of the hype and inflated prices from some of the more famous tax havens, Starchild gives you the benefit of his many years hands-on experience in setting up trusts in many countries around the world.

ISBN 0 906619 39 4

The Tax Haven Report is available from Scope International Ltd., Forestside House, Forestside, Rowlands Castle, Hampshire PO9 6EE, UK. Price £60 UK Sterling (or equivalent) by credit card, cash, check or banker's draft. Price includes postage and packing, and please allow 6-8 weeks for surface delivery outside UK. For quicker air mail service add £15 or equivalent (allow 3-4 weeks for delivery). Ordering details and order form are supplied on the last two pages of this Report.

REMEMBER: Consultations with specialists, including Adam Starchild, are available to all purchasers and our no nonsense money back guarantee applies to all our publications.

THE AUSTRIA AND LIECHTENSTEIN REPORT

1st Edition 1994

Dr Reinhard Stern

Few people are aware that banks in Austria offer all the same advantages of their Swiss counterparts – plus the only true remaining bank secrecy laws in Europe. Now a new Scope report introduces Austria, the small country with the reputation as one of the world's most popular tourist destinations.

The first part of the book profiles Austria and gives you background information you should have at your fingertips if you plan to visit the country Its government, its social system and language, its people and their concerns, and much more. You'll be prepared with information on everything from phone calls to vineyards. The report then moves to specifics for those interested in staying in the country longer. It will help you decide whether Austria is the second residence or retirement haven you've been looking for, and if so, whether to avoid residence requirements or officially apply for a residence permit.

The second part turns to business and delivers newly-available information, some of it has never been published before, on important aspects of banking, investment and economics in Austria. Dr Stern outlines the numerous advantages of investing here, the accounts available to foreigners, and how the policy of banking super-secrecy can enable you to open accounts or purchase securities, future options and bullion coins anonymously. He discusses the best banks to approach for the services you might need and perhaps more importantly, he warns his readers of the mistakes most frequently made by the unwary when undertaking *private* business here.

Additionally, he introduces two secret enclaves, not known to the public, where Austria's best banks are to be found. Detailed maps included in this section explain how to get to those out-of-the-way secret enclaves. A special section deals with the Vienna stock market, which was the world's top performer several years ago and is likely to be a very attractive market in the near future.

Favourable tax laws allow foreigners wishing to reside here low tax or even zero-tax residence status plus tax-free income. Inside information, virtually unknown to the public, is thoroughly discussed.

What kind of businesses exist in Austria, how are they structured, and what status do they have? Should you consider forming a company here. You'll want to know about the corporate taxes and learn your way in and out of the loopholes on the real-estate scene, where restrictions on newcomers can otherwise be a barrier. This report makes it a whole lot simpler.

Liechtenstein is similar to Switzerland in many ways. However, there are also distinctive differences of which investors should be aware. The sections on Liechtenstein answer vital questions on this Principality, including setting up accounts, attractive fund management plans and bank secrecy. It advises on taxes, and how to avoid them by setting up private trusts and anonymous commercial *Anstalts.* You will have information on everything from purchasing real estate anonymously to secret tax loopholes between Austria and Liechtenstein which can be used by PTs and potential offshore investors alike. Clear, easy to understand examples will show you how to establish your heirs and beneficiaries, thereby protecting your assets from potential disaster. The Liechtenstein sections also include a discussion of the most favourable banks to administer your affairs.

HERE ARE A FEW EXAMPLES OF THE QUESTIONS THE AUSTRIA/LIECHTENSTEIN REPORT WILL ANSWER FOR YOU

- What are the basic dos and don'ts of investments in Austria?
- Austrian bank secrecy: how safe and how secret is it really?
- How do I go about establishing and maintaining anonymity?
- Where are the best banks?
- Which accounts are available to foreigners?
- How can I establish my heirs and protect my assets?
- Where are the super secrecy bank enclaves and how do I use them?
- Exactly what kind of tax breaks does Austria offer foreigners?
- How can I live and do business in Austria without paying taxes?
- Should I establish a business or a holding company in Austria?
- How can I move cash anonymously and cross borders safely and discreetly?
- How high is the cost of living in Austria?
- How can I establish residency?
- Should I consider Austria as a place to retire?
- What should I know before buying real estate?
- I'm a PT – Is Austria really for me?
- How does a Liechtenstein Anstalt (commercial trust) work?
- Can a Stiftung provide the anonymous asset management I need?
- What are the secret tax loopholes between Austria and Liechtenstein?
- What are the differences between banks in Austria, Liechtenstein and Switzerland?

. . . and many other questions are answered in this unique report.

Order today using the priority order form at the back of this report.

ISBN 0 906619 44 0

HOW TO ORDER:

Each individual sumptuously bound report is £60/$100 or equivalent in any currency. Please allow £5.00 p&p for UK and surface delivery. All orders are despatched promptly, but please allow 6-8 weeks for surface delivery outside UK and 28 days within the UK and overseas DHL before querying non-delivery. For quicker service add £15/$25 for courier service.
Bank drafts, travelers cheques made payable to SCOPE INTERNATIONAL LTD. or currency may be sent. **Or** quote credit card number and expiry date. Telephone and fax orders will be accepted on the numbers given below. If you are not satisfied, your money will be refunded to you in full if you return the undamaged report(s) to us within 28 days of receipt. **Please use the order form on the reverse side of this page.**

Post, Fax or Telephone your order to:-

SCOPE INTERNATIONAL LTD,
Forestside House, Forestside,
Rowlands Castle, Hants. PO9 6EE, Great Britain.
Telephone: 0705 631751
Fax: 0705 631322
Tel outside UK - Dial: International Code + 44 705 631751
Fax outside UK - Dial: International Code + 44 705 631322

SPECIAL OFFER
Save up to £480

SPECIAL OFFER TO READERS OF THIS REPORT!

Order any 3 or more of our Special Reports and you may deduct £60 off the total cost, order 6 and you may deduct £135, order 9 and you may deduct £225, order 12 and deduct £315 or take all 16 and save £480.

None of Scope International's Special Reports are subsidized, authorized or encouraged by the organizations, countries or institutions written about. All the author has to sell is good, objective information. Satisfaction is guaranteed. If these reports do not deliver as advertised, they may be returned for a refund.

AVOID DELAY
POST, FAX OR PHONE YOUR ORDER TODAY.

LEARN THE SECRETS OF THE SUPER-RICH

PRIORITY ORDER FORM

Mr/Mrs/Miss/Ms ....
(Block Letters Please)

Address ....

....

....

..........................Post/Zip Code ....

Tel: .... Fax: ....

SPECIAL OFFER TO READERS OF THIS REPORT!

Order any 3 or more of Dr Hill's Special Reports and you may deduct £60 off the total cost. Simply mark your choice of Reports and deduct £60 from the total cost of your order. Order 6 and you may deduct £120. Order 9 and you may deduct £225. Order 12 and deduct £315 or take all 16 and save £480.

Please Tick	Title	Author	Published price	Total
☐	**Banking in Silence**	**WG Hill**	**£60**	
☐	**The Austria & Liechtenstein Report**	**Dr R.M. Stern**	**£60**	
☐	**The Albania Report**	**WG Hill**	**£60**	
☐	**Sex Havens**	**WG Hill**	**£60**	
☐	**Think Like A Tycoon**	**WG Hill**	**£60**	
☐	**The Andorra & Gibraltar Report**	**WG Hill**	**£60**	
☐	**PT 1**	**WG Hill**	**£60**	
☐	**PT 2**	**WG Hill**	**£60**	
☐	**The Passport Report**	**WG Hill**	**£60**	
☐	**The Lloyd's Report**	**WG Hill**	**£60**	
☐	**The Monaco Report**	**WG Hill**	**£60**	
☐	**The Campione Report**	**WG Hill**	**£60**	
☐	**The Swiss Report**	**Marshall Langer**	**£60**	
☐	**The Tax Exile Report**	**Marshall Langer**	**£60**	
☐	**The Channel Island Report**	**Scope International**	**£60**	
☐	**The Tax Haven Report**	**Adam Starchild**	**£60**	

Please charge my (delete as necessary):
Visa/Access/Mastercard/Eurocard/AMEX/Diners

Signature ....

My card number is:

IMPORTANT Please quote expiry date: ....

Order Summary

TOTAL GOODS	
LESS £60, £135, £225, £315 OR £480 SPECIAL OFFER DISCOUNT	
SUB-TOTAL	
AIRMAIL CHARGE £15 ($25) (SURFACE & UK - £5)	
TOTAL	
CHEQUE ENCLOSED PAYABLE TO SCOPE INTERNATIONAL LTD	

POST OR FAX YOUR ORDER TODAY, DETAILS OVERLEAF OR RING RICHARD OR STEWART AT SCOPE INTERNATIONAL ON +44 (0) 705 631751